'This book is simply brilliant, an outstanding contribution to the field. It is difficult to imagine a better introduction to the ethics of consent. The text is well-structured, thoroughly argued, and highly engaging.'

– *Peter Schaber, University of Zurich, Switzerland*

The Ethics of Consent

We borrow and lend possessions, sign up to social networking sites, agree to sexual advances, and undergo medical procedures—all by giving consent. Without consent, these acts would be rights violations. With it, they can be made permissible. Consequently, questions about consent are controversial and ethically fraught.

The Ethics of Consent is a clear and much-needed introduction to this fundamental topic. In Part I, the authors examine conceptual and theoretical questions surrounding consent, providing an accessible overview of topics such as validity, competence, the informational requirements for consent, coercion, manipulation, and deception. In Part II they examine consent to medical care, clinical research, online data use, sex, and government.

The book addresses important and controversial subjects, including the involuntary treatment of patients in healthcare, the payment of healthy volunteers in research, the use of data-collecting technology in public education, the ethics of intoxicated sex, and the authority of referendums.

An excellent starting point for anyone studying the ethics of consent, this book will be valuable for those working in philosophy, applied ethics and philosophy of law, as well as related disciplines such as medicine, public policy, and gender studies.

Joseph Millum is a Senior Lecturer in Philosophy at St. Andrews University, UK.

Danielle Bromwich is an Associate Professor of Philosophy at the University of Leeds, UK.

The Ethics of...

When is it right to go to war? What are the causes of poverty? Are human intelligence and machine intelligence the same? What is cyber-terrorism? Do races exist? What makes a person a refugee?

Each engaging textbook from *The Ethics of...* series focuses on a significant ethical issue and provides a clear and stimulating explanation of the surrounding philosophical discussions. Focusing on moral debates at the forefront of contemporary society they have been designed for use by students studying philosophy, applied ethics, global ethics and related subjects such as politics, international relations and sociology. Features to aid study include chapter summaries, study questions, annotated further reading and glossaries.

The Ethics of Sex
An Introduction
Neil McArthur

The Ethics of War and Peace
An Introduction
Third Edition
Helen Frowe

The Ethics of Pandemics
An Introduction
Iwao Hirose

The Ethics of Climate Change
An Introduction
Second Edition
Byron Williston

The Ethics of Humanitarian Intervention
An Introduction
Jonathan Parry

The Ethics of Surveillance, second edition
An Introduction
Kevin Macnish

The Ethics of Consent
An Introduction
Joseph Millum and Danielle Bromwich

For more information about this series, please visit: https://www.routledge.com/The-Ethics-of-/book-series/ETHICSOF.

The Ethics of Consent

An Introduction

Joseph Millum and Danielle Bromwich

Routledge
Taylor & Francis Group
LONDON AND NEW YORK

Cover image: Alessandra Indino / Getty Images

First published 2026
by Routledge
4 Park Square, Milton Park, Abingdon, Oxon OX14 4RN

and by Routledge
605 Third Avenue, New York, NY 10158

Routledge is an imprint of the Taylor & Francis Group, an informa business

British Library Cataloguing-in-Publication Data
A catalogue record for this book is available from the British Library

ISBN: 978-1-032-26256-7 (hbk)
ISBN: 978-1-032-26254-3 (pbk)
ISBN: 978-1-003-28739-1 (ebk)

DOI: 10.4324/9781003287391

Typeset in Times New Roman
by codeMantra

For Ritika and David

Contents

Acknowledgements

Our collaborative work on consent began over a decade ago when we were both working in the Department of Bioethics in the Clinical Center of the US National Institutes of Health. Many of the ideas in this book trace their origins back to that time.

Our work would not have been possible without the support of this and our various other academic communities. Joe thanks his colleagues at the Clinical Center Department of Bioethics and in the Department of Philosophy at University of St Andrews. Danielle thanks her colleagues at the Clinical Center Department of Bioethics, the Department of Philosophy at the University of Massachusetts Boston, IDEA: The Ethics Centre, and the School of Philosophy, Religion, and History of Science at University of Leeds.

Over the years, many people have given us invaluable feedback. In particular, we would like to thank: Adam Beresford, Robyn Bluhm, Larry Blum, Kirstin Borgerson, Joe Bowen, Maria Brincker, Luke Brunning, Tom Dougherty, Annette Dufner, Michael Garnett, Christine Grady, Steve Levine, Doug Mackay, Tash McKeever, Frank Miller, Collin O'Neil, Annette Rid, Ben Sachs-Cobbe, Léa Salje, Peter Schaber, Seema Shah, Jeremy Wanderer, Marika Warren, Dave Wendler, Alan Wertheimer, and two anonymous reviewers for Routledge who gave extensive comments on the draft manuscript. Thanks also to Tony Bruce and Adam Johnson at Routledge and to Jorren Dykstra for research assistance.

Finally, we thank our families for their love and support. Joe thanks Ritika, Trevor, Tony, both Sylvias, Danny, Jenny, and the rest of the family. Danielle thanks David and Bramble, Mum and Dad, Toby and Lya, Mrs. E, Zoe and Steve. Toby, there will be a quiz, so make sure Lya reads this to you!

1 Introduction

Why this book?

1. The ubiquity of consent

Joe just went to the barber's. As a long-time customer, he greeted the barber and they shook hands. Joe sat in the chair, allowed the barber to put a towel around his neck and said, "A clean shave on top please, and the usual beard fade." Half an hour later he got up and paid at the register. Later, Joe would sign up for a food delivery service. First, he was asked to consent to the use of cookies. This was annoying. He went through the list and ticked "No" to everything except essential cookies. Then he could finally access the website, where he signed up for the service and agreed to the terms and conditions without reading them. Joe's friend, Sam, comes to the door and he invites her inside. Sam has come to borrow Joe's bike for the weekend.

Danielle just went to the doctor's. At reception, she was asked to read and sign a form giving permission for the practice to access her records and share medical information with other providers. The check-up itself was less formal. After Danielle described her complaint, Dr. Ranasinghe picked up her otoscope, and said "Let's take a look." Before examining Danielle's ear, she said, "Just let me know if anything is uncomfortable." "Okay, I will," replied Danielle. Last week, Danielle was taking part in a research study led by a professor at her university. That involved her signing another form to say that she had had the study explained to her and understood her rights, even though it was just a questionnaire about her daily habits. She looks at the news. The leader of a political party she did not vote for is talking about his mandate from the people as he makes dramatic cuts to foreign aid. Did I agree to this, she wonders?

For most adults, consent is a ubiquitous and essential part of life. We allow physical contact (sexual or otherwise), sign up to online services, borrow and lend possessions, and undergo medical procedures—all by giving consent. Sometimes the consent process is formalized and documented, as with the terms and conditions Joe agrees to or the consent form used in Danielle's research study. But much of the time consent is more casual. We might give consent through speech, as when Sam is invited inside, or through a gesture, like putting out a hand to shake or proffering a credit card to pay. We might even—tacitly—consent by doing nothing at all, as Danielle would if she did not object to the medical examination after her exchange with Dr. Ranasinghe. Such consent exchanges are unremarkable. Yet they are

DOI: 10.4324/9781003287391-1

vitally important: consent allows us to direct our own lives. By giving consent, Joe can host his friends. Because no one is allowed in his house without consent, Joe can also protect his home, property, and privacy.

2. Recent controversies

Acts that would be permissible with valid consent may be ethically very wrong without it. In August 2023, the Spanish women's football team had just won their first ever World Cup. During the medal ceremony Luis Rubiales, president of the Royal Spanish Football Federation, forcibly kissed one of the players, Jenni Hermoso, on the lips. Initially described by Rubiales as an "unimportant gesture of affection,"[1] the incident became emblematic of sexism in Spanish football and wider society. Rubiales was ultimately found guilty of sexual assault when the court determined that Hermoso had not, in fact, consented. Responding to the verdict, Irene Montero, who was Minister of Equality at the time of the incident, said: "Not long ago, it was unthinkable that a court would recognise a kiss without consent as a sexual assault. Feminism is changing everything: Only 'yes' means 'yes'."[2]

In 2013, British surgeon Simon Bramhall successfully transplanted a liver. When the liver failed shortly afterwards and the patient returned to hospital for another transplant, the new surgeon discovered the initials "SB," had been burned into their liver with an argon beam coagulator after the conclusion of the surgery.[3] Subsequent investigations showed that Bramhall had done this to at least one other patient. He was convicted of two counts of assault, even though the liver was not harmed by his actions. Tony Badenoch QC, the prosecutor, said: "This case is about his practice on two occasions, without the consent of the patient and for no clinical reason whatever, to burn his initials on to the surface of a newly-transplanted liver."[4]

In these cases, consent was neither requested nor received. But in others, the very question at issue is whether consent was *successfully* given. The transformative power of consent—from a wrongful rights violation to a permissible act—means that this matters enormously.

In September 1999, eighteen-year-old Jesse Gelsinger was given an experimental gene therapy as part of a clinical study to treat ornithine transcarbamoylase (OTC) deficiency, a rare X chromosome-linked metabolic disorder.[5] Gelsinger had an unexpected and severe immune reaction to the viral vector used to deliver the corrective OTC gene. He died four days later. Gelsinger had been an enthusiastic volunteer in the research—wanting to help develop treatments for patients with his condition. The subsequent investigation turned up a number of facts that he apparently had not been told, including side effects in two previous volunteers, deaths in primate studies of a different gene therapy, and a potential financial conflict of interest for the principal investigator, Dr. James Wilson.[6] Gelsinger certainly did not know some important information. Did that mean he did not give valid consent? Does it matter if knowing those facts would not have affected his decision to enroll in the study?

In 2014, Cambridge University researcher Dr. Aleksandr Kogan developed a Facebook app called "This Is Your Digital Life."[7] Several hundred thousand Facebook users were paid to use this app to take a personality test as part of an academic study. In fact, not only did the app use their information, it also harvested profile data and private messages from all these users' friends. Detailed data on tens of millions of users was sold to the company Cambridge Analytica, where it was used for targeted political ads in high-profile campaigns, including Donald Trump's 2016 election. The data collected by the app was all consistent with Facebook's terms and conditions at the time, to which users had agreed. Nevertheless, members of the public and government officials regarded this as a massive breach of privacy. In what sense had users given meaningful consent to their data being collected by this private company?

Many of the cases that emerged during the #MeToo movement beginning in 2017 clearly involved unconsented sexual contact. An anonymous story of a date gone wrong with comedian Aziz Ansari prompted conflicting reactions. According to his accuser's account, Ansari pressured her into various sexual acts and persisted in making advances even after they had been refused.[8] Was this sexual assault or just miscommunication and bad sex?[9]

3. Philosophy and the ethics of consent

Controversial cases like these often implicate questions of law or professional practice. We can ask, for example, whether the gene therapy researchers disclosed everything required by the regulations governing human subjects research or whether Cambridge Analytica was in violation of Facebook's terms of service. There are also important questions of fact—concerning, say, what data was actually harvested or whether Ansari actually did what was reported. But answering all these legal and factual questions would not suffice to answer our questions about the validity of consent or the rightness and wrongness of people's actions. Those questions are matters of philosophical ethics. They are the topic of this book.

It will be helpful at the outset to say something about philosophy and the philosophical method. Philosophy is the study of fundamental questions about the nature of reality and our place within it. The philosophical method does not involve the collection of data. Philosophy is therefore unlike the sciences. Instead, philosophers try to make progress by analyzing concepts, generating and reflecting on intuitions, and constructing arguments. A philosopher might take the concept of "voluntary," for instance, and analyze what it means. What are the necessary and sufficient conditions for an act to count as voluntary? They will try out different conceptions of voluntariness and test them against their intuitions. They might ask: does *this* proposed way of understanding voluntariness make sense of cases where all would agree an act was voluntary and rule out those that are clearly involuntary?

For those who are not philosophers, it may appear mysterious, at first glance, how philosophy can answer questions of ethics. Ethics is about values—what is right and wrong, good and bad. But values cannot be seen or touched or measured. This means that we cannot use the scientific method to answer ethical questions. So, then, what do we do if we disagree about a matter of ethics or if we, as individuals, do not know what is the right thing to do?

We ask the reader to set aside wholesale skepticism about whether there is any such thing as being right or wrong about ethics. That is a whole different topic.[10] Everyone, we hope, starts with some values. We invite anyone who doubts this to reflect on the public reaction to the recent consent controversies. Most people had no trouble reaching a verdict on the ethics of Rubiales's kiss. This would be hard to explain without assuming that most people have an "everyday moral sense"[11]—a capacity to make ethical judgements using general, often rudimentary, principles that reflect their values.

Our starting point are these values. A convincing argument in philosophical ethics is one that shows someone that in order to be consistent with their most deeply held values, they ought to also believe a particular ethical view. This involves subjecting their values to critical scrutiny—attempting to identify and jettison those that are unreliable. Sometimes, it will involve clarifying what their values really are. Other times, it will involve rejecting an ethical view that they previously held because it cannot be made consistent with their other deeply held values. Or it will involve changing their values in the light of insights about what they imply.[12]

To illustrate, over the years, both authors of this book have come to believe that the consumption of meat from factory-farmed animals is ethically wrong. In part, this change in our ethical views has come about through learning more about the conditions under which animals are kept and killed. That, in itself, can provoke ethical insight. In part, however, it is the result of reflecting on our values. We believe that it is wrongful to cause suffering unnecessarily or for trivial reasons. We believe, after considering the possibilities, that it is speciesist to treat the suffering of humans differently than the suffering of non-humans. We believe that the pleasure of eating meat is a trivial benefit, given the alternatives. The results of philosophical inquiry can be surprising—we both grew up eating factory-farmed meat and, before subjecting this practice to critical scrutiny, we each had the unreflective intuition that our diets were ethically benign. Consistency compelled us to admit that we were mistaken and admit that we have reasons for *not* acting as we previously did. This change is the result of philosophical reflection on our existing values. It is an example of how progress in philosophy can be made.

This brings us to the philosophy of this book. Our central question—as we critically survey the major views in the ethics of consent literature—is: what would a convincing philosophical theory of consent look like? To answer that question, we look to the function of consent. As we have seen, consent plays a morally transformative role in our lives when it is valid, and it explains why people are wronged when it is not. We need a theory of consent that can explain that moral transformation and how it can go wrong. That theory should also help us make sense of the hard cases in which we are uncertain about whether valid consent was successfully given.

Many theories aim to do this, so how do we judge whether they succeed? We think progress can be made by appeal to two uncontroversial standards. First, we should expect a convincing philosophical theory of consent to get the right answer for cases in which we are confident about our considered judgements. Hermoso did not consent to Rubiales's kiss and Bramhall's patients did not consent to his scarring them. Any view that does not give the right answer in straightforward cases like these should be rejected. Second, any good theory must be able to explain the verdicts it entails. The reason why we *need* a philosophical theory is because there is something that needs explaining—in this case, it is the normative phenomenon of valid consent. Without an explanation, the view will not be able to help with difficult cases, where we are not certain what ethical verdict we should reach. So, if any view makes claims about some condition being necessary or sufficient for valid consent it must be able to explain why. Many views in the consent literature entail plausible verdicts about cases, but they are of little use to us *unless* they can also explain those verdicts.

4. Structure of the book

This book aims to provide a comprehensive philosophical introduction to the ethics of consent for students, academics, and lay readers.

The first part of the book—on *theory*—examines the conceptual and theoretical questions that philosophers and ethicists have raised with regard to consent. We introduce key terminology, describe areas of consensus, and outline significant disagreements. Though mostly philosophical, the four chapters that constitute this part assume no background in philosophy. We try to give an accessible overview of key concepts such as validity, competence, coercion, manipulation, and the like, which the reader can then apply to their own philosophical puzzles.

The second part of the book—on *practice*—considers how the theoretical discussions so far are relevant to specific areas of life where consent is particularly important. We examine consent to medicine, clinical research, the provision of personal data online, sex, and the purported relationship between consent and legitimate government. For each of these domains, we show how the earlier theoretical discussion applies and where disagreement in the literature has important implications for practice. Each chapter also includes a detailed analysis of two difficult cases where consent is at issue but the right policy or action is not easily settled by existing theories.

We aim to give an overview of current thinking on each topic. However, we also have our own views on many questions. We do not shy away from presenting arguments for these views and we leave it to the reader to judge whether those arguments are convincing. In later chapters, in particular, you will see how our views about theoretical questions have a direct bearing on the conclusions we draw regarding policy and practice. If you disagree with us about an aspect of theory, we hope you will consider whether that disagreement also has practical implications.

5. How to use this book

The remainder of this introduction summarizes the book's nine other chapters. Since the later chapters refer back to and sometimes build on earlier arguments, the easiest way to engage the book is by reading them in order. However, we have written each chapter so that it can stand alone. So, if you are interested in a particular topic, you can skip straight to that chapter. It will refer you to other relevant sections of the book, which you can then read if needed. In some cases, it may be most valuable to read a pair of chapters—one on theory and one on practice. For example, if you are interested in decision-making capacity in medicine, Chapter 3 on competence and Chapter 6 on consent to medical care will be a complementary pair.

6. Chapter summaries

Chapter 2: What is consent?

The first theory chapter addresses fundamental questions about the nature of consent and its ethical and legal significance. We approach what consent is by looking at what consent does. Consent, when *valid*, involves the waiving or transferring of a right. We argue that validity is the foundational concept for thinking about the ethics of consent. Next, we turn to the structure of rights and present a common terminology for talking about them. Consent is one of our so-called "normative powers," along with promising, commanding, forgiving, and the like. For all these normative powers, we can ask what grounds or justifies them. Doing so can help us make progress with challenging philosophical questions regarding the powers. Along with some ideas about how the power to consent is grounded in the value of autonomy, we address what the act of consenting is, how the scope of what someone has consented to is determined, and what effects consent has. We close the chapter by discussing how bad nonconsensual acts are and whether there are any limits to what competent adults can consent to.

Chapter 3: Competence

It is widely agreed that consent is valid when, and only when, the following conditions are met:

(1) the person giving consent is *competent*;
(2) appropriate information has been *disclosed* to them;
(3) they have sufficient *understanding*;
(4) their decision is *voluntary*; and
(5) they *token* consent.

This chapter covers competence (or "decision-making capacity," as it is sometimes labeled). The following theory chapters cover the informational requirements (disclosure and understanding) and the voluntariness requirement.

Someone who is competent to consent for themselves has the right to do so and others should not make that decision for them. Someone who is not competent lacks that right and a surrogate decision-maker should make decisions on their behalf. It therefore matters a great deal whether judgments of competence are accurate.

We outline the major conceptions of competence, starting with the widely endorsed four abilities model. According to this view, competence has four components: (i) the capacity to communicate a choice; (ii) the capacity to understand relevant information; (iii) the capacity to appreciate one's situation; and (iv) the capacity to reason about one's options. The four abilities model has sometimes been criticized for ignoring the relevance of emotions or values to decision-making. We consider a couple of ways in which it might be supplemented to take account of these criticisms. We then raise the concern that the model is too demanding—it wrongly prohibits some individuals with marginal autonomy from consenting for themselves. We consider ways to deal with this problem. More liberal views would allow individuals with marginal autonomy to make their own decisions, but at the risk of not protecting them from the harmful consequences of those decisions. Views that adjust the threshold for competence according to the risk of the decisions can protect people from bad choices, but they no longer seem to capture what competence is. We close with our own *separate grounds* view which resolves this problem in a principled way. Competence actually comprises two separate rights each of which require different capacities. One is the power to waive one's rights by giving consent, which requires quite minimal decision-making abilities. The other is a claim against others paternalistically interfering with one's decisions. Only persons with quite extensive decision-making abilities have this right against interference.

Chapter 4: The informational requirements: understanding and disclosure

The disclosure and understanding requirements are usually regarded as closely related: the reason for disclosing information to someone who is making a decision is to enable their understanding of it. This chapter therefore examines the two concepts together. We begin by assessing different views of what must be understood for valid consent, before discussing how what is understood relates to the *scope* of consent. On some views—those that are widely held in medicine and clinical research—what ought to be disclosed is derived from an analysis of what needs to be understood for consent to be valid. These views imply that the informational requirements for valid consent are conceptually connected *and* that a lot of information must usually be disclosed and understood. Despite being widely held, we argue that these views are false: the disclosure and understanding requirements have distinct grounds. After exploring the obligations on the part of the recipient of consent to disclose relevant information, we argue that only one of these obligations is tied to validity. The consent receiver has a duty to avoid exercising illegitimate control over the consent giver and this often entails substantive duties of disclosure. However, this does not imply that the consent-giver needs to understand all those facts that ought to be disclosed. They only need to understand how to waive their rights through consent. We close the chapter by considering how different forms of ignorance—on the part of the giver and the receiver of consent—affect validity.

Chapter 5: Voluntariness: coercion, manipulation, and deception

If consent is involuntary, then it is not valid. But what makes an action involuntary? If a nursing home resident only takes their medication because the staff threaten to withhold privileges, does that count? What about someone who is enticed to participate in a research study by the promise of a big payout? Or someone who is guilt-tripped into acquiescing to sex?

The chapter begins by asking what it means for an action to be voluntary in general. This involves distinguishing voluntary actions from reflexive, accidental, and forced motions. We then move onto voluntariness in the specific context of consent. Non-voluntary motions do not count as tokens of consent and so cannot be morally transformative. For other acts, whether or not they count as voluntary depends on who ultimately controls the act and how. Consent proffered as the result of *illegitimate control* will be involuntary in this sense and so invalid. The remaining sections address coercion, deception, and manipulation—the major ways in which others can illegitimately influence us. For each case, we provide an overview of how philosophers think about the concept and consider whether and when it involves illegitimate control.

Chapter 6: Consent to medical care

The first chapter on consent in practice looks at clinical care. We begin this chapter with the history of consent requirements in medicine. We then describe current practice in Western countries, where it is now expected that clinicians will obtain the informed consent of their patients. We address several open questions concerning the informational and competence requirements. After considering how clinicians ought to obtain valid consent to treatment from willing competent adults, we turn to the question of how treatment decisions should be made for incapacitated adults. We then consider two hard cases. The first is a perennial problem in medicine: the presentation of information to patients who face difficult treatment decisions. Clinicians have a professional duty to promote their patient's interests and the consent process represents an opportunity to help a patient make a good decision. To what extent are clinicians permitted to persuade, manipulate, or deceive in order to improve their patient's choice? The second hard case considers the treatment of patients who refuse to consent to treatment. Many jurisdictions permit the involuntary detention and treatment of patients who are thought to pose a risk to themselves or others. When is this ethically justified?

Chapter 7: Consent to clinical research

Early clinical research was frequently characterized by indifference about whether subjects were aware of or agreed to their participation in experiments. This chapter briefly describes some important episodes in the history of clinical research that led to changes in norms or laws concerning informed consent. These include early controlled human infection studies, Nazi wartime experimentation, and the Tuskegee syphilis experiment. As a result of the scrutiny given to research and the incorporation of detailed consent requirements into policy and guidance, the consent process has been more formalized and better studied in the context of clinical research than anywhere else. We describe in some detail current practice for obtaining informed consent, the standard view on what is required, and describe how decision-making capacity is assessed for potential research participants whose competence is in question. We close with two cases. The first concerns what research participants understand about the studies in which they are enrolled. Data from numerous studies suggest that understanding is highly variable and often inadequate according to the standards laid out by current guidance. Are these standards mistaken or is the dominant view of what is required for valid consent in error? The second case concerns the payment of healthy volunteers for high-risk research. Some argue that paying participants substantial sums is coercive or constitutes "undue influence," which may undermine the quality of their consent. We consider whether these charges have merit.

Chapter 8: Consent online

Whether it is agreeing to the terms and conditions for a new app, signing up on a social networking site, or simply accepting the use of cookies on a website, we regularly assent to the collection and use of our personal data online. For social networking sites, like Facebook and Instagram, users' personal data is a core component of the business model—allowing the sites to precisely target advertisements and tweak their content to encourage people to stay on the site. Recent scandals, such as the sale of Facebook user data to the consulting firm Cambridge Analytica for use in political advertising, have raised questions about exactly what users consent to with regard to the collection and use of their personal data.

We begin this chapter with a discussion of privacy, since the right to control one's personal information is the main right implicated in online consent. We briefly summarize some key legal regimes governing data privacy. The complexity and ubiquity of online transactions have motivated some scholars to question whether traditional models of consent apply in this domain. We defend the applicability of our view against more radical attempts to rethink consent in this domain. Then we consider the competence problem before discussing two hard cases that concern opacity and voluntariness. The first hard case analyzes the use of lengthy terms and conditions. We assess the ethical significance of signing up to a digital service after struggling to parse complicated and incomplete terms of service. The second concerns the voluntariness of online consent in the context of modern education. We outline the growing industry of educational technology and consider whether it is possible to opt out of its use or data collection while also accessing publicly funded education.

Chapter 9: Consent to sex

The #MeToo movement has drawn attention to the shockingly high prevalence of unwanted sexual advances and non-consensual sexual acts. In this chapter, we explore consent to sex. Starting with the law, we outline the way in which modern thinking about sexual autonomy coupled with civil rights, feminist, and LGBTQ+ activism has transformed Western attitudes towards permissible sexual relations. Turning next to ethics, we consider the radical view that valid consent is not necessary for permissible sexual relations. Against this view, we argue that consent is necessary, but not sufficient. Some important questions about the ethics of sex are not primarily about consent. We then turn to the necessary conditions for valid consent. We explore current debates that concern the understanding and voluntariness conditions, before exploring the disclosure and competence conditions in two hard cases. Our first hard case concerns sex and deception. Whereas in other contexts, deception renders consent invalid, it is commonly thought that lying about one's profession, age, or marital status to get someone into bed is at worst bad behavior. We consider whether deceiving someone into sex invalidates their consent and what implications this has for the disclosure of private information. The second case addresses consent given by adults who are voluntarily inebriated. Intoxicated sex is common, but alcohol and drugs impair our decision-making capacity. We explore whether an intoxicated person can give valid consent to sex.

Chapter 10: Consent to government

Within political philosophy there has been considerable debate about what—if anything—justifies the authority of governments to regulate the lives of the people within a state. One popular response is that governments have authority by virtue of the consent of the governed. This chapter introduces the reader to the problem of political obligation, traces the modern Western notion that consent can solve this problem from John Locke to the present, and explains the various challenges for the view. These challenges invoke familiar concepts from the analyses given earlier in this book—of understanding, voluntariness, and the tokening of consent. Some modern political philosophers have attempted to revive the consent theory of political authority. We argue that they fail to show that most individuals have actually given consent to the state in which they live. In order for consent to ground state authority substantial reforms would be necessary to obtain consent and render it morally transformative.

This chapter's first difficult case takes the best case for government authority on the basis of consent—a referendum—and asks whether the results of a referendum have special authority because they directly express the will of the governed. We consider the UK's referendum on European Union membership in the light of concerns raised about misinformation, which might in other contexts be thought to invalidate consent. The second difficult case concerns a rather different issue: whether it is possible to give consent when threatened with legal sanctions for refusal. We focus on laws requiring drivers to agree to blood alcohol tests. Does the fact that agents of the state issue the threat mean that consent to such a test can be valid?

Notes

1 News.com.au. "'Not OK': Outrage over 'horrific' unsolicited World Cup kiss." August 21, 2023. Available at: www.news.com.au/sport/football/world-cup/not-ok-outrage-over-unsolicited-world-cup-kiss/news-story/1e49784a6324bcde1e57748d92381b20.
2 Pinedo, Emma. "Spanish ex-soccer boss Rubiales sentenced to pay fine over kiss without consent." *Reuters*. February 20, 2025. Available at: www.reuters.com/world/europe/spanish-court-sentences-ex-soccer-boss-rubiales-pay-fine-over-kiss-without-2025-02-20.
3 Gibson, Richard. "The unique harm of Bramhall's liver branding." *Prindle Post*. March 22, 2024. Available at: www.prindleinstitute.org/2024/03/the-unique-harm-of-bramhalls-liver-branding.
4 BBC News. "'Liver branding' surgeon Simon Bramhall fined £10,000." January 12, 2018. Available at: www.bbc.co.uk/news/uk-england-birmingham-42663518.
5 Rinde, Meir. "The death of Jesse Gelsinger, 20 years later." *Distillations Magazine*. June 4, 2019. Available at: www.sciencehistory.org/stories/magazine/the-death-of-jesse-gelsinger-20-years-later.
6 Wilson, Robin Fretwell. "The death of Jesse Gelsinger: New evidence of the influence of money and prestige in human research." *American Journal of Law & Medicine* 36.2–3 (2010): 295–325.
7 Wagner, Kurt. "Here's how Facebook allowed Cambridge Analytica to get data for 50 million users." *Vox*. March 17, 2018. Available at: www.vox.com/2018/3/17/17134072/facebook-cambridge-analytica-trump-explained-user-data.
8 Way, Katie. "I went on a date with Aziz Ansari. It turned into the worst night of my life." January 13, 2018. Available at: https://babe.net/2018/01/13/aziz-ansari-28355.
9 Crary, David and Tamara Lush. "Has #MeToo gone too far? Ansari story sparks debate." *The Washington Post*. January 18, 2018.
10 For an accessible introduction to foundational questions of ethics, we recommend Rachels, James, and Stuart Rachels. *The elements of moral philosophy*, 7th edition. McGraw Hill, 2012.
11 Voorhoeve, Alex. *Conversations on ethics*. Oxford University Press, 2009: 3.
12 The philosophical method we describe here is called reflective equilibrium. After subjecting our intuitions and values to critical scrutiny and eliminating those that are obviously biased or otherwise unreliable, this methodology brings together our considered judgements and our values and attempts to bring them into an acceptable coherence. One of us has described and defended this philosophical methodology elsewhere, but we are both disciples of it in this book. See DeGrazia, David, and Joseph Millum. *A theory of bioethics*. Cambridge University Press, 2021: ch. 2.

Part I Consent theory

2 What is consent?

1. Introduction

By giving consent, we change our rights and others' duties—making it permissible for them to do something that was previously forbidden. To some, this ability to transform our normative situation with such a simple act has seemed "magical."[1] Heidi Hurd writes:

> consent turns a trespass into a dinner party; a battery into a handshake; a theft into a gift; an invasion of privacy into an intimate moment; a commercial appropriation of name and likeness into a biography.[2]

It is natural to wonder about the nature of this extraordinary ability.

Once we start thinking about the nature of consent, a number of distinct questions arise. Some concern what is *possible.* Are there limits to what someone can give consent to? Or can we waive every one of our rights? Some others concern *scope.* How do we know what we consent to when we give consent? Is it just whatever we intend to permit? Or could I accidentally give consent? Others concern *ontology*. Is consent an act? If so, what sort of act—is it purely mental or must we communicate to give consent? Still others concern moral *force*. Does consent always make an act permissible? How bad are non-consensual acts?

These are philosophically perplexing questions, as we will see. But they are not only of philosophical interest; they have practical implications too. Take the question of what it is possible to consent to. In 1990, a group of men in the UK were convicted of offences, including for assault, as a result of their participation in sado-masochistic sexual acts. The accused argued that everyone involved had consented to these acts, but their arguments were dismissed. Their consent to harm was treated as irrelevant. This judgment was affirmed on appeal by the House of Lords, which agreed that consent was not a valid defense to assault.[3]

This chapter aims to make progress on the overarching question—what is consent?—by examining different answers to all the above questions. While we leave some open for the reader's judgment, we commit to answers on others that will inform how we approach the rest of the book. In particular, we argue that consent is the performance of an act which signifies the waiving of a right (or sometimes its alienation or transfer). Consent is *valid* when it successfully waives (or alienates

DOI: 10.4324/9781003287391-3

or transfers) that right. The question of what makes consent valid or invalid will occupy us throughout the rest of the book.

We begin by distinguishing two ways in which the term "consent" gets used and clarify our focus on it as a way of giving permission. We then explain validity and argue that this is the foundational concept for thinking about the ethics of consent. Since giving valid consent involves exercising a right, we turn next to the structure of rights and present a common terminology for talking about them. Consent is one of our so-called "normative powers," along with promising, commanding, forgiving, and the like. For all these normative powers, we can ask what grounds or justifies them. Doing so can help us make progress with challenging philosophical questions regarding the powers. Along with some ideas about how the power to consent is grounded in the value of autonomy, we address what the act of consenting is, how the scope of what someone has consented to is determined, and what effects consent has. We close the chapter by discussing how bad nonconsensual acts are and whether there are any limits to what competent adults can consent to.

2. What does consent do?

The best place to start, in working out what consent *is*, is to clarify what it does. The language of consent is ambiguous between two main meanings, which have quite different ethical and legal implications.[4] One meaning of consent is to take on duties. For example, if you "consent" to give a toast at someone's wedding, then you have effectively promised to do so. This *promissory consent* is not the main subject matter of this book, but it is worth bearing it in mind, since one's linguistic intuitions about consent may be led astray by it. The other main meaning is to give someone else permission. For example, when a patient gives consent to an appendectomy, he permits the surgeon to perform acts that she was previously forbidden to perform. This *permissive consent* is what we are interested in.

When permissive consent is successfully given, the person giving it exercises a right. For example, our patient exercises his right over his body to permit the surgeon to cut and sew his abdomen. Consent often constitutes temporarily *waiving* a right. This means that the permission granted can be revoked when the consent giver chooses.[5] For example, someone who has consented to sex can decide against continuing at any point and revoke the permission they gave. But not all permissions can be revoked like this. I might lend you a book for a week—in which case I would have to ask permission if I wanted it back earlier. At the extreme, sometimes we *alienate* or *transfer* our rights over something. If I gift you the book, then I lose all my rights over it and you gain the rights of ownership that I once had. This transfer of rights is also sometimes described as consent.[6]

3. Validity as a foundational concept

When permissive consent is successful, we label it as valid. Valid consent successfully *waives* (or *alienates* or *transfers*) the consent giver's right. Some writers question the importance of validity. For example, Franklin G. Miller and Alan Wertheimer argue that what matters in consent transactions is whether they are *morally transformative* and that can come apart from whether the consent is valid. They illustrate their view with the following example.

> *Lawn Blower.* A asks B whether he can borrow B's lawn blower, about which (unbeknownst to A) B is quite proprietary. B mistakenly thinks that A has asked to borrow [her] lawn mower, about which [s]he is not proprietary. B says, "Sure, it's in my garage; help yourself when you need it."[7]

In cases like this, Miller and Wertheimer say, our intuitions about the validity of consent can go either way—we might think consent was valid or we might think consent is invalid. Nevertheless, we are likely to agree that A—who we will call Alexei—is permitted to borrow the lawn blower. Either consent is valid and so Alexei can take it, or consent is invalid, but Alexei is innocent of the invalidity and so can take it. The validity of consent is not what does the work here, what matters is the permissibility of Alexei proceeding. Miller and Wertheimer propose an alternative model of consent transactions, which they call the *fair transactions* model:

> A is morally permitted to proceed on the basis of a consent transaction if A has treated B fairly and responds in a reasonable manner to B's token or expression of consent or what A reasonably believes is B's token or expression of consent.[8]

We remain convinced that talk of validity should not be jettisoned. The concept of validity is foundational, even in cases like those Miller and Wertheimer describe. To see this, consider an alternative explanation for why Alexei is permitted to take the lawn blower: he has good reason to think that B—who we will call Beatriz—gave valid consent. If Alexei knew that Beatriz had misheard, then he would not have permission to take the blower. Why? Because Beatriz's consent would not have been valid. Though Alexei's evidence—what he has reason to believe—is what determines the permissibility of his action, the evidence is evidence *about* whether Beatriz's consent was valid.

The centrality of validity to our ethical thinking about consent can be seen even more clearly when we think about cases in which the effects of consent can be reversed. Suppose that Alexei asked to keep Beatriz's lawn blower and Beatriz agreed. Later, she realizes the mistake and points out that he misheard the request and wants her blower back. Whether Alexei or Beatriz is the rightful owner clearly turns on whether the consent was valid in the first place.

Validity is the foundational concept around which our discussion centers throughout this book. We explore the theoretical question of what is required for valid consent by analyzing ways in which consent can be rendered invalid: through incompetence, through incomplete or misleading information, and through involuntariness. The picture that emerges of what is required for valid consent then informs our discussion of the ethics of consent in practice.

4. The structure of rights

If consent is the exercise of a right, it is important to know how rights work. This issue, in various forms, will occupy us throughout the book. For now, it will be helpful to lay out a common way to understand the structure of rights. This will allow us to state precisely what consent does.

Start with an example with which we are all familiar—owning a physical object. Suppose you own a bicycle. Your property right over the bicycle can be broken down into a number of component rights. First, you are permitted to ride the bicycle on public roads. Other people do not have this privilege. Indeed, second, you have a claim against everyone else that they not ride your bike. Except, third, you can allow other people to ride it. In other words, you have the power to give other people permission to ride your bike—you can lend it to someone. Finally, you are protected against other parties interfering with your rights—there are laws that prevent the bicycle from being confiscated unless due process has been followed.

This way of analyzing the structure of rights was formalized by the legal scholar Wesley Hohfeld.[9] The Hohfeldian system has since been widely adopted by scholars working on legal and moral rights. It analyzes rights as combinations of four types of *incident*: privileges, claims, powers, and immunities. These are defined as follows:[10]

- *A* has a *privilege* to φ if and only if A has no duty not to φ (you are permitted to ride the bike).
- *A* has a *claim* that *B* φ *if and only if B* has a duty to *A* to φ (others are not permitted to ride the bike).
- *A* has a *power if and only if A* has the ability to alter her own or another's Hohfeldian incidents (you can lend other people the bike).
- *B* has an *immunity if and only if A* lacks the ability to alter *B*'s Hohfeldian incidents (the police cannot arbitrarily confiscate the bike).

It is worth noting that the examples given do not exhaust the incidents associated with my property right. For instance, I also have the privilege to paint my bike, the power to sell my bike, and many more. The contours of my property rights are also not as simple as these examples suggest. My privilege to ride the bicycle on public roads, for example, is limited to when I am sober, I am not evading arrest, my brakes are working, and so on.

This vocabulary can help us to state precisely what is going on when someone gives valid permissive consent. *Valid consent* is the exercise of a power in order to waive a claim. So, when the patient gives valid consent to a tooth extraction, they permit their dentist to remove a tooth, where before the consent they had a claim that she not touch them.

5. Normative powers

In the language of the previous section, valid consent involves exercising a power: it changes the consent giver's rights and someone else's duties. The ability to give consent is therefore what philosophers call a *normative power*. Normative powers are "capacities to create normative reasons by our willing or say-so."[11] So, for example, when I consent to you borrowing my bike for the afternoon, I remove a reason you previously had *not* to take my bike for the afternoon. After receiving my consent, the normative situation has changed—you are free to use it. Promising is also a normative power—when you promise to have the bike back to me by 6 p.m., you create a reason you did not have before. After receiving your promise, the normative situation has changed again—you are required to return it by a specific time.

Other normative powers include commanding, whereby one person creates duties in another by virtue of their authority, abandoning, whereby one person relinquishes their rights over something, and forgiving, whereby the wronged party releases the wrongdoer from specific obligations, such as the duty to make amends. All involve acts whose successful performance changes our moral relationships to others. Successful performance involves meeting certain conditions, such as acting voluntarily, possessing necessary mental capacities (competence), and knowing what acts constitute exercising the normative power. It will prove helpful to keep in mind other normative powers when we are discussing consent, since they provide useful analogies and points of comparison.

Regarding all of these normative powers, we can ask what grounds them. In virtue of what do we have this magical ability to alter our normative relationships simply because we decide to do so? Asking this question is not an invitation to skepticism about whether we have such normative powers. At least for the purposes of this book, we assume that competent adults have the power to give consent. Rather, by looking at what justifies ascribing a normative power to someone, we hope to make progress on specific questions about when consent is valid, what is wrong about acting without valid consent, and so on. For example, in Chapter 3, we discuss competence (decision-making capacity). We argue that an account of what makes someone competent to make her own decisions can be defended by looking at what is valuable about making one's own decisions. A person's interest in making their own decisions grounds the power.

Views about what grounds normative powers—like consent—often look at what important values are promoted by the power.[12] In other words, they treat the power to consent as *instrumental* to some other good or goods. Many philosophers appeal to the value of autonomy. For example, Massimo Renzo argues:

> Being able to control the consent-sensitive duties that others owe us is valuable because it increases our capacity to exercise our self-determining agency

> and shape our life as we wish. For example, I can realize the plan of staying healthy by consenting to surgery; I can realize the plan of keeping plants in my apartment by consenting to my neighbor watering them while I'm away; I can realize the plan of feeding my child by consenting to you taking my money in exchange for pizza.[13]

When we are capable of giving consent, we can direct our lives in important ways—ways that protect or further our interests or align with our personal conception of the good. Sometimes we have an interest in protecting ourselves from others, so by refusing to consent, we can leave valuable normative barriers in place. But just as often we want to remove these barriers and allow interactions that further our goals, including in ways that are risky or altruistic—and we can do that by giving consent. In this way, we need to be able to give and refuse consent to live an autonomous life.[14]

Note that in order to facilitate competent individuals directing their own lives, consent must play two roles. The first is that it must support *agency*—people need to be able to give other people permission when it suits them (and refuse permission when that is what they prefer). The other, complementary role, is *publicity*. By communicating my consent to another party, I not only free them from a duty not to interfere with me, I also give them reassurance that it is safe for them to do so. By giving a doctor consent to draw my blood, I both make it permissible for her to do so *and* free her of the risk of wronging me.[15]

As our arguments in other parts of this book show, thinking in terms of the values that ground normative powers, like consent, can be very helpful in making progress on some tricky theoretical and practical questions. However, doing so is unlikely to resolve all the controversial questions regarding that power. That is because there will still be disagreement about exactly how autonomy relates to well-being, how the value of agency should be balanced with that of publicity, and other normative questions. There is no foundational ethical theory that philosophers agree on and so can be use as bedrock for the rest of our ethical judgments. Instead, an account of what grounds the power to consent will be one consideration among others. We will still have to rely on careful conceptual analysis, appeal to intuitions, and the other components of critical thinking about ethics.[16]

6. The act of consenting

So far we have talked about consent as an act. But what sort of act? Here there is a debate between those who think that consent is purely mental (the attitudinal view) and those who think that it requires some sort of behavior outside of the consent giver's mind (the performative view).[17]

Proponents of the attitudinal view vary with respect to what sort of mental state they think consent consists in. Some say that the consent giver must *intend* that the consent receiver engage in the act to which he consents, others that he *acquiesce* in it, and others that he mentally *waives his right* against it.[18] In any case, it is key to the view that no external indication need occur in order for the moral transformation to take place. What would have been a wrongful battery can be made a permissible surgery simply by thinking it so. Of course, there are often external signals that tell others whether consent has been given. It is on the basis of those signals that the recipient of consent can infer whether she is permitted to proceed. But signing a form, nodding agreement, or saying "I consent," are just evidence.

Proponents of performative views deny that these external acts are merely evidence about whether consent has been given. For them, it is essential that some sort of public performance take place. Someone who says "No," has not given valid consent, even if they sincerely hope, intend, or will that the refused act be performed.

How should we decide between the attitudinal and performative views? We will look now at three argumentative strategies that have been used. As well as helping us to decide what the act of consenting consists in, they serve as useful exemplars of types of philosophical argument. The same types of argument will recur throughout this book.

The first way in which supporters of these different views attempt to argue their side is by appeal to cases. Here is one from Larry Alexander:

> … suppose D propositions V for sex within earshot of TP [third party]. V, a foreigner, understands D's request and wants to signify her consent, but her mastery of D's language is poor. She responds to D with a term that in her language means "do it" but which in D's language means "don't." D, believing he lacks V's consent, nonetheless starts fondling V. He is surely culpable for doing so, but he is doing nothing that is without V's consent and therefore wrong. And TP, who understands D's and V's confusion, should not try to stop D.

Setting aside the implausibility of the scenario (how is D not surprised by V's response to his action?), people tend to have quite different reactions to these cases. Philosophers like Alexander think the verdict is obvious (consent is valid) and so treat the case as evidence for attitudinal views; but others endorse the contrary view and deny that V has given valid consent. Since the disputants do not agree about the case, such cases cannot move their discussion forward.[19] Only when there is agreement about the correct verdict to draw can a case be used as evidence in favor of one view over another.

The second argumentative strategy used by both sides is to draw analogies with other normative powers. Defenders of attitudinal views sometimes point to the legal phenomenon of "abandonment," whereby someone relinquishes ownership of a possession without transferring it to anyone else. For example, someone might leave a box of old books on the pavement where they can be taken by anyone who wants them. Abandonment, it is argued, requires no more than the intention to relinquish.[20] Other normative powers seem to require outward performance. Promising, for example, requires not just that the promiser make the promise but arguably that the promise gets uptake. If I am alone in a room and say, "I promise to make Sharon dal and rice for dinner," I acquire no duty to cook. But if I say it to Sharon and she accepts, then I acquire a duty to her. A mental promise is just an intention—it does not do anything normative.

The question then becomes—is consent more like abandonment or more like promising? We think that the analogies approach favors the performative view. First, consent and promising do seem similar. Both are typically dyadic—that is, they involve the rights and duties that two parties have with respect to each other. With consent, the consent giver starts with a right against interference and the receiver a duty not to interfere. By giving consent, she exercises a power to waive that right and so releases the receiver from the duty. With a promise, the promiser creates a duty in themselves and a claim in the promisee. The promisee also acquires a power to release the promiser from the duty. Consent and promises seem like counterparts.[21] By contrast, abandonment does not involve any directed rights or duties—to abandon something is to relinquish one's rights, but there is no one to whom one transfers those rights. In addition, abandonment, unlike consent and promising, only seems to apply to property. Given that the rules around property are primarily a matter of law, which determines what counts as property and what rights we have in what we own, we might be suspicious of whether our ethical intuitions regarding it are to be trusted. Even worse, for attitudinalists who use the abandonment analogy, it is not even true that in the law abandonment is only a mental state. The legal abandonment of property requires both the intention to relinquish ownership and some physical act of relinquishment.[22]

The final strategy for adjudicating between performative and attitudinal views is to look at the function of consent.[23] In the previous section, we talked about how the normative power of consent might be grounded in some important value that it serves. Perhaps consent can best play its role of enabling us to act autonomously or control our normative relationships if it requires a public act. Or perhaps it can best play that role if consent involves only a mental act or state of mind.

The challenge in looking to the function of consent to decide between performative and attitudinal views is twofold. First, proponents of performative views make a compelling case for the importance of other parties knowing whether one has given consent (as noted in the previous section). It is really important, for example, that a surgeon have a reliable signal to tell her she can ethically proceed. But attitudinalists do not need to deny this. Of course, the communication of consent has an important *epistemological* role to play—that is, it helps the consent receiver work out if consent was given.[24] And, of course, the surgeon would be culpable if she proceeded despite lacking evidence of consent. But, they may argue, that tells us nothing about the underlying *ontology*—that is, what really is the case.[25] Second, both views can tell a plausible story about how consent plays an important normative function and promotes important values. Perhaps it is better able to play some role on one view than another. But that will only be decisive if we know how important the various values are. Does it matter more that people are able to waive their rights and so give permission—building relationships and intimacy? If so, perhaps this favors an attitudinal view. Or, does it matter more that people are protected against unauthorized trespasses on their persons and property (and from mistakenly trespassing)? If so, perhaps this favors a performative view.[26]

Our view is that performative views are—on balance—more plausible. We find little appeal in the cases cited by attitudinalists. We find the analogies to other speech acts favor a performative view. We find it very plausible that signaling consent is essential to consent playing its normative role. There seems no particular reason to separate the signaling from the act of consent, except a prior theoretical commitment to an attitudinal view. We also find linguistic intuition favors a performative view. It is striking that the verb "to consent" is applied specifically to the act that signifies consent, not to the mental state that accompanies it.[27]

On this point, as elsewhere in the book, you may disagree with us. We invite you to consider where we may have made errors. Is it that we start from different verdicts about cases or different intuitions about what counts as consent? Is there some error of reasoning that we have committed in laying out the arguments on either side? Or, are we giving too much or too little weight to one type of argumentative strategy over another?

7. Tokening consent

If consent *is* the performance of an act, it is natural to ask next—what act? A moment's reflection suggests that there is no single act that constitutes tokening consent. We can consent by saying, "I consent." But we do not need to be so explicit. If you ask to borrow my bike, a simple "Yes," or just a thumbs up might be sufficient. Consent can be a question—"Would you like to come in?" Or it can be a command—"Come in!" In the right circumstances, it is even possible to token consent by doing nothing. The Chair of a meeting might ask if there are any objections to a proposed change in their society's rules, pause, and then say, "Hearing none, I'll take that as consent." Here the members present, assuming that they are aware and voluntarily silent, have given *tacit consent*.[28]

What we can say is that one tokens consent through a speech act that signifies consent in the context in which it is performed. *Speech act* is a technical term. A speech act is, roughly, an act that is performed by doing something with a particular *meaning*, where that meaning is conventionally defined. Speech acts do not have to be spoken. So, for example, "I quit!" said in a sincere tone to one's boss is an act of resigning; equally, waving a white flag in a context of war is a request to parley. But they only have their specific meanings because of the conventions of communication mutually understood by the parties involved. There is no reason why waving a white flag could not mean "I quit!" except that by convention it does not. The examples given in the last paragraph are all examples of speech acts which signify consent. All have this significance only because of convention and in the specific context in which the convention gives them the meaning of "I consent." For example, "Yes," is only a token of consent when it is a response to a question.[29]

Note that when giving consent we sometimes also perform other speech acts at the same time. For example, someone might make a request that also tokens consent, such as "Kiss me!" or "Please come in!" They might even exercise other normative powers through the same speech act. For example, I might agree to the terms of a contract that involve the assignment of both rights and duties. If I describe the act of signing the contract as giving "consent" I am then using consent in two different senses—the promissory and the permissive (section 2) and exercising two corresponding normative powers.

8. Does the act of consent require uptake?

A final contentious question regarding the nature of the act of consenting concerns *uptake*. In the normal case, a promise is effective only if it gets uptake from the promisee. Muttering, "I promise to take Michael dancing," in a room on one's own does not create a duty; the promise must be successfully communicated to Michael. Does the same apply to consent? That is, does the recipient of consent need to know that consent has been given?

The same argumentative strategies can be applied to answering this question as with the debate between attitudinal and performative views. We can look at cases, at analogous powers, and at the function that would be served if valid consent required (or did not require) uptake. However, we think that these strategies yield a less certain verdict than they do when applied to the previous debate.

Consider the following pair of cases. First, suppose Ms. Gardener puts a sign on their grass that says, "Walking on this lawn permitted." Someone fails to read the sign, but still walks across the lawn. Have they trespassed?[30] It is natural to say that they have not. Certainly, we would want the law to treat this as though Ms. Gardener had unilaterally given permission to the public. Now, consider instead a medical example. Suppose a dentist started a routine filling only to discover that several teeth are rotten and need extraction. She asks: "Are you okay with me pulling them right now while you're numb? Or should we wait and talk over the options later?" "Go ahead now," croaks her patient, but the dentist is rattling her instruments and doesn't hear. Clearly, the dentist ought not to proceed without checking again, since she does not have *evidence* that the patient has consented. In addition, it seems natural to say that the attempt to give consent failed—it was not successfully communicated.[31]

It is also possible to find analogies to support either view. Promising, as noted, seems to be a normative power where uptake is required. At the very least, a promise must be successfully communicated to the promisee; arguably, they also have to accept it. Commanding also seems to require uptake. On the other hand, it is definitely possible to abandon one's possessions without anyone knowing about it.

Likewise, looking at the function of consent will give different verdicts depending on which functions we judge most valuable. The interest people have in agency might support saying that uptake is not required. The interests people have in public accountability and intimate relationships might support saying that it is.[32]

One possibility is that uptake is needed for some consent acts but not others.[33] For example, it would be consistent with our examples to say that consent must be successfully communicated when it is directed at identifiable individuals and not when directed to the public at large. Or, it might be that there are ways one can consent to the use of property that do not apply to the use of one's body.

Though we are inclined to the view that uptake is required, we are less confident in this case, since the arguments either way seem more evenly balanced. At the very least, however, we are confident that consent requires some sort of public expression.[34] And someone who acts without good evidence that they have valid consent will typically act wrongly, since they will not have evidence that they have permission, even if they in fact do.

9. The scope of consent

Suppose someone has successfully performed a speech act that signifies giving consent. Valid consent to *something* may have been given, but the exact scope of that consent may still be debatable. For example, medical researchers often take biological samples from their participants and store them for later experiments. At the time of collection, they might not have known what they would want to do with the samples in the future. In fact, sometimes novel experiments have only become possible because of technological advances that were not foreseen at the time of sample collection. Getting specific consent for these new experiments might be difficult or impossible. It is therefore important to know what decides the scope of the original consent.

One view on scope is that it is a matter of intention. I consent to all and only those acts that I intend to consent to.[35] If this were right, we would have to investigate what research participants intended to allow the researchers to do with their samples. Of course, the participants could not have intended the exact experiments, since no one knew about those experiments at the time of consent. But perhaps their intentions could be more general—intending that the researchers carry out research on their disease, or for the greater good, or, maybe, intending that the researchers carry out whatever studies they liked!

However, fixing the scope of consent according to the intentions of the consent giver will not work. Innocent mistakes can lead to someone giving valid consent to an action whose scope is outside what they intend. For example, you ask if you can borrow my mandolin for a week and I say yes. I intend to have the mandolin back before my aunt's birthday so that I can play for her, but I am mixed up about the dates—her birthday is only five days away. Nonetheless, I agreed to a week and when you do not drop off the mandolin before her birthday I have only myself to blame. Here my intentions are inconsistent, but the scope of my consent is clear—it is determined by what I told you, not what I meant to permit.

Some alternative views hold that the scope of consent is fixed by conversational, social, or cultural conventions.[36] As conventions are public, these views avoid the problems that plague intentions views, but they get into difficulty when the conventions that determine the scope of consent are not shared by consenting parties. Imagine that upon moving to a different country, Sacha invites their new colleagues over for dinner. While they prepare the appetizers, they say to their guests, "Just make yourselves comfortable." One of their guests does so by lighting up a cigarette. Let us suppose that regional conventions imply that you may smoke indoors, but Sacha may not have known this, and not intended it or thought that they were implicating it when they issued their invitation. If a conventions view is correct, then Sacha has consented to something without understanding the scope of their consent.

We think that a closely related view is correct. The scope of consent is fixed by what is successfully communicated by the consent giver.[37] The meaning of a word is not decided by an individual speaker—it depends on how the word is used within a community of language users. We suggest, therefore, that the scope of consent is fixed by the *meaning* of the speech act through which consent is given and not the speaker's intentions. This might lead to some surprises, as it does when Sacha comes to realize that "Just make yourselves comfortable" includes a wider range of permissible activities than they had intended to permit. Upon seeing the guest pull out their cigarettes, Sacha may need to redraw the contours of consent—"Actually, would you mind smoking on the balcony?"—or, if the guest suspects that the conventions differ, then they should check what has been permitted—"Are you okay with me smoking indoors?" The meaning of the speech act is determined by the linguistic community of which the individual is a part. In the case of the mandolin, saying "Yes" to the question "May I borrow your mandolin for a week?" means "You may borrow my mandolin for a week." That is therefore the scope of the permission given. In this way consent is no different than other speech acts. What we promise or command is not a matter of what we intend, but a matter of what our acts *mean*. If I know the conventions around promising and voluntarily say, "I promise to play 'Happy Birthday' for you," then I acquire a duty to play "Happy Birthday" for you. What I *intend* is neither here nor there.

We say more about the conditions for successful communication in Chapter 4, when we discuss what needs to be understood in order to give valid consent. There we engage the question of broad consent to the use of biological samples at greater length.

10. The effects of consent

We have considered what consent is and what determines its scope. But what does it do? Consent can transform the moral status of an act. But even valid consent does not always do this. Suppose a married man agrees to sex with someone who is not his spouse. He is not in an open relationship. His new lover's consent may then be valid but he should still not have sex.[38] Or suppose a patient finds himself very attracted to his psychotherapist and proposes sex.[39] Whatever her inclinations, the psychotherapist ought to decline. By taking on the individual as a patient she has acquired a professional obligation to refrain from acts like this that may be harmful to her patient or impede the therapy.[40]

These examples suggest two types of case in which valid consent can fail to make an act permissible. One is where there are duties owed to third parties. The other is where there are duties owed to the person giving consent, which cannot be waived.

In both types of case, we can explain what is going on in the same way. Valid consent waives a claim-right. That right no longer stands in the way of the act being permissible. But an act may be impermissible for multiple reasons.[41] It would be wrong to kiss someone without their permission and it would be wrong if doing so would break a promise. Valid consent to the kiss only removes the possible wrong to the consent giver, not the wrong to his spouse. Likewise, a patient cannot waive his psychotherapist's professional obligation, since that is grounded in the patient-clinician relationship. He can only waive his bodily rights against being touched and that is not enough to render sex with his therapist permissible.[42] As Onora O'Neill puts it: "Informed consent is one tip of the ethical iceberg: those who think otherwise overlook the rest of the iceberg."[43] In brief, valid consent suspends one duty and in many cases—but not all—thereby gives someone permission.

11. How bad are non-consensual acts?

Non-consensual penetrative sex and non-consensual kissing are both wrongful. Yet the first is surely worse than the second. What explains this difference?

One answer is that rape is normally much worse for its victim than an unwanted kiss. The traumatic experience of rape and its aftermath dwarfs any discomfort, annoyance, or sense of violation that might accompany a kiss. The harm experienced by the victim is surely part of the explanation of why one act is more wrongful than the other. Yet, it cannot be the whole picture.

To see why, consider how we would judge an act of unconsented sex of which the victim had no experience and no knowledge even after the fact.[44] They experience no harm and yet we would be loth to say that no wrong was done. Indeed, we may think that the wrong is still worse than some quite aversive experiences—such as receiving an unwanted slap on the buttocks, for example. This difference needs to be explained or some argument given for why our initial response to the cases is mistaken.

One possibility is that what makes a particular act wrongful is not the actual harm that results but the harm that is *expected* to result.[45] Attempted murder, it might be argued, is just as wrongful whether it succeeds or not. Since the perpetrator of an unconsented act cannot know that his actions will be harmless—cannot reasonably expect that his victim will never find out and never experience negative consequences—he does not get off the hook if matters turn out that way. But this still does not solve the problem. We can at least imagine cases where the perpetrator is justifiably very confident about the likely effects of his actions. Consider, for example, someone who is alone with a patient in a persistent vegetative state. He may be confident that there will be no traces of the undignified things he does to their body, yet we would likely still judge them wrongful.

One way to explain what is going on here is to say that someone can be harmed without experiencing the harm. We might think, for example, that it is bad for someone if she is secretly despised by her so-called friends or if she is remembered after her death only for her misdeeds. Her life goes worse, even if she never knows about it. It goes worse because she has interests in close friendships and in having a good reputation. Along these lines, it is plausible that we have interests in bodily integrity and sexual integrity that are independent of our beliefs about them.[46] Unconsented infringements of our rights can be harmful because they set back these interests, independent of other harms that are caused.

Non-consensual acts could also be wrong because they are disrespectful (or degrading). If someone is autonomous and so has the right to make their own decisions, then it is disrespectful to ignore their choices. It is wrong to override a competent person's decisions for their own good—to act paternalistically (see Chapter 3). Doing so treats them like a child. To override someone's decisions in a way that disregards their well-being or harms them is even worse. Doing so treats them like they do not matter morally at all. This failure of respect is a serious wrong, in addition to any harms it causes.[47]

This brief discussion allows us to identify what makes non-consensual acts wrong. It also gives us a framework for analyzing the gravity of the rights violation involved—that is, how wrong they are. Non-consensual acts are *prima facie* wrongful because they violate rights. These violations are worse when more harm accompanies the rights violation. The harm can be intrinsic to the violation—for example, because it sets back the person's interest in bodily integrity. But the act can also cause other harms that exacerbate the wrong—for example, pain, distress, and fear. Non-consensual acts are also worse insofar as they are more disrespectful. They will be more disrespectful the more they imply a devaluation of the other's status (treating them as a child or as an object).[48] Finally, some rights are more important than others. For example, bodily rights are, on the whole, more important than property rights. How bad a violation is will also vary with the importance of the right—either because that makes the harm intrinsic to the rights violation bigger or because the disrespect of the violation is therefore greater.[49]

This framework can explain why non-consensual sex is worse than a non-consensual kiss. Not only will the experiential harm usually be greater, but the intrinsic harm involved in violating someone's sexual integrity through unconsented penetrative sex is greater. Moreover, it matters much more to a person whom they have sex with than who kisses them. That fact makes the failure to respect their decision about sex much worse than the failure to respect their decision about kisses.

The framework can also be helpful in thinking about when it is justifiable to act without someone's consent. Most people think that at least some rights have thresholds.[50] This means that it can sometimes be justifiable to override someone's right if the consequences of doing so are sufficiently important.[51] For example, consider laws that require doctors or laboratories to report diagnoses of infectious diseases, such as syphilis.[52] Even though this involves overriding a patient's right to control their medical information, these laws might be justified if they help track the spread of diseases and so protect other people.[53] The framework is relevant to identifying the threshold for permissibly infringing someone's rights: it will be higher, the worse it would be to violate the right.[54]

12. The limits of consent

Thus far, we have discussed only acts for which valid consent is possible. But are there some acts that one simply cannot give consent to—that is some rights that one cannot waive? Take the case of Armin Meiwes, who was convicted of murder in 2006 for killing and partially eating another man.[55] Meiwes had a defense: the victim had consented to being eaten and there was a videotape to prove it.[56] This argument ultimately failed in court, but should it have been allowed?

Some scholars argue that our interests somehow limit what we can consent to. For example, David Owens thinks that consent and other normative powers are grounded in our *normative interests*—interests in being able to control whether we and others have particular duties or permissions. For instance, sometimes it is good for me to be able to decide whether a particular action will wrong me. Owens illustrates:

> Think of the difference between a lover's bite and a rapist's. Purely qua physical injury, they are on a par but one exacerbates the wrong of rape whilst the other may enhance the good of sex. Since for many lovers being able to control whether you are bitten is a good thing, their choice turns the bite into a good thing. By contrast, lobotomization or (voluntary) enslavement can't be good in the same way whether chosen or not.[57]

On a view like Owens's, it is only possible to consent to an act, if doing so could be in one's interests. But it cannot be in your interests to make it permissible for someone to lobotomize or enslave you. That limits the possible scope of consent.[58] Recall the men prosecuted for sado-masochism that we mentioned in the introduction. On a view like this, whether they were innocent of wrongful harm depends on whether the harms could be overall in their interests. This would depend on both how valuable it is to be able to let others hurt one for sexual gratification and how bad the injuries would be. There would eventually be a point at which an injury would be too serious for consent to permit it.[59]

One challenge for these interest-based views is that they tie what someone can consent to very closely to what is good for them. However, there are many cases in which people appear to act autonomously in ways that are contrary to their interests, including through giving or refusing consent. Consider, for example, someone who recognizes the good they could do through donating their wealth to charity and decides they ought to do what they can to alleviate suffering. They sell most of their possessions and adopt a life of relative poverty so that they can give away as much money as possible. Their actions might be excessively altruistic and contrary to their own well-being, but there seems no reason to question the validity of their consent to transfer property. Or, consider the sincere religious believer who refuses a life-saving blood transfusion because they think it is forbidden. Provided that they are competent, informed, and unpressured, such refusals are typically respected.[60] Further, interest-based views struggle to explain bad decisions. We typically think that competent adults can give valid consent, even when by doing so they are making a mistake. I might regret the enormous tattoo I request—and that regret might be fully predictable by the tattoo artist who agrees to ink me—yet by giving me the tattoo she does not violate my rights. Consent in such cases seems valid, even when it is a bad idea.

One possible response would be to distinguish between the value to someone of having a choice and the value of any particular option chosen. It is beneficial to be able to decide what to do with one's money, for instance, even though some uses of that freedom might be contrary to one's interests. This response might deal with some cases. However, it will struggle with cases of extreme altruism or piety—these decisions seem self-sacrificing even if we think there are benefits to having the freedom to make them. Cases like these therefore lead us to doubt that considerations of wellbeing (or interests) put substantive limits on consent.

Though we do not think that what we can consent to is limited by our interests, we do think there are conceptual limits: there are some acts that it simply would not make sense to say someone consented to.

First, and most obviously, someone can only give consent when they have a claim right to exercise. I cannot lend someone your bike because I do not have rights over the bike to begin with. (One religious objection to suicide or euthanasia runs along similar lines: I cannot give up my life because it is not mine to give.)

Second, there are ways that rights cannot be exercised because it would be physically impossible. I cannot give away my blood to someone while it is in my body, since they could not exercise their new property rights without violating other rights of mine. There is no such problem with giving away a blood sample once it has been removed. So, I cannot alienate parts of myself that are still attached.[61] We might be able to contract to give them away at some future point, of course (agreeing to give blood, or to act as a gestational surrogate). But such contracts are a matter of promissory consent, not just permissive consent. There may be many promises that we cannot make or that third parties should not enforce.

Third, there are some acts whose normative status cannot be changed by consent. Suppose I have a right against you that you not treat me unfairly. It makes no sense to say that I could waive that right: the result of the rights waiver would be that I give you permission to treat me unfairly. But that means that the treatment would still be unfair! To illustrate, consider a case of price gouging. I might agree to pay someone £100 for an umbrella when caught in a downpour on the way to an important interview. This, let us assume, is an exploitative price. It might be that my consent to the transaction is valid.[62] Yet the consent does not and cannot make the exchange a fair one.

Further, even if it is possible to consent to some act, it does not follow that the act is ethically unproblematic. As we noted in section 10, some acts are impermissible, even with valid consent. Moreover, if someone agrees to a very harmful act, and if we cannot make sense of why she would agree, that in itself seems like evidence something has gone wrong with the consent process.[63] Perhaps she has misunderstood what is proposed or actually lacks the capacity to make her own decisions. And finally, what is ethically possible is not the same as what should be legally permitted or enforced. There may be good reasons to have laws that protect some people, even if they also involve paternalistic interference.[64] For example, we have laws restricting what medicines can be sold and by whom. These impede some people from taking drugs that they might freely choose to take; but many people think that their protective effects justify any restrictions on liberty.

Taking all these points on board, could someone give valid consent to be cannibalized? We think, in principle, yes. Each act by the cannibal involves a rights-waiver that could be voluntarily and knowingly agreed to. This includes the disposition of their body after death. Being killed and eaten would be very bad for the victim, but that is not sufficient to show that the consent would be invalid. Nevertheless, that does not settle the matter for cases like Meiwes. Given what he agreed to, we should be very worried that Meiwes's victim did not actually have capacity to make this decision himself. Even if he could, it might still be wrong of Meiwes to take advantage of him and kill him as he did. And laws against consensual cannibalism might be a very good idea (despite the interference with the autonomy of would-be cannibals and their dinners). Here, again, you may disagree with us. We invite you to consider why.

13. Conclusions

This chapter has covered a lot of ground. We looked at the structure of rights, the values that underlie our normative power to consent, and the nature of the act that constitutes giving consent. We then considered what fixes the scope of someone's consent, what effects it has, and how bad it is to act without someone's consent. Finally, we asked whether there are some rights that cannot be waived by giving consent.

Throughout, we have been focused on the question of *validity*—whether a speech act successfully waives (or transfers or alienates) someone's rights. In the chapters that follow, we analyze the conditions under which consent is rendered valid or invalid. We begin with the capacities that an individual must have if they are to be able to give consent.

Notes

1 Hurd, Heidi M. "The moral magic of consent." *Legal Theory* 2.2 (1996): 121–146.
2 Hurd, Heidi M. "The moral magic of consent." *Legal Theory* 2.2 (1996): 123.
3 *R v. Brown* [1993] 2 All ER 75.

4 Cf. Healey, Richard. "Consent, rights, and reasons for action." *Criminal Law and Philosophy* 13.3 (2019): 499–500; Simmons, A. John. "Tacit consent and political obligation." *Philosophy & Public Affairs* (1976): 275–276.
5 Cf. Sun, Angela. "Can consent be irrevocable?" *Philosophers' Imprint*, forthcoming.
6 Hallie Liberto labels these "authority-retaining," "authority-suspending," and "authority-extinguishing" forms of consent. Liberto, Hallie. *Green light ethics: A theory of permissive consent and its moral metaphysics*. Oxford University Press, 2022: 35–38.
7 Miller, Franklin G., and Alan Wertheimer. "Preface to a theory of consent transactions: Beyond valid consent." In Franklin G. Miller and Alan Wertheimer (eds.), *The ethics of consent: Theory and practice*. Oxford University Press, 2010: 85–86.
8 Miller, Franklin G., and Alan Wertheimer. "Preface to a theory of consent transactions: Beyond valid consent." In Franklin G. Miller and Alan Wertheimer (eds.), *The ethics of consent: Theory and practice*. Oxford University Press, 2010: 81.
9 Hohfeld, W. *Fundamental legal conceptions*, ed. W. Cook. Yale University Press, 1919.
10 Wenar, Leif. "Rights." *The Stanford Encyclopedia of Philosophy* (Spring 2023 edition), ed. Edward N. Zalta and Uri Nodelman, section 2.1.
11 Chang, Ruth. "Do we have normative powers?" *Aristotelian Society Supplementary Volume* 94.1 (2020): 275.
12 The alternative route, which we do not pursue here, is to ground autonomy rights in respect for our status as self-governing entities. See, e.g., discussion in Schaber, P. "Consent and wronging a person." In Andreas Müller and Peter Schaber (eds.), *The Routledge handbook of the ethics of consent*. Routledge, 2018: 59f.
13 Renzo, Massimo. "Defective normative powers: The case of consent." *Journal of Practical Ethics* 10.1 (2022): 52.
14 Compare Dougherty, Tom. "Yes means yes: Consent as communication." *Philosophy & Public Affairs* 43.3 (2015): 224–253. While most philosophers who ground normative powers in the value of autonomy do so in the way we describe, some identify even more specific interests. For example, David Owens hones in on a very specific interest that he thinks normative powers are uniquely able to promote—*normative interests*, which are interests human persons have in controlling the normative relationships in which they stand to other people. According to Owens: "What grounds the power of consent is our interest in having control over the normative situation and in particular our permissive interest, our interest in its being the case that such things as rape and trespass wrong us unless we declare otherwise." (Owens, David. *Shaping the normative landscape*. Oxford University Press, 2012: 2.) Identifying this permissive interest, for Owens, allows us to make sense of how we can be wronged by someone who acts without our consent, even if they do not harm us.
15 Bolinger, Renée Jorgensen. "Moral risk and communicating consent." *Philosophy & Public Affairs* 47.2 (2019): 179–207.
16 For more discussion of problems with the "appeal to values" approach, see Liberto, Hallie. *Green light ethics: A theory of permissive consent and its moral metaphysics*. Oxford University Press, 2022: 19–25.
17 Both have alternative labels, e.g., the attitudinal view may also be called a "mental state view" (e.g., Renzo, Massimo. "Defective normative powers: The case of consent." *Journal of Practical Ethics* 10.1 (2022): 49) or a "subjective view" (e.g., Wertheimer, Alan. *Consent to sexual relations*. Cambridge University Press, 2003: 144), the performative view may also be called a "behavioral view" or a "communicationist" view (Goodin, Robert E. "Consent as an act of commitment." *European Journal of Philosophy* 32 (2024): 194–209). A third possibility is a hybrid view according to which consent comprises both a mental state and some external behavior. For example, Victor Tadros claims that "X's consent typically involves an attempt to communicate to Y that Y is released from their duty not to do some of those things, where that attempted communication involves an intent to permit Y to be released from those duties." (Tadros, Victor. "Beyond the scope of consent." *Philosophy & Public Affairs* 50 (2022): 433.) Since valid consent is impossible without certain mental states, as we will see over the course of this book, we treat performative and hybrid views as falling under the same category (cf. Schnüriger, Hubert, "What is consent?" In Andreas Müller and Peter Schaber (eds.), *The Routledge handbook of the ethics of consent*. Routledge, 2018: 21–31).

18 Alexander, Larry. "The ontology of consent." *Analytic Philosophy* 55.1 (2014): 107.
19 Millum, Joseph, and Danielle Bromwich. "Understanding, communication, and consent." *Ergo* 5.2 (2018): 62–63.
20 See, e.g., Ferzan, Kimberly Kessler. "Consent, culpability, and the law of rape." *Ohio State Journal of Criminal Law* 13.2 (2016): 403–404.
21 For extensive discussion of this analogy, see Dougherty, Tom. "Yes means yes: Consent as communication." *Philosophy & Public Affairs* 43.3 (2015): 232–236.
22 For the US, see citations in Ferzan, Kimberly Kessler. "Consent, culpability, and the law of rape." *Ohio State Journal of Criminal Law* 13.2 (2016): 404, n30. For the UK, see, e.g., *Robot Arenas Ltd & Anor v. Waterfield & Anor* [2010] EWHC 115 (QB) (08 February 2010).
23 Cf. Bolinger, Renée Jorgensen. "Moral risk and communicating consent." *Philosophy & Public Affairs* 47.2 (2019): 179–207.
24 Epistemology is the study of knowledge.
25 For discussion, see Schnüriger, Hubert, "What is consent?" In Andreas Müller and Peter Schaber (eds.), *The Routledge handbook of the ethics of consent*. Routledge, 2018: 26–28.
26 Cf. Liberto, Hallie. *Green light ethics: A theory of permissive consent and its moral metaphysics*. Oxford University Press, 2022: 23–25.
27 Millum, Joseph, and Danielle Bromwich. "Understanding, communication, and consent." *Ergo* 5.2 (2018): 62.
28 Simmons, A. John. "Tacit consent and political obligation." *Philosophy & Public Affairs* (1976): 278–281.
29 "As a first approximation, speech acts are those acts that can (though need not) be performed by saying that one is doing so. On this conception, resigning, promising, asserting and asking are all speech acts, while convincing, insulting and growing six inches are not." Green, Mitchell. "Speech acts." *The Stanford Encyclopedia of Philosophy* (Fall 2021 edition), ed. Edward N. Zalta.
30 The example is due to Tom Dougherty (*The scope of consent*. Oxford University Press, 2021: 79–81). Dougherty also raises a concern that if uptake is required then this raises a problem for refusing consent in some circumstances (p. 79). Following Rae Langton, they argue that if men believe the rape myth that women are not genuinely refusing when they say "No," to sex, then it may be impossible for women to communicate refusal. (Langton, R. 1993. "Speech acts and unspeakable acts," *Philosophy and Public Affairs* 22.4: 293–330.) If uptake is required to refuse, then this means that they cannot successfully refuse. That implication would be very troubling. We do not pursue this idea here, since we think it is problematic in several ways. First, it suggests that the default is that a man is permitted to have sex with a woman, unless she refuses. But this gets matters the wrong way round—there is a duty not to have sex unless consent has been given. Second, even if applied only to women who gave consent and then changed their mind, we are not convinced that men who state this myth really think that consent cannot be revoked. Rather, we think they are engaged in highly motivated reasoning in order to justify behavior that they know is wrongful. Third, as we discuss in the next section, what is meant by a speech act is not up to individuals, but depends on the community of speakers. "No," means no, even if an individual denies that it does. If that refusal is communicated then consent will be revoked. Cf. Jacobson, Daniel. "Freedom of speech acts? A response to Langton." *Philosophy & Public Affairs* (1995): 64–79.
31 Compare Millum, Joseph, and Danielle Bromwich. "Understanding, communication, and consent." *Ergo* 5 (2018).
32 Raty, Anni. "The value of uptake." *Journal of Ethics & Social Philosophy* 27 (2024): 424–442.
33 Raty, Anni. "The value of uptake." *Journal of Ethics & Social Philosophy* 27 (2024): 435–436, 439–440.
34 Suppose that Ms. Gardener wrote the sign, but forgot to put it out and left it in the shed. In that case, it seems to us that she has not granted permission and anyone walking on the lawn would still be trespassing.
35 Dougherty, Tom. "Sex, lies, and consent." *Ethics* 123.4 (2013): 734. Cf. Hurd, Heidi M. "The moral magic of consent." *Legal theory* 2.2 (1996): 125–126.
36 See, e.g., Tilton, Emily C. R., and Jonathan Jenkins Ichikawa. "Not what I agreed to: Content and consent." *Ethics* 132.1 (2021): 127–154.
37 Millum, Joseph, and Danielle Bromwich. "Understanding, communication, and consent." *Ergo* 5 (2018).

38 Hurd, Heidi, "The normative force of consent." In Andreas Müller and Peter Schaber (eds.), *The Routledge handbook of the ethics of consent*. Routledge, 2018: 39.
39 Wertheimer, Alan. *Consent to sexual relations*. Cambridge University Press, 2003: 123.
40 Perry, Clifton, and Joan Wallman Kuruc. "Psychotherapists' sexual relationships with their patients." *Annals Health L.* 2 (1993): 35–38. See also the literature on the ethics of professor student relationships, for example, Srinivasan, Amia. "Sex as a pedagogical failure." *Yale LJ* 129 (2019): 1100–1146.
41 Cf. Healey, Richard. "Consent, rights, and reasons for action." *Criminal Law and Philosophy* 13.3 (2019): 499–500.
42 This analysis can be extended in a straightforward way to consent given on someone else's behalf, such as when a surrogate decision-maker decides on behalf of a non-competent patient (Chapter 6). There may be duties owed to third parties or to the patient that cannot be waived by the surrogate decision-maker and which thereby stop consent alone from making an act permissible.
43 O'Neill, Onora. "Some limits of informed consent." *Journal of Medical Ethics* 29.1 (2003): 5.
44 Gardner, John, and Stephen Shute. "The wrongness of rape." In Jeremy Horder (ed.), *Oxford essays in jurisprudence, fourth series*. Clarendon Press, 2000: 196–197. The case of unconscious sex that someone never becomes aware of is probably very rare. However, there may be many cases in which someone is deceived into sex and so, on our view, gives invalid consent without ever finding out about the deceit (see Chapter 9).
45 Wertheimer, Alan. *Consent to sexual relations*. Cambridge University Press, 2003: 102.
46 Cf. Archard, David. "The wrong of rape." *The Philosophical Quarterly* 57.228 (2007): 378–380.
47 Shafer, M., and M. Frye. "Rape and respect." In M. Vetterling-Braggin, F. A. Alliston, and J. English (eds), *Feminism and Philosophy*. Littlefield, Adams, 1977: 333–346.
48 Liberto, Hallie. *Green light ethics: A theory of permissive consent and its moral metaphysics*. Oxford University Press, 2022: 104–109.
49 David Archard endorses the first of these explanations (Archard, David. "The wrong of rape." *The Philosophical Quarterly* 57.228 (2007): 378–380); Shafer and Frye endorse the second (Shafer, M., and M. Frye. "Rape and respect." In M. Vetterling-Braggin, F. A. Alliston, and J. English (eds), *Feminism and Philosophy*. Littlefield, Adams, 1977: 333–346). Both argue that what makes rape particularly bad is that it violates something core to a person's identity. For others with a similar view, see the list in Archard's article (pp. 388–389).
50 It is possible that some do not, or at least that there are never any actual cases in which the right can permissibly be overridden on the grounds that doing so will promote good consequences. For discussion, see DeGrazia, David, and Joseph Millum. *A Theory of Bioethics*. Cambridge University Press, 2021: 71–77.
51 DeGrazia, David, and Joseph Millum. *A Theory of Bioethics*. Cambridge University Press, 2021: 54–55.
52 Marcus, U., V. Bremer, and O. Hamouda. "Syphilis surveillance and trends of the syphilis epidemic in Germany since the mid-90s." *Eurosurveillance* 9.12 (2004): 9–10.
53 A justified rights infringement must still be the most minimal infringement necessary to achieve the goal in question. So, if the beneficial consequences do justify mandatory reporting of a disease, then it should still be done anonymously and the information reported only to those government departments that need it.
54 We use Judith Jarvis Thomson's vocabulary here, where any intrusion into the domain of someone's rights is an "infringement" but only wrongful infringements count as "violations." Thomson, Judith. "Self-defense and rights." In *Rights, Restitution, and Risk*. Harvard University Press, 1986: 33–48.
55 Harding, Luke. "German court finds cannibal guilty of murder." *The Guardian*, May 10, 2006.
56 Harding, Luke. "Victim of cannibal agreed to be eaten." *The Guardian*, December 4, 2003.
57 Owens, David. *Shaping the Normative Landscape*. Oxford University Press, 2012: 180.
58 Compare Keith Hyams: "paternalist reasoning is well suited to the explanation of several intuitions about substantive limits to consent's capacity to legitimise, like the putative limit preventing agents from consenting to be tortured. Such intuitive limits can be explained by paternalist considerations as preventing agents from consenting to things which are never, or extremely rarely, beneficial for them." Hyams, Keith. "When consent doesn't work: A rights-based case for limits to consent's capacity to legitimize." *Journal of Moral Philosophy* 8.1 (2011): 117.

59 Notably, some of the judges in the case thought there was a threshold of harm above which consent failed to exculpate. See Archard, David. "The wrong of rape." *The Philosophical Quarterly* 57.228 (2007): 378.

60 Note that whether the refusal is respected is *not* regarded as a matter of what the religious patient believes about the post-mortal consequences of refusal. Someone who refuses treatment because otherwise they will be punished in the afterlife is treated just the same as someone who refuses it because they think it forbidden by God irrespective of consequences.

61 Similar points explain why it is not possible to consent to enslavement. The individual consenting would remain an agent—they physically could not transfer their agency to the other party. That means that any time the other party wanted them to do something the enslaver would have to command it and the enslaved would have to decide whether to do it. Unsurprisingly, slavery is only possible against a background of enforcement backed up by violence.

62 For discussion, see Wertheimer, Alan. *Exploitation*. Princeton University Press, 1999.

63 Bromwich, Danielle, and Annette Rid. "Can informed consent to research be adapted to risk?" *Journal of Medical Ethics* 41.7 (2015): 521–528.

64 Miller, Franklin G., and Alan Wertheimer. "Facing up to paternalism in research ethics." *Hastings Center Report* 37.3 (2007): 24–34.

3 Competence

1. Introduction

In the last chapter we argued that *validity* is the foundational concept for thinking about the ethics of consent. When consent is valid the consent giver successfully waives (or alienates or transfers) their right; when it is invalid, they do not. So, what conditions need to be in place for consent to be valid?

Scholars generally agree that valid consent requires that the following necessary and jointly sufficient conditions are met:

1. the person giving consent must be *competent*;
2. appropriate information must be *disclosed* to them;
3. they must have sufficient *understanding*;
4. their decision must be *voluntary*; and
5. they must *token* consent.

We discussed the last condition—tokening consent—in the previous chapter (section 7). In this chapter we discuss the competence condition. Chapter 4 addresses disclosure and understanding—the informational requirements. Chapter 5 addresses voluntariness.

Competence—or decision-making capacity, as it is sometimes called—refers to a person's ability to make autonomous decisions.[1] Someone who can make autonomous decisions can direct their own life in certain ways, and this ability grounds their *right* to do so, including by giving or withholding consent. For example, it is widely agreed that a competent adult can consent to get married, enlist in the armed forces, enroll in a first-in-human clinical trial, or refuse to consent to life-saving care. Others are not permitted to make those decisions on their behalf or otherwise interfere with their sphere of agency *even if* they judge the decision risky, unwise, irrational, or ill-informed.[2] But someone who is not competent has no right to make their own decisions. Legally recognized third parties make the important decisions about their lives on their behalf. For example, a child's parents or guardians make most decisions for them concerning their living arrangements, education, and medical care (provided that the decisions meet certain criteria[3]). The difference between how competent and non-competent individuals have a right to be treated makes it

DOI: 10.4324/9781003287391-4

very important that the line distinguishing them is drawn correctly. After all, we ought to respect a person's autonomy if they have the capacity to make their own decisions, yet we also ought to protect the non-autonomous from the harms of poor decision-making.

Determinations of competence require answers to both *metaphysical* and *epistemological* questions. The metaphysical questions concern what competence *is*. What capacities underlie autonomous decision-making? Are they general in nature or task-specific? Do they vary with the risks or stakes of the activity? Do they come in degrees and, if so, what difference, if any, does that make to the rights of those on the margins? The epistemological questions concern how we can *know* if someone is competent to consent. Can we determine whether and when decision-making competence has been compromised? Can we be confident that an intervention really facilitates autonomous decision-making?

A recent UK adult safeguarding case illustrates the stakes. In 2014, a local authority intervened with a married couple who were seeking fertility treatment.[4] CH—who we will call Colin—had Down syndrome. After being assessed by a consultant psychiatrist in accordance with the Mental Capacity Act, he was judged incapable of giving valid consent to sex. The local authority ordered him to attend a sex education course before being reassessed, and informed his wife, WH—who we will call Wen—that having sex with her husband would be a serious criminal offence that would result in him being removed from the home. The couple complied with the order—Wen moved into a separate bedroom and reduced acts of physical affection so as not to arouse or confuse Colin. However, the required course was not made available to him until over a year after the initial assessment. In mid-2016, Colin completed the course and was deemed competent to consent to sex with Wen. In 2017, the couple received a formal apology for the delay, and £10,000 in damages.

We will return to this case over the course of the chapter as we explore the concept of competence to consent. We begin by outlining the major conceptions of competence. The most widely endorsed and operationalized view is the four abilities model. It is generally agreed, however, that this model is not protective enough of those with emotional or affective impairments while being overly protective of individuals with marginal autonomy. It wrongly prohibits some individuals from consenting for themselves. Two alternative conceptions exist to rectify these problems. The first are liberal views of competence. These solve the over-protectiveness problem but potentially at the expense of some people jeopardizing their welfare when they should be protected from harm. The second are risk-adapted views. These succeed in giving us the correct verdict on cases in which most people would agree that an individual either should be allowed to consent for themselves or should be protected from harm. However, these views fail to capture what competence *is*. We close the chapter by diagnosing a shared and, we think, mistaken assumption that all existing views of competence make. Once this assumption is rejected it is possible to resolve the problem in a principled way. We sketch a way of doing this with our own view according to which competence comprises two separate rights each of which require different capacities.

2. Threshold and scope

Before proceeding to different views about the nature of competence, two practical issues are worth addressing.

The first concerns the *threshold* for competence. The capacity for autonomous decision-making comes in degrees, but consent is a binary notion—either it is valid or it is not.[5] This means that there is some threshold of ability above which a person has the right to make their own consent decisions and below which they do not. In practice, a decision also needs to be made about how high to set the bar for evidence that someone meets or does not meet the conditions for competence (for example, when assessing a patient for their ability to consent to medical care). Set it too high, and someone who possesses the capacities for autonomous decision-making is wrongfully denied their right to consent. Set it too low, and someone who lacks these capacities is vulnerable to the consequences of their poor decision-making.

Precisely where the threshold lies is a matter of debate—as we will see in the following sections. But there are constraints on any plausible answer. Scholars agree that most mentally mature adults are competent to consent and most toddlers, persons with severe dementia, and persons with profound learning disabilities are not.[6] Any view that implies otherwise ought to be rejected.

The second issue concerns the *scope* of competence judgments. When we say that someone is competent, should we aim to make a global judgment (they are *generally* able to make their own decisions) or a local judgment (they are simply competent to make *this specific* decision)?[7]

In many jurisdictions, the law reflects global judgements of competence with wide scope. For example, when someone reaches 18 years of age, unless they have been judged incompetent on other grounds, a person in England and Wales becomes a legal adult with full autonomy rights. This renders them legally competent to consent to and refuse medical care and treatment, including refusing life-saving interventions. In other situations, the scope is restricted. For example, the law in England and Wales recognizes 16-year-olds as legally competent to consent to medical care and treatment, but not legally competent to refuse treatment that is in their best interests. Sometimes the scope is narrower in a different respect: an authority may find a person legally incompetent to make certain types of decisions, but not others. When the local authority judged Colin not competent to make sexual decisions—and, consequently, certain medical decisions—based on the psychiatrist's expert judgement, he was not found *generally* non-competent. For instance, he might still be permitted to make certain financial decisions, like exchanging money for goods on his weekly food shop.

Ethically speaking, while the *threshold* issue is a matter of debate, the *scope* issue is mostly settled.[8] Consent decisions are specific. As illustrated in Chapter 2, when a person succeeds in giving valid consent to some act, they exercise their power to waive a *specific* right in a *specific* way in a *specific* context. Depending on the right exercised, the act might only require minimal decision-making capacities—for example, when your partner asks, "Would you like a hug? You seem upset." Others require more sophisticated capacities. Unlike a hug, deciding whether to agree to a 10-year fixed rate mortgage is more complicated both in terms of precisely what you are waiving your rights against and the factors relevant to your interests—such as, the uncertainty of future interest rates, the stability of your employment, and the possibility of hefty exit fees. It is widely agreed, therefore, that the kind of competence implicated in consent transactions is *local*.

3. The four abilities model

When a person is *competent* to consent, they have the ability to waive a specific autonomy right, and when that rights waiver is successful it has the normative effect of releasing another person from a duty not to interfere with them. But what capacities does a person need to possess to have this ability?

The most widely held view of what competence consists in is the four abilities model. This model is widely accepted in medical practice and clinical research.[9] According to the version of this view implemented in capacity assessments in the United States, a person can validly consent to some act if and only if they can (i) communicate a choice; (ii) understand relevant information; (iii) appreciate their situation and the consequences for them of different choices; and (iv) reason about their options. Variants on this model are used to assess capacity in other jurisdictions too, such as Canada and the UK.[10] For example, the consultant psychiatrist who examined Colin would have assessed his ability to understand, retain, use, and weigh relevant information, as well as whether he had the ability to communicate a decision.

The four abilities model seems to protect those with impaired decision-making capacities from harmful decisions without smuggling in value judgements or resorting to discriminatory stereotyping. The model is purely procedural: it assesses a person's ability to perform cognitive tasks that are widely agreed to be necessary for autonomous decision-making. This ensures that it is value- and diagnosis-neutral.[11] Colin is not found incompetent *because* he has Down syndrome or *because* he is making a decision that his assessor considers unwise, risky, or ill-informed. He is found incompetent simply because he does not possess sufficient ability to understand, reason, or weigh relevant information about sexual relations.[12]

While the four abilities model protects those like Colin with *cognitive* impairments, some worry that it fails to protect those with *emotional* or *affective* impairments. To see the problem, consider Jennifer Hawkins's example of Terence, a patient diagnosed two years ago with anorexia nervosa.[13] After a period of relative stability, Terence has declined rapidly. His weight is now dangerously low and if he is not fed medically, he will likely die. Despite this, he refuses treatment.

He tells his clinical team that he knows he has an illness, he understands that he could die if he is not medically fed, "but, he insists, he would rather die than put on weight."[14]

Although many patients with this condition who refuse lifesaving treatment lack capacity on the four abilities model, Terence would not be one of them:

> Terence counts as having capacity because he understands the basic facts about his situation and accepts that this information applies to him. It is significant that he says he knows he is ill, for this means he has what psychiatrists call "insight." He can reason well enough to grasp the different paths open to him, and what the results of each path might be. He knows there is a high chance of death without treatment. Finally, given his stated preference for avoiding weight gain, even at the risk of death, his choice is, broadly speaking, instrumentally rational—it makes sense given the values he currently has and the priority he gives them.[15]

This verdict might unsettle us. Terence might not currently see successful treatment as a potential benefit, or a future in which he potentially does not value death over weight gain as desirable, but from the outside he seems mistaken not to do so. Scholars and practitioners have long worried that some people in emotional turmoil (because of shock, trauma, grief, or illness) are rendered incapable of seeing value in a future that *is* likely to be subjectively valuable to them.[16] A view—like the four abilities model—that ignores the role emotions, values, or disordered affective states can make to our ability to make autonomous decisions seems to miss something important.

4. More demanding views

Assessing the decision-making competence of people with potentially disordered affective states may require an even more substantive conception of autonomy.[17] Those who offer such views tend to agree that the four abilities—understanding, appreciation, reasoning, and choice—are necessary, but just not sufficient for decision-making competence.

Some think that a radical reconceptualization of competence is required to arrive at the correct view. For example, Hawkins offers a view of decision-making capacity in medicine that starts with the goals of that enterprise. A clinician has a professional obligation to balance two values: patient autonomy and patient wellbeing. While some competent patients make medical decisions that have a negative net effect on their overall well-being, their decisions are respected because they are *capable* of protecting their subjective interests. However, "the individuals we need to protect are those who are less able to look after their own interests than most ordinary people are, individuals who are more likely than others to make serious prudential mistakes."[18] This leads Hawkins to reconceptualize decision-making capacity in medicine along welfarist lines.[19]

Hawkins argues that, even when they possess the four abilities, someone can be deemed to lack decision-making capacity with respect to a particular decision when two conditions are met: (i) there is good evidence that they are making a serious prudential mistake with their decision; and (ii) they have a condition that is known to make those with it make prudential mistakes. It is because Terence was only recently diagnosed with anorexia that:

> his chances of full recovery with treatment are still high. It is against that background that his choice looks like a serious prudential mistake because it seems that he is throwing away many years of life that would be quite good for him from his perspective if he lived them.[20]

Moreover, "in the context of anorexia nervosa refusing life-sustaining treatment that involves weight gain is both predictable and the result of the rigid evaluative outlook characteristic of the disorder."[21] This more demanding view of competence would find Terence incapable of refusing life-saving medical care.

Others think that it is possible to assess whether emotional or affective disorders impair autonomous decision-making without abandoning a purely procedural approach to decision-making capacity. For example, Lauren Harcarik, Scott Kim, and Joseph Millum argue in favor of adding a fifth criterion to the four abilities model: the ability to value.[22] A person possesses this ability if they (i) have values; (ii) can access those values; (iii) can engage in practical reasoning with those values; and (iv) can act on the result of that reasoning. Including the ability to value in capacity assessments provides additional resources for exploring what has gone wrong for patients like Terence. It is possible that Terence retains the ability to value; but it is also possible that he is struggling to access his real values or bring them to bear on his decision-making.

More demanding views have the advantage of providing additional conceptual resources for understanding some cases that the standard four abilities model struggles with. However, they, like the four abilities model, also appear *overly* demanding in some cases. To see this, consider Colin again.

If Colin was unable—without specialist assistance—to reason probabilistically or appreciate how he might think or feel in different circumstances, it is likely that the four abilities model would find him incapable of waiving any of his bodily rights with a romantic partner. He was, on this view, as incapable of consenting to kisses and hugs, as he was to sex. Yet that verdict seems implausible. Wen's decision to protect Colin by moving into a separate bedroom and reducing acts of physical affection makes sense for acts that would have confused him (for example, if kissing in bed had become the couple's shorthand for initiating sex). But other acts may have preserved a mutually desired intimacy without communicating the commencement of sexual relations. It seems very plausible to think that Colin and Wen should have been permitted to engage in those acts, when both of them were agreeable. The four abilities model appears too demanding in such cases.

5. Liberal views

In response to cases like these, some writers have proposed *liberal* views of competence.[23] According to these views, decision-making capacity requires only a minimal capacity for autonomous action. For instance, Agnieszka Jaworska argues that the capacity for autonomy is best understood as the capacity to value.[24] A person capable of valuing:

> thinks she is correct in wanting what she wants; achieving what she wants is tied up with her sense of self-worth; and the importance of achieving what she wants is, for her, independent of her own experience.[25]

A person who possesses the capacity to value can set normative standards for their own life. For example, if Colin thinks that fertility treatment to conceive a biological child is the right course of action for him and Wen, is disposed to feel upset or saddened by difficulties in conceiving, and can remove himself from his immediate emotions and reflectively judge the achievement of this goal to be worthwhile, then he is capable of valuing it.[26]

Through the lens of Alzheimer's disease, Jaworska provides extensive empirical evidence to show that it is possible for a person to have the capacity to value while having other cognitive impairments.[27] These impairments might make it difficult for a person to put their values into action.

Colin does not have dementia, but he may rely on Wen and his clinicians to assist him in understanding and reasoning through the steps involved in having a biological child given the couple's fertility issues. However, just because he might struggle to operationalize his life plans without their assistance, does not imply that he cannot govern his own life.

We often need help putting our plans into action.[28] Perhaps Esme realizes that she needs to set boundaries at work if she is ever going to achieve a reasonable workload, but she might have no idea how to implement this in practice. When she asks for her manager's assistance, asks a friend whether she should agree to work on a new project, or puts that question to her "Just Say No" WhatsApp group, she does not reveal that she is incapable of making decisions about her work. She just reveals that she needs social support to live an autonomous life.[29] Just like Colin, sometimes those of us who are cognitively unimpaired need help to understand and reason through how to operationalize our values.

The virtue of liberal views of competence is that they take marginal autonomy seriously. They recognize the tremendous value of self-governance and the wretchedness of having one's life run by others. It is for these reasons that they set the threshold for autonomy at the lowest point at which it is plausible to suppose that a person could direct their own lives by setting normative standards for their own actions. With the limited information we have, it is likely that Colin had the capacity to value, and so on a liberal view, he had the capacity to consent to both sexual relations and medical treatment.

However, few scholars hold a liberal view of competence without caveats.[30] After all, while this view protects the exercise of autonomy, it fails to protect those on the margins from likely or serious harms or the burdens of certain decisions.

Suppose that Colin and Wen both have Down syndrome. While both have the capacity to value, they have trouble understanding complex information, they have problems with their short-term memory, and they have considerable difficulty making decisions that align with their values when those decisions involve multiple steps and require evaluating alternatives with distinct risk-benefit profiles. They both want a biological child. They are informed that, were Wen to become pregnant, there would be an increased chance that their child would also have Down syndrome, and potentially require additional social, caring, and educational support. They live independently but rely on substantial familial support. Their elderly parents are too old to care for a new child. A liberal view would imply that, as valuers, Colin and Wen have the right that other parties not interfere with their decisions—if they decide to pursue IVF it should be up to them. But it seems negligent to claim that they are competent enough to accept the burdensome consequences of decisions when their capacity to protect their own interests is exceeded.

Moreover, while Colin and Wen seem to have a loving relationship, the idea that the capacity to value is sufficient for competence is more troubling if we consider potentially exploitative relationships. Intellectual disability renders a person more vulnerable to manipulation, exploitation, and coercive control. However, if the right to make one's own decisions is grounded in minimal capacities, then those with marginal autonomy are offered little protection against malevolent attempts to get them to do the bidding of others.[31]

6. Risk-adapted views

The four abilities model appears too demanding in some cases, so that people with mild decisional impairments are prohibited from making decisions that it intuitively seems they should be permitted to make. Meanwhile, liberal views appear too lax in other cases, where they would allow these vulnerable individuals to make very poor decisions. One solution to this dilemma is to adopt a risk-adapted view of competence.

Some consent decisions are riskier than others. It is riskier to consent to an experimental vaccination than a blood draw. Some are more momentous than others. There seems to be more at stake when a person in a monogamous relationship consents to sex with someone who is not their partner than when they consent to sex with their partner. We might think, then, that our competence to consent varies with the risks or the stakes of the activity being authorized.

Allen Buchanan and Dan Brock hold a version of this view. They claim that:

> No single standard of competence is adequate for all decisions. The standard depends in large part on the risk involved, and varies along a range from low/

> minimal to high/maximal. The more serious the expected harm to the patient from acting on a choice, the higher should be the standard of decision-making capacity, and the greater should be the certainty that the standard is satisfied.[32]

Although Buchanan and Brock developed their view for medical decision-making, we can illustrate it by returning to Colin's capacity assessment. The risks of sex using contraception are lower than those of unprotected sex in addition to the couple receiving reproductive treatment that increases the likelihood of pregnancy. Hence, the capacities that Colin would need to validly consent to the first kind of sexual activity are lower on this view than those he would need to waive his right against the second.

Risk-adapted views seem able to balance respect for autonomy with the protection of well-being. If competence varies with the risks or stakes of the activity, then marginal autonomy is recognized and respected when these are low, but persons with borderline decision-making capacities are protected when these are high. In this way, risk-adapted views appear to solve the problem that plagued both the more liberal and more demanding views we have considered. There is no need to hold a fixed view that prioritizes either autonomy or wellbeing as the threshold for competence can vary with risk.

However, even though these views often give us plausible verdicts about whether a person should be allowed to make their own consent decisions without interference, they do so at a cost. They no longer seem to be talking about the concept of *competence*. Consequently, it is not clear that they can explain their verdicts about cases.

To see the problem, think about what competence *is*. It is the ability to perform a specific task. Some tasks are harder, more complicated, more advanced than others. Someone might be competent to drive an automatic car, but not a manual. You might be competent to sew a button, but not a buttonhole. The reason that some tasks are more difficult than others is not in virtue of their being riskier or more momentous; it is just in virtue of their being more complex. The possible harm of botching a button replacement on your best suit is far higher than that of making a mess of a buttonhole on a piece of scrap fabric. Nonetheless, the former is a much simpler task than the latter.

Of course, *if* risk reliably tracked complexity, there would be no problem with risk-adapted views of competence. There would be good reason to think that as a task became riskier it also becomes more complex and vice versa. However, that is not the case, not even when we focus exclusively on consent decisions.

Some high-risk consent decisions are simple. Suppose that Hafsha has a severe peanut allergy. After being exposed to peanuts, she goes into anaphylactic shock, and her sister pulls an adrenaline auto-injector out of her bag. She asks Hafsha if she should administer it. The risks of refusing this intervention are very high: death. The benefits of accepting this intervention are also very high: life saved. However, the consent decision itself is simple.[33]

Other low-risk consent decisions are complicated. Suppose Adefolake's doctor has just suggested that she schedule a mammogram. She decides to think about it.

After a week's research, she is finding it hard to make the decision. She is 41 years old, with no family history of breast cancer, but she is a moderate drinker. She had a mammogram last year, and her insurance company only covers this screening every *other* year, and so she would be paying for this out of pocket. She can afford to do this, and she likes the idea of knowing her situation. This is a low-risk decision—neither accepting nor declining the screening is especially risky in this case. But it is a complicated decision. Adefolake is trying to understand and weigh the following considerations: the base rate of disease (low in women in their early forties), her individual risk (family history, age, lifestyle factors), the accuracy of the screening, the efficacy of early treatment should cancer be detected, the probability of misdiagnosis and the associated stress, costs, and additional interventions, and the other uses she could put her money to if she declined this screening.

7. The components of competence

Existing accounts of what capacities are needed for someone to be competent face a challenge. If the threshold for decision-making competence is set low, the power to consent is recognized in those with marginal autonomy. This means that others have a duty not to interfere with such an individual's consent decision even if there is good reason to think it represents a serious setback to the agent's wellbeing. And yet, many people who *just* pass the low threshold will lack the capacities a person needs to adequately protect their own interests. This is troubling: people with borderline decision-making capacities are forced to suffer the consequences of decisions that they are unable to grasp adequately.

More demanding views—such as the four abilities model and those that build on it—protect those with borderline decision-making capacity but now seem to rule too many people incompetent. If we raise the threshold, individuals who would have passed a low one are offered greater protection, but at the cost of denying the limited autonomy that some of them likely possess. And, *because* the threshold for decision-making capacity is set high, those who *just* fail to pass it are not only denied their freedom; they are effectively sentenced to live lives directed—and so, dominated—by others *even when* they are likely to be able to set normative standards for themselves.

In the previous section, we considered whether a risk-adapted view would resolve this apparent tension between the values of well-being and autonomy. We suggested that risk-adapted views face a different challenge. Since risk fails to track difficulty, they no longer seem to be philosophical accounts of *competence*.

To develop a principled solution to the problem, we think it is helpful to return to a foundational question—what grounds the right to make decisions for oneself? A first step in answering this question is to note that there are actually two component rights involved here. When Colin was judged to lack the capacity to give valid consent to sex, he was not *only* judged to lack the power to exercise an autonomy right, he was also judged to lack a claim against others interfering with his life on paternalistic grounds. In effect, the psychiatrist's assessment found him lacking *two features* of agential control with regards to his sex life: he lacked the capacity to consent to sex and he lacked a claim against others preventing him from engaging in a sexual relationship with his wife. These features of agential control are rarely distinguished in the literature. The less obvious question, then, is: are the capacities that ground the power to waive a right through consent the same as those that ground a claim against others paternalistically interfering with one's consent decisions?

On the views of competence we have considered so far, these rights are assumed to have the *same* grounds. That is, whatever capacities ground the power to waive a right through consent are the same as those that ground a claim against paternalistic interference. Everyone who has the power to waive a right through consent therefore has a claim against others that they not interfere with their consent decision (and vice versa). In contrast to these *common grounds* views, we think that these two rights have *different* normative grounds. The capacities that a person needs to consent for themselves are more minimal than those they need to have a claim against paternalistic interference. This means that someone like Colin—someone with marginal autonomy—may have the power to consent and yet not the right to demand that others respect their consent decisions when there are weighty paternalistic reasons to interfere. We call this the *separate grounds* view. In the final two sections of this chapter, we sketch the view and show how it could deal with the challenges to the common grounds views.[34]

8. The grounds of the power to consent

Turn, first, to the grounds of the power to consent. Scholars agree that to be competent to exercise an autonomy right, like the power to consent, you need to be capable of *autonomous* decision-making.[35] Most mentally mature adults are—or at least are under ordinary circumstances. But the same cannot be said for all rights-holders. For example, a toddler is unable to alienate their property rights. She cannot exchange her new unicorn scooter with her older brother, no matter how good an offer he makes.

To see why the power to consent is thought to be grounded by this capacity, it is useful to think about the value of autonomy to beings like us. There is a good we can only realize if we can direct our own lives—the good of directing our lives in accordance with reasons that are derived from our values. This is a *prudential good*—one which contributes to a person's wellbeing.[36]

It is also intimately related to consent. One way we go about directing our own lives is by giving and refusing consent. When we can give consent, we can exercise a degree of control over our own lives by doing the things we want—such as, engaging in intimate acts with others, exchanging money for goods, authorizing needed medical care—and refusing the things we do not want. This not only explains why the capacity for autonomy is thought to underlie the power to consent, it also explains the value of consent itself: it allows us a degree of control over our own lives, and that is something *deeply* valuable to the person whose life it is. We can see this clearly in the case of Colin and Wen (if we make some assumptions about the health of their relationship). Colin was denied a very important good by being denied the option of agreeing to sexual relations with Wen. It is not that the sensations of sexual relations in themselves would be particularly good for Colin. Rather, by agreeing to sex he is able to express his love for his partner and to create and deepen a meaningful relationship with her.

The answer to the question of what makes giving consent valuable, helps us answer the question of what a person needs to be capable of to exercise their autonomy through consent. If achieving the distinctive good of directing one's own life through autonomous action requires that one's interests, projects, relationships, or goals are a source of reasons for action, then someone just needs to be capable of valuing. Once someone has values concerning an area of their life, be it their career, their finances, their health, or sex, they can give consent to acts within that area. Thus, we agree with liberal common grounds theorists like Jaworska that the capacities needed to give consent are relatively minimal.

9. The grounds of the claim against paternalistic interference

It is also widely held that the right against paternalistic interference is grounded in autonomy. Once again, we agree. However, the way in which autonomy enters the picture is quite different on our separate grounds view. The conception of autonomy that grounds the right to consent is welfarist—the right is grounded in the prudential value of autonomy. But that could not also ground a right against paternalism. If it did, the paternalist *would* be justified in interfering with a consent decision anytime it had a negative impact on the consent giver's overall well-being. This would not only fail to protect the autonomous person's right to make *imprudent* decisions; it would fail to make normative sense of our responses to paternalism. We do not object to paternalism because the would-be paternalist has not considered the benefit we get from making our own decisions. We *demand* that they respect our agency by not interfering with our consent decisions *even* if those decisions are unwise, risky, instrumentally irrational, or uninformed.

At what point can someone legitimately make this demand? After all, we are comfortable with interfering with the decisions of many valuers when we judge that they are making bad choices. For example, despite a 6-year-old's objection, their parents might insist that they receive a second dose of their MMR vaccination because it is in their best interests. Likewise, despite a 13-year-old's decision to sign up for Instagram, their parent might deactivate that account after seeing evidence of the negative impact social media has on mental health. Few object to these instances of paternalism. Why, then, is the typical 20-year-old permitted to refuse recommended travel vaccines before a trip and sign up to whatever social media they like?

The answer, we suggest, is that the 20-year-old is capable of being responsible—and so held responsible—for their own actions. Unlike the 6-year-old or the 13-year-old, this agent can take responsibility for the harms that might befall them as a result of making an unwise, risky, or otherwise poor decision. In effect, they can say to the paternalist—"I'll take responsibility for those harms, so don't interfere on that basis."

The idea that competence is linked to responsibility is not new to us (though it has been neglected in the philosophical literature). Carl Elliott makes exactly this point:

> what we really want to know when we ask if a person is competent is whether that person is able to make decisions for which he can be legitimately judged accountable. If a person is accountable for his decision, the credit for that decision justifiably rests with him. Any praise, blame, merit, or demerit that the decision carries can be reasonably said to belong to him, because the decision was truly his.[37]

This brings us to a final question: what capacities does a person need to be held responsible in this way? The answer will depend on one's specific conception of responsibility. However, on most views of responsibility, the capacities are far more substantial than those required for valuing. For example, according to one standard account, a person must meet two conditions to be responsible for an action.[38] The first is that the person must have acted *voluntarily*. The second is *epistemic*—since ignorance is sometimes an excuse, the person must either be aware of certain facts or blameworthy for their ignorance. For example, they know (or should know) what they are doing, what the possible consequences are, and whether the act is justified or not. In short, they must be *able* to make a good decision (whether or not they actually make it).

Clearly, meeting the epistemic condition for responsibility requires more than just being a valuer. In fact, we think that the capacities needed to be responsible for one's consent decision are much closer to the those enumerated by more demanding views of competence, like the four abilities model. To work out the normative status of an act someone needs to be able to understand the relevant information, appreciate how it applies to their situation, and reason through what to do on the basis of that information and their values.

Even with just a sketch of what it means to be a valuer and what is needed in order to be held responsible for one's actions, it is possible to see how this analysis can make sense of cases like Colin's. Colin is clearly a valuer, so he can give consent and thereby permit Wen to have sex with him. However, it is possible that he lacks the capacity to be responsible for at least some of his actions—such as those involved in deciding to have a child. If that is correct—and we don't know enough details of the actual case to be sure—some sort of paternalistic intervention could be justified. When Colin lacked the capacity to be held responsible, and where he was making risky decisions, other parties could permissibly intervene in order to ensure that he made decisions that aligned with his interests and values.

10. Conclusions

Determinations of competence are of enormous practical significance. If someone is deemed incapable of making their own decisions about some area of their life—be it medicine, finances, or sexual relations—other parties can step in and make decisions for them. If they are in fact capable, this denies them a core right. On the other hand, if someone who lacks capacity is allowed to make important decisions for themselves, they may cause themselves harm or be taken advantage of by others. It is therefore vitally important that both false positives and false negatives be avoided as much as possible. Deciding whether someone is competent requires that we have a clear conception of what competence is. This is a matter of debate. This chapter has outlined a number of different views of competence and considered their pros and cons. We diagnosed the existing views as sharing a mistake. All assume that the power to give consent and the claim against paternalistic interference have the same grounds, so that someone who can give their own consent can also demand that others not interfere, even when they are making a very bad decision. We suggested that a separate grounds view of competence provides a plausible alternative. It allows us to respect the autonomy of those with marginal decision-making capacity, while still protecting their interests.

Notes

1 Buchanan, A. E., and D. W. Brock. *Deciding for others: The ethics of surrogate decision making.* Cambridge University Press, 1990: 82. Note that some writers use "competence" to refer to the *legal* capacity and thereby distinguish it from "decision-making capacity." Since such a usage is not consistent within law or ethics, we do not follow this practice. Where the context does not already make it clear, we say explicitly if we are referring specifically to the legal power.
2 In many jurisdictions, a competent person's right to make unwise decisions is legally protected, and it is unlawful to treat a person as incompetent merely because their decision is considered unwise. For example, in England and Wales, principle 4 of the Mental Capacity Act states: "A person is not to be treated as unable to make a decision merely because he makes an unwise decision." Mental Capacity Act 2005, 1(4). Available at: www.legislation.gov.uk/ukpga/2005/9/section/1 (accessed March 10, 2025)
3 These criteria typically involve limits to parental authority based on the child's welfare. For example, we are not aware of any jurisdiction in which parents are legally permitted to decline beneficial and life-preserving care on their child's behalf.
4 *CH v. A Metropolitan Council* [2017] EWCOP 12.
5 Buchanan, A. E., and D. W. Brock. *Deciding for others: The ethics of surrogate decision making.* Cambridge University Press, 1990: 26.
6 Cf. The "inclusivity" criterion—the requirement that most mentally mature adults are competent—in Hawkins, Jennifer, and Louis C. Charland. "Decision-making capacity." *The Stanford Encyclopedia of Philosophy* (Fall 2020 edition), ed. Edward N. Zalta.
7 Most scholars hold a local view, but Ronald Dworkin is a notable exception. He says, "competence in the sense in which it is presupposed by the right to autonomy is a very different matter. It means the more diffuse and general ability I described: the ability to act out of general preference or character or conviction or a sense of self. There will, of course, be hard cases in which we cannot know with any confidence whether a particular dementia patient is competent in that sense. But we must make that overall judgment, not some combination of judgments about

specific task capability, in order to decide whether some mentally incapacitated patient has the right to autonomy." Dworkin, Ronald. *Life's dominion: An argument about abortion, euthanasia, and individual freedom*. Knopf, 1993: 235.

8 For example, the authors of the SEP entry on decision-making capacity say, "decision relativity refers to the now almost universally accepted idea that an individual's decisional capacity should be assessed relative to a specific decision, at a particular time, in a particular context." Hawkins, Jennifer, and Louis C. Charland. "Decision-making capacity." *The Stanford Encyclopedia of Philosophy* (Fall 2020 edition), ed. Edward N. Zalta.

9 Grisso, Thomas, Paul S. Appelbaum, and Carolyn Hill-Fotouhi. "The MacCAT-T: A clinical tool to assess patients' capacities to make treatment decisions." *Psychiatric Services* 48.11 (1997): 1415–1419. This model was originally developed by Paul Appelbaum, Thomas Grisso, and colleagues and is based on reviews of US statutory and case law, as well as clinical experience and ethical analysis (see, e.g., Grisso, Thomas, and Paul S. Appelbaum. *Assessing competence to consent to treatment: A guide for physicians and other health professionals*. Oxford University Press, 1998).

10 The functional test used in England and Wales also understands the capacity for autonomy in terms of abilities—in this case, the ability to understand, to retain, to use or weigh relevant information and to communicate one's decision. Despite the overlap with the four abilities model, the Mental Capacity Act's functional test does not assess the ability to appreciate. See Kim, Scott Y. H., et al. "Broad concepts and messy realities: Optimizing the application of mental capacity criteria." *Journal of Medical Ethics* 48.11 (2022): 838–844.

11 It is widely agreed that tests of decision-making competence ought to be value neutral and independent of mental health diagnosis. See Hawkins, Jennifer, and Louis C. Charland. "Decision-making capacity." *The Stanford Encyclopedia of Philosophy* (Fall 2020 edition), ed. Edward N. Zalta. However, some argue that individual rights in a liberal society—such as, the right to consent or the right against paternalistic interference—require a substantive—and so value-laden—conception of autonomy. See, for example, Freyenhagen, Fabian. "Autonomy's substance." Journal of Applied Philosophy 34.1 (2017): 114–129.

12 See Mental Capacity Act 2005, 3(1). Available at: www.legislation.gov.uk/ukpga/2005/9/section/1 (accessed March 10, 2025).

13 Hawkins, Jennifer. "Affect, values and problems assessing decision-making capacity." *The American Journal of Bioethics* 24.8 (2024): 71–82.

14 Hawkins, Jennifer. "Affect, values and problems assessing decision-making capacity." *The American Journal of Bioethics* 24.8 (2024): 73.

15 Hawkins, Jennifer. "Affect, values and problems assessing decision-making capacity." *The American Journal of Bioethics* 24.8 (2024): 73.

16 Cf. Halpern, Jodi. *From detached concern to empathy: Humanizing medical practice*. Oxford University Press, 2001: 1–13; Elliot, C. Caring about risks: Are severely depressed patients competent to consent to research? *Archives of General Psychiatry* 54.22 (1997): 113–116; and Hope, T., J. Tan, A. Stewart, and J. McMillan. "Agency, ambivalence and authenticity: The many ways in which anorexia nervosa can affect autonomy." *International Journal of Law in Context* 9.1 (2013): 20–36.

17 See, for example, Freyenhagen, F., T. O'Shea. "Hidden substance: Mental disorder as a challenge to normatively neutral accounts of autonomy." *International Journal of Law in Context* 9.1 (2013): 53–70.

18 Hawkins, Jennifer. "Affect, values and problems assessing decision-making capacity." *The American Journal of Bioethics* 24.8 (2024): 76.

19 However, with that said, this reconceptualization is not, nor is it intended to be, a radical overhaul of the standard view. Hawkins accepts that the four abilities are necessary for decision-making competence.

20 Hawkins, Jennifer. "Affect, values and problems assessing decision-making capacity." *The American Journal of Bioethics* 24.8 (2024): 75.

21 Hawkins, Jennifer. "Affect, values and problems assessing decision-making capacity." *The American Journal of Bioethics* 24.8 (2024): 76.

22 Harcarik, Lauren, Scott Y. H. Kim, and Joseph Millum. "The ability to value: An additional criterion for decision-making capacity." *Bioethics* 39.3 (2025): 288–295.

23 Jaworska, Agnieszka. "Respecting the margins of agency: Alzheimer's patients and the capacity to value." *Philosophy & Public Affairs* 28.2 (1999): 105–138; and Shiffrin, Seana. "Autonomy, beneficence, and the permanently demented." In Justine Burley (ed.), *Ronald Dworkin and his critics*. Wiley, 2004: 195–217.

24 Contrast, then, Jaworska's view that the capacity to value is more or less *sufficient* for someone to be competent with Harcarik, Kim, and Millum's argument that it should be an *additional necessary* criterion for competence.

25 Jaworska, Agnieszka. "Respecting the margins of agency: Alzheimer's patients and the capacity to value." *Philosophy & Public Affairs* 28.2 (1999): 116. Note that Jaworska means something different by "capacity to value" than Harcarik et al. mean by the "ability to value." This is because Jaworska is aiming to articulate what valuing *is*, while Harcarik et al. are more concerned with how values fit into a model of decision-making.

26 This interpretation is consistent with widely accepted views of valuing. See, for example, Scheffler, Samuel. "Valuing." In *Equality and tradition: Question of value in moral and political theory*. Oxford University Press, 2010: 29; and Theunissen, L. Nandi. *The value of humanity*. Oxford University Press, 2020: 95.

27 See, for example, Souren, Liduin, and Emile Franssen. *Broken connections: Alzheimer's disease, part I*, trans. R. M. J. van der Wilden-Fall. Swets & Zeitlinger, 1994: 52; Damasio, Antonio R. *Descartes' error: Emotion, reason, and the human brain*. G. P. Putnam's Sons, 1994: 70–71; and Braak, H., and E. Braak. "Staging of Alzheimer's disease-related neurofibrillary changes." *Neurobiology of Aging* i6.3 (May 1995): 274–275.

28 In fact, many of us need help forming these plans in the first place, even those of us who are presumed competent.

29 Socially supported decision-making is common both for competent and non-competent persons. For example, many competent persons use therapy to explore what they value and to help them make better *life decisions*—ones that align and further their interests. The same kinds of support can help those with marginal autonomy pass a threshold of decision-making capacity. See, for example, Wilkinson, Dominic, and Neil Levy. "Scaffolding informed consent." *Journal of Medical Ethics* (2024), online ahead of print. Available at: https://jme.bmj.com/content/early/2024/12/20/jme-2024-110105. There is a growing body of empirically informed scholarship in philosophy of mind that supports the view that our autonomy is socially constituted; even that our minds *extend* beyond our body into our environment. See, Andy, Clark, and David Chalmers. "The extended mind." *Analysis* 58.1 (1998): 7–19. And, for practical application, see Nine, Cara. "The wrong of displacement: The home as extended mind." *Journal of Political Philosophy* 26.2 (2018): 240–257; and Carter, Matilda. "The person as environmentally integrated: Dementia, loss, and extended cognition." *J. Ethics & Soc. Phil.* 28 (2024): 53–82.

30 For example, even Jaworska might be interpreted as offering a view about the nature and value of autonomy, rather than a view about competence to consent.

31 Despite the paucity of unified and good quality data, studies support the worry that those with impaired or marginal decision-making capacities are especially vulnerable to exploitation and forms of coercive control. See Abubakar, Aisha M., Rowland G. Seymour, Alison Gardner, Imogen Lambert, Rachel Fyson, and Nicola Wright. "Cognitive impairment and exploitation: Connecting fragments of a bigger picture through data." *Journal of Public Health* 46.4 (December 2024): 498–505.

32 Buchanan, A.E., and D.W. Brock, *Deciding for others: The ethics of surrogate decision making*. Cambridge University Press, 1990: 52.

33 One might follow Buchanan and Brock in judging that refusing the injection in this case is highly risky and so should require a high degree of decision-making capacity, while accepting it is low risk and so requires relatively little in the way of decision-making capacity (Buchanan, A. E., and D.W. Brock. *Deciding for others: The ethics of surrogate decision making*. Cambridge University Press, 1990: 52). This view has come under considerable criticism by those who think that it does not make sense to say that someone is competent to agree to something but incompetent to refuse it. See, e.g., Wicclair, Mark R. "Patient decision-making capacity and risk." *Bioethics* 5.2 (1991): 91–104.

34 The remainder of this chapter draws heavily on Bromwich, Danielle and Joseph Millum. "The separate grounds of competence." Unpublished manuscript.

35 See Hawkins, Jennifer, and Louis C. Charland. "Decision-making capacity." *The Stanford Encyclopedia of Philosophy* (Fall 2020 edition), ed. Edward N. Zalta.

36 Many consent scholars have argued that the value of consent lies in the prudential value of autonomous action. See, e.g., Ferzan, Kimberly Kessler. "Consent, culpability, and the law of rape." *Ohio State Journal of Criminal Law* 13 (2015): 404–406; Owens, David. *Shaping the normative landscape*. Oxford University Press, 2012: 172–176; Renzo, Massimo, "Defective normative powers: The case of consent." *Journal of Practical Ethics* 10.1 (2022): 50–54; Shiffrin, Seana Valentine. "Promising, intimate relationships, and conventionalism." *Philosophical Review* 117.4 (2008): 500–502; Tadros, Victor. *Wrongs and crimes*. Oxford University Press, 2016: 219–222; Wertheimer, Alan. *Consent to sexual relations*. Cambridge University Press, 2003: 124–127. For a dissenting view, see Healey, Richard. "Consent, interaction, and the value of shared understanding." *Legal Theory* 28.1 (2022): 35–58.

37 Elliott, Carl. "Competence as accountability." *The Journal of Clinical Ethics* 2.3 (Fall 1991): 169.

38 Rudy-Hiller, Fernando. "The epistemic condition for moral responsibility." *The Stanford Encyclopedia of Philosophy* (Winter 2022 edition), ed. Edward N. Zalta and Uri Nodelman. This is an account of "responsibility as accountability."

4 The informational requirements

Understanding and disclosure

1. Introduction

As we noted in the last chapter, scholars generally agree on five necessary and jointly sufficient conditions for valid consent:

1. the person giving consent must be *competent*;
2. appropriate information must be *disclosed* to them;
3. they must have sufficient *understanding*;
4. their decision must be *voluntary*; and
5. they must *token* consent.

Most of the disagreement about consent lies in how these conditions should be understood. This chapter is dedicated to the *informational requirements* for valid consent: disclosure and understanding.

It should be evident that the person giving consent needs to understand *something*. If someone says, "Yes," without knowing that they are being asked for consent, then it is hard to make sense of them authorizing something with that speech act. And yet there must be a limit on what someone has to know to give valid consent. It must be possible to consent to activities we have not experienced before (like a kiss, an eyebrow wax, or a lumber puncture) and to acts with unknown risks (like an experimental drug being studied in a clinical trial). So, what *exactly* does someone need to understand to waive their rights through consent? The answer to this first question needs to explain how and why consent is invalidated when the person giving it does not have the requisite understanding.

A similar question arises for disclosure. The person receiving consent is often in possession of information that could make a difference to a consent decision. Perhaps you would not retain Minh as your investment portfolio manager if you knew she had been convicted of fraud, would decline sexual relations with Safa had you known that she was a virgin, or would have opted for a Caesarean section if the doctor had communicated your elevated risks of a life-threatening obstetric emergency.[1] What exactly is the person requesting or receiving consent required to tell the person giving consent? Are they required to disclose information already in the public domain, such as a criminal conviction? Or personal information, such

DOI: 10.4324/9781003287391-5

as their sexual history, if they think it might be relevant? And how specific should the information disclosed be? Are the duties of disclosure properly discharged if an obstetrician merely outlines a general increased risk of birth complications, or do they need to give likelihoods and magnitudes? An account of the disclosure requirement should not only help us answer these questions, it should explain why consent is invalidated when duties of disclosure are not properly discharged.

Although we pose these questions about the understanding and disclosure requirements separately, it is natural to think that the informational requirements are related: the reason why we disclose information to a person making a consent decision is to enable them to understand it. The final question, which is addressed as we explore the first two, is: what is the relationship between the understanding and disclosure requirements for valid consent?

This chapter starts by assessing different views of what must be understood for valid consent. Within medicine and clinical research it is widely held that what ought to be disclosed can be derived from what needs to be understood. This view implies that the informational requirements for valid consent are *conceptually* related. Despite being widely held, we argue that this view is false: the disclosure and understanding requirements have distinct grounds. We argue that the consent receiver has a duty to avoid exercising illegitimate control over the consent giver and this often entails substantive duties of disclosure. However, this does not imply that the consent giver needs to understand all the facts that ought to be disclosed. We close the chapter by considering how different forms of ignorance—on the part of the giver and the receiver of consent—affect validity.

2. The understanding requirement

Accounts of the understanding requirement vary in terms of the amount of information the consenter needs to understand to give valid consent. However, in determining its content, we have already ruled out *everything* and *nothing*. The reasons for doing so are instructive. First, unless we are willing to give up on the possibility of valid consent, the content of the understanding requirement must be limited to only those facts that the consenter *can* understand. Second, since valid consent *just is* the exercise of one of our normative powers, the minimum information the consenter must understand is that they are exercising their rights to give consent to some act or acts.

A minimal view of the understanding requirement

One way to determine the content of the understanding requirement is to think through a case in which someone's ignorance makes it so that we cannot make sense of them giving valid consent.[2] Imagine that Zoltán is listening to a podcast with his earphones in. His husband, Faizan, passes by, points to the garage and asks, "Can I take yours today?" Zoltán catches the gesture, but not the request, and assumes Faizan is just telling him that he is leaving. He nods to acknowledge his departure. Set aside the question of whether, given the miscommunication, Faizan would be justified in taking Zoltán's car. What explains the intuition that Zoltán has not given valid consent?[3]

The answer is simple: Zoltán does not understand *that* his nod communicates consent. He thinks Faizan is just informing him that he is leaving, so he nods in acknowledgement. His nod is not even a token of consent in this context, let alone an invalid one. We can derive the first condition of a minimal understanding requirement from this observation: to give valid consent, the consenter must understand *that* they are tokening consent.[4]

We can derive a second condition from this observation too: to understand *that* one is giving consent, one must understand *how* to exercise one's right to give consent.[5] Had Zoltán heard the request, he could not consent by shouting "Zamboni!," blowing his nose, or wiggling his toes. None of these acts would have the normative effect of waiving his rights.[6]

The speech acts that signify consent are context dependent. Sometimes a written signature is required to authorize certain medical procedures, legal waivers, or financial contracts. In less formal settings, a verbal or non-verbal affirmation—or actions that are understood by the parties to communicate that—will suffice. A thumbs up when asked if you want chocolate sprinkles on your cappuccino, rolling up your sleeve when the phlebotomist approaches you with the needle, and leaning in when your date asks if they can kiss you good night can all signal consent when you understand the context of communication.

This analysis is fine as far as it goes, but it does not tell us much about what the consenter needs to understand about the specific act to which they are giving consent. Imagine that Zoltán hears Faizan's request, and understands *that* he is giving consent by nodding, we can still ask: what does Zoltán need to understand to give consent to this act (Faizan borrowing his car for the day) rather than some other one (Faizan repainting his car in pink and purple stripes)?

Plausibly, we might think that he needs to understand the act regarding which he is waiving his rights—borrowing the car. The trouble is that there are *many ways* in which any act could be accurately described. Some descriptions are simple. Others detail what is going on at a molecular level. Some are brief. Others include the purpose of the act, the associated risks and benefits, and the alternatives to the act. So, what is the correct way to describe the act for the purposes of valid consent?

Once again, we think that the way to determine the minimal content of this third condition is to identify the type of description, or level of understanding, at which we could not make sense of the consenter waiving their rights against *this* act rather than some other one. Out of curiosity, Zoltán might ask ChatGPT to explain what is going on at a sub-atomic level when someone else drives his car, but we generally succeed in giving valid consent without any grasp of the quantum mechanics at play. Likewise, he might ask Faizan why he needs to use it today, but again we can make sense of him waiving his rights against its use without caring to know the answer. What we cannot make sense of, however, is Zoltán being asked, "Can I take yours today?," agreeing to that request, and not understanding what "yours" refers to. When he lacks *this* understanding it is unclear to everyone—including himself—*what* he is waiving his rights against.

This brief analysis gives us a minimal view of the understanding requirement for valid consent. The consenter just needs to understand (i) *that* they are giving consent, (ii) *how* to give consent, and (iii) to *what* they are giving consent.

This third condition could still be interpreted in different ways, some of which will be more minimal than others. For example, if someone understands that they are agreeing to knee surgery, presumably they have to know which knee will be operated on. But do they also need to know who the surgeon is or how long the surgery will last? If someone gives consent to sex, do they know what they are consenting to if they are mistaken about their partner's true identity?[7]

We can make some progress on answering this question by looking at the ways that what is communicated goes beyond what is literally said. When Zoltán understands Faizan's familiar request, and consents with a nod, the normative effect on the standing rights and responsibilities is precise. *Faizan* is released from the duty not to drive his car. Others are not—his daughter is not now free to drive it. Faizan is not released from *other* directed duties—he is not now free to get the car repainted. And the release is temporary—if Faizan wants to use the car next week, he will need to ask again. None of this is explicitly stated by Zoltán, and yet it is successfully communicated when he nods in response to Faizan's request.

What explains this is a general feature of successful communication. When Faizan points to the garage and asks, "Can I take yours?" he implies—or *conversationally implicates*—"your car," but he does not say so explicitly. Likewise, given the context, it is implied that he will just be *borrowing* the car, since getting permission for more than just that common request would require some more explicit clarification of what he was up to. Successful communication would be all but impossible if meaning were determined by what is *literally* said or if we had to share exactly the same mental images or descriptions.[8] For example, if Zoltán nods, and says, "Use the new car keys," he can communicate that *these* are the new car keys even if he hands Faizan a smart key when Faizan was expecting a key he would insert. No-one would think that they had failed to communicate simply because they had a different mental picture of the keys or because "new key" was too vague a descriptor to rule out a smart key. We succeed in communicating with each other in virtue of understanding what is conversationally implicated by what is literally said given the conversational context, the background norms of communication, and a common ground established by our past interactions.[9]

These norms explain how a simple nod can communicate consent that is both extensive (i.e., allows a lot of different actions) while also being restrictive. Zoltán does not delineate the precise boundaries of his consent, but his consent does not restrict Faizan's route, playlist, or parking options. No such idiosyncratic restrictions are implicated by a nod. They would need to be made explicit to be communicated—"Yes, you can take my car, but just stay off the Otley road," "Fine, but don't park in that lot downtown," "Taylor Swift is absolutely forbidden!"

However, while it is extensive in certain respects, a nod that successfully gives consent does not communicate that anything goes either. Faizan is not now permitted to use the car as a getaway vehicle, or as transport for a pack of muddy, badly behaved dogs, or as a motor in a demolition derby. Upon being caught doing any one of these things, we would have no trouble identifying his cynical misinterpretation of the communicative norms at play here if he were to protest: "I don't see the problem. You said I could use it!"

Maximalist views of the understanding requirement

Someone might agree that these three conditions tell us what, *at the very least,* the consenter needs to understand. But is that *all* that needs to be understood? In bioethics—an area of scholarship that has thoroughly analyzed the understanding requirement—most writers and guidelines claim that the consenter must know much more about the act to which they consent.[10]

Three views in the consent literature would ground a more substantial content. On the first—the *interests view*—consent is only valid if the consenter understands all the true facts about the act that are relevant to their interests.[11] On the second—the *inducements view*—the consenter needs to understand all the true facts that are relevant to their consent decision.[12] On the third—the *context understanding view* —the consenter needs to understand enough to be in a sufficiently good position for giving consent.[13] For instance, "to be in a sufficiently good position for making a choice, they need to know the action's possible consequences and know about the alternative courses of action."[14]

The reason why more maximalist views think that this additional information needs to be understood takes us back to the relationship between consent and autonomy. When we are capable of giving or refusing consent, we can direct our lives in ways that protect or further our interests or align with our personal conception of the good. This enables us to protect ourselves from others' interference, but also remove these normative barriers when interaction would benefit us. However, we can only meaningfully do this if we are in possession of information that enables us to protect our own interests or make subjectively correct decisions for ourselves. Hence, we need to understand these facts in order to make autonomous decisions.

The difficulty for such views is that there are many cases in which valid consent appears to be given but understanding of the allegedly essential facts is absent. For example, someone may have sex without being able to grasp the emotional impact it will have on them. Someone may enroll in the military ignorant of the *specific* risks of *this* deployment in *this* region. Someone may choose to donate a large sum to charity without thinking through the consequences. Where the other party is innocent of coercion, deception, or manipulation—that is, when the consent was given voluntarily by a person with decision-making capacity—there seems no reason to question the consent's validity. And yet it would be hard to deny that these facts—some of which no-one knows or could know at the time of consent—are relevant to the consenter's interests or to making a good decision.

In the next section, we return to these more maximalist views when discussing the disclosure requirement. There we consider whether they could be adapted so that what must be understood depends not just on the consent giver's interests or motivations, but on what the consent receiver knows.

3. The disclosure requirement

We turn now from the understanding requirement to the disclosure requirement.[15] In what follows, we analyze three strategies for determining the content of the disclosure requirement for valid consent. We assess these strategies against the same standards with which we assessed the understanding requirement. First, any plausible account of the disclosure requirement should render the intuitively correct verdicts for cases where we are confident that consent is valid or invalid. However, we turn to theory not only for accounts that entail the right verdict, but ones that give us a principled explanation of it. That gives us confidence that an account's verdicts for controversial cases can be relied upon. Second, then, an account of the disclosure requirement should explain why consent is invalidated when the person receiving or requesting consent fails to disclose the facts that they ought to. We think that only one account can meet both standards.

First strategy: derive disclosure from understanding

The most common strategy is to derive the disclosure requirement from the understanding requirement: the consent receiver should disclose certain facts to the consenter because valid consent requires that all this information be understood.[16] This not only gives us a clear answer to the question "what ought to be disclosed?," but a principled one. All the facts that ought to be disclosed ought to be disclosed *because* they must also be understood.

This strategy makes sense and gives intuitively plausible results for those with more maximalist views of the understanding requirement. Such views are common in medicine and clinical research.[17] For example, according to the interests view, patients and research participants need to understand all the information about a consent decision that is relevant to their interests. On the inducements view, patients and research participants need to understand all the information that is relevant to their decision. All that information should therefore all be disclosed in an understandable way. Such views can explain why the risk of a treatment or research procedure, for example, ought to be disclosed: the risks of the activity to which the patient or participant is giving consent is typically the kind of information that they need to understand to protect their interests or make decisions on the basis of what matters to them.

In section 2, we argued that maximalist views of understanding from which the standard view of disclosure is derived are false. Still, you might disagree with us about the understanding requirement. Even so, we think that this strategy for deriving the content of the disclosure requirement has serious problems.

To see why, return to Zoltán and Faizan. Imagine that the couple own a kayak and a removable roof rack to transport it. Suppose that there are four associated hazards. If not properly secured, the roof rack can (a) detach or (b) dent the roof of the car. These issues are known by the manufacturer, outlined in the product manual, and were disclosed by the salesperson when the couple purchased it. However, the roof rack also (c) can cause damage to the car's paintwork if the foam padding wears thin and (d) has a major design fault that will see it recalled in three years' time. At the time of purchase, however, these additional issues are unknown to all and so not disclosed by anyone.

Imagine that earlier that morning, Faizan promised to take their daughter out kayaking. He asks Zoltán if he can borrow his car to transport the kayak. Zoltán agrees. His consent seems valid.

Now consider a variant on the case. Faizan has noticed that the padding on the roof rack has perished in places. He suspects that when the weight of the kayak is added it will scratch the car's paintwork. He decides not to mention it. Once again, Faizan makes his request and Zoltán agrees. This time it seems implausible to think that he has given valid consent.

What explains the normative difference between the two cases? It cannot be *understanding* because Zoltán understands the same information in both cases—he understands that he is waiving his rights against Faizan using his car with the removable roof rack and kayak securely attached, he understands risks (a) and (b), and in neither case does he know about risks (c) and (d). The only difference, then, is that in the second case Faizan withholds something that he knows—namely, that the roof rack has deteriorated and is likely to cause damage to Zoltán's car if used. This suggests that there is a problem with disclosure, not understanding.

It seems clear that the fact that Faizan knows about risk (c) is relevant here. That is why Zoltán's consent is undermined when Faizan does not mention risk (c) but not when he does not mention risk (d)—the one that no one knows about. The proponent of an interests or inducement view of understanding might be tempted to adapt their view to say that the person giving consent must understand everything that the consent receiver knows and is relevant to their interests or inducements. The problem, though, is that the view then gives us the right verdict, but loses its ability to explain that verdict. The explanation was supposed to be in terms of what was in Zoltán's interests or what mattered to him. But why think that he succeeds in protecting his interests or deciding based on what matters to him when he understands *not* the set of facts that includes all those true propositions (a) – (d) about the roof rack, but *just* the set of facts that precisely mirrors what Faizan understands? This revised view seems to get the right answer but for the wrong reason. Disclosure is not just about understanding, but about the actions of the recipient of consent.

Second strategy: derive disclosure from positive duties

The second strategy is to work out what positive duties—that is, duties of assistance—the recipient of consent owes the consenter and use these to derive the disclosure requirement.

Tom Dougherty adopts this strategy. They argue that the recipient of consent has a positive duty "to put the consent-giver in a suitably good position for giving consent."[18] If the consent receiver breaches this duty and thereby obtains a token of consent, that consent will be invalidated.[19]

Unlike the views that derive disclosure from the understanding requirement, this one can explain what is going on in the roof rack cases. There are two intuitions that need to be explained. First, that Zoltán's consent is valid in the first case, but not the second. Second, that the problem is one of disclosure. Dougherty's view accounts for both: it is because Faizan fails to discharge a positive duty of *disclosure* in the second case—that is, not informing Zoltán that the roof rack is damaged and risks scratching up his car—that he cannot justify his treatment of Zoltán. He breaches no such duty in the first case.

However, the challenge for proponents of this strategy is that in order to work out whether the disclosure requirement has been met, we need to know what positive duties someone has. That will matter when it comes to resolving cases in which we are unsure what information ought to be disclosed or how much effort needs to go into the disclosure. This leads to difficulties.

To illustrate, Dougherty claims that the relevant duty is "at least partly grounded in [the consent giver's] interest in making an informed decision about whether to consent."[20] Later, they say that, "we should consider what, in light of everyone's interests, can reasonably be demanded of consent-receivers to help consent-givers make their choices."[21]

Two problems immediately suggest themselves. One is that on this view whether consent is valid depends on a balancing of interests. It is only because it is not a big hassle for Faizan to tell Zoltán about risk (c)—a risk he knows would matter—that he has a duty to do so. However, imagine that Zoltán rarely does his fair share of parenting. He was supposed to take their daughter out today, but he has been called into work yet again. So, Faizan is doing Zoltán a big favor by taking on all the parenting. Due to the last-minute change of plans, Faizan is now in a rush to get their daughter to her kayaking lesson on time. Meanwhile, though a scratch to his car might be relevant to Zoltán's decision, it is not a huge deal. Expecting Faizan to pause and start a conversation about the risks of attaching the roof rack would be adding yet another burden to him. On the balance of interests, it is unclear why Faizan would be under this obligation since he is already doing Zoltán a big favor. The point generalizes: for any example, we can imagine a version in which the balance of interests is such that the recipient of consent no longer has a duty of disclosure. This seems implausible: whether someone's consent is invalid should not be a matter of weighing up their interests versus those of another party.

The second problem is that if the duty to disclose is a positive duty grounded in the consent giver's interests, we can no longer explain why the duty is *directed* (i.e., why the duty is owed by the person requesting consent). This becomes clear when we consider acts that are in the interests of the consent giver rather than the recipient of consent. For example, we would expect a volunteer health care worker to disclose relevant information to patients, even when the procedures that the patients will undergo are very much in their interests and the volunteer is acting altruistically. Further, even if there is information that these patients would benefit from being told before agreeing to a procedure, and even if receiving that information is important enough to ground a duty of beneficence, why does the burden of disclosure fall on the person who is going to carry out the procedure? Why not a third party? Or why not think that the person giving consent—the beneficiary in this case—has a duty to find out information themselves?

Third strategy: derive disclosure from negative duties

The third and final strategy is to work out what negative duties the recipient of consent owes the consenter and use that to derive the duties of disclosure. This is our strategy.[22] Unlike the previous strategy, it has the advantage that the duties in question are relatively clear. As negative duties—duties not to harm or violate rights—they will also pick out the correct duty-bearer to fulfil the duty of disclosure.

We start, as always, with the function of consent. When valid, consent waives a specific right, and releases another from a specific duty. However, sometimes the interference of another party—whether it be the recipient of consent or someone else[23]—impedes that rights waiver. The strength and nature of that interference can be sufficient to vitiate consent.

Coercion is the obvious example. If Theo threatens to post intimate pictures of Milly online unless she gives him the passcode to her phone, he exercises the kind of illegitimate control that can invalidate her consent. His threat is illegitimate because the decision about who gets to access her phone is exclusively hers to make and he is proposing to violate her rights. It is controlling because he possesses those images and she, let us suppose, has every reason to believe that he will use them as he is threatening to do. As we explain in the next chapter, when a threat is illegitimate *and* controlling, it undermines the voluntariness condition for valid consent.

This is relevant to our current discussion because coercion is not the only way to illegitimately control a consent decision. Another way is by providing or withholding information that is relevant to that decision. Suppose Theo wants access to Milly's phone. As he leaves for work, he takes her phone instead of his. He then sends an email from his work computer explaining the "accidental" mix-up. Later on, he sends another email. He invents an emergency that requires him to phone his parents *immediately*—he hates asking but there is no-one else in the office, he is freaking out, he needs her passcode *now*. She sends it along and assents to him using her phone.

Just like before, he exercises illegitimate control over her consent decision. His deception is illegitimate (given that, we are assuming, it is wrongful). Plus, he *succeeds* in controlling her. By way of deception, he gets her to share her passcode. Her consent to his use of her phone is the direct result of his elaborate deceptive manipulation. Whether it is via coercion or deception, when one person illegitimately controls another's decision about something over which they have an autonomy right, they undermine the voluntariness of that decision.

Deceptive disclosure can illegitimately control someone's consent decision when the deception successfully motivates them to consent. But information can be disclosed in a manner that deceives even when no literal untruths are stated. For example, if a doctor knows about a common and serious side-effect of a medication and does not mention it, that will be deceptive. Patients have good reason to expect that their doctors will tell them about such side effects and so will assume that these side effects are not present if they are not mentioned. They are deceived by implicature.

We think that this deceptive implicature explains the normative difference in the roof rack cases. Faizan has good reason to think that what he knows about the poor state of the roof rack would be relevant to whether Zoltán would consent to it being fastened to his car. Given their relationship, Zoltán has good reason to expect Faizan would disclose such a risk. By voluntarily withholding it, Faizan exercises illegitimate control over Zoltán's consent decision, thereby undermining the voluntariness of his consent. What explains why Zoltán's consent is valid in the first case, but not the second, is not a fact about understanding, but voluntariness. He understands enough to exercise his rights in both cases. Faizan's deceptive withholding undermines the voluntariness of his decision in the second case. However, in the first, there is no control exercised because Faizan does not know about the problem with the roof rack either. We get the right verdict about cases *and* we can explain why consent is invalidated when the recipient of consent fails to disclose what they ought to.

The content and manner of disclosure

One reason why we are interested in a philosophical account of what underlies the understanding and disclosure requirements is that such an account can help us work out what needs to be understood and what needs to be disclosed in particular contexts. For example, if the disclosure and understanding requirements were derived from the interests of the consent giver, we could work out what a patient needs to be told by looking at what interests were at stake in their decision. As discussed, we think that the disclosure requirement is grounded in the recipient of consent's duty not to exercise illegitimate control over the consent decision. We now show how that insight can be used to derive the content and manner of the disclosure requirement.[24]

First, the recipient of consent can only exercise illegitimate control by way of information if they know that information. If Faizan had not noticed the perished foam, he would be in no better epistemic position than Zoltán. What puts him in a position to exercise illegitimate control is his knowledge.[25] This explains the normative significance of what the recipient of consent knows and what they ought to disclose.

Second, to invalidate consent, the information provided or withheld must be controlling. Even when the recipient of consent knows certain facts, they are only able to exercise illegitimate *control* with that information if the facts are relevant to the decision being made. Faizan might notice that the roof rack's logo looks like the logo for Olympiacos FC, but unless Zoltán is a die-hard fan of a rival team, it is hard to see how this fact could be dispositive of his consent decision. In addition, it must be the case that the giver of consent does not already know the information. If Zoltán has already noticed that the padding on the roof rack has worn through, then Faizan cannot control his decision by withholding that information.

Finally, to invalidate consent, the use of information must not *only* be controlling but illegitimate. Deception on the part of the recipient of consent is illegitimate, and there are many ways in which information can be provided or withheld deceptively. As we saw in the roof rack example, deception can occur through withholding or omission. If Zoltán would expect Faizan to mention the possibility of the worn roof rack damaging his car, then not mentioning it implies—or conversationally implicates—that he has noticed no such issues. Deception can also occur through bald-faced lies or even misrepresentations.

The way in which deception invalidates consent is outlined in more depth in chapter 5—the chapter on voluntariness. The relationship between privacy and potentially deceptive withholding is explored in a hard case in Chapter 9.

This brief analysis enables us to derive the content of the disclosure requirement. In order to avoid exercising illegitimate control, the recipient of consent must disclose a piece of information if and only if: (1) they believe it; (2) they have reason to think it is relevant to the consenter's decision; and (3) they judge the consenter would reasonably expect to be told it. Now, of course, sometimes the recipient of consent will be unsure what is relevant. For example, perhaps Faizan knows that Zoltán has the same lackadaisical attitude to car care and maintenance as he does, and so he might be genuinely unsure whether Zoltán would care about a couple of scratches. In this, and similar cases of uncertainty, the recipient ought to disclose all those facts that it would be reasonable to expect would be relevant. The state of the roof rack is one of those facts. The goal should be to come as close to a consenter-specific standard as possible.

Even when the recipient of consent discloses all the information they ought to, they still risk exercising illegitimate control over the consenter's decision if they do not pay attention to the manner in which that information is disclosed. Imagine that Faizan says "This roof rack risks damaging the paintwork on your car" in Urdu when he knows Zoltán only speaks English. He might have disclosed everything he ought to, but disclosing it in a language he knows Zoltán does not understand controls the information Zoltán receives just as surely as if he did not tell him at all. Likewise—and more plausibly—if the product manual discloses known risks of the roof rack, but is written in high-level technicalese, then the manufacturers fail to make information understandable to their customers. In some contexts—like the informed consent context in medicine or research—scientific jargon makes it impossible for most patients or potential research participants to understand information that is relevant to their consent decisions. The recipient of consent therefore ought to pay close attention to the manner of disclosure and ensure that relevant information is disclosed in a way they have reason to think the consenter is able to understand.

4. Ignorance and error

Sometimes we token consent despite being ignorant of important facts. Someone may click the box to indicate that they have read the terms and conditions without having done so and then indicate consent. Someone may assign another person the right to make financial or medical decisions on their behalf without knowing which decisions they will make. Or someone might agree to the use of their genetic samples in future research without knowing what that research might be about. How does this ignorance affect the validity and the scope of consent?[26] On the other side, sometimes the person *receiving* consent is ignorant. The researchers requesting permission to use genetic samples likely do not know what scientific questions the samples will ultimately be relevant to answering. A doctor might not know and so may fail to disclose all the risks of a procedure that they are recommending. Does this undermine consent?

Start with broad consent—consent that is given to a range of acts that are not yet fully defined, such as the future use of genetic samples.[27] Is broad consent possible? We think so. Just as we can be extremely specific about the ways in which we will permit someone to act, so we can be very general about it too. Provided that the communication about what is permitted is successful, I can give you permission only to stick me with a particular needle in a particular place, or give you permission to use any needle you like, or, indeed, to stick me anywhere that you judge will be safe and give you the blood sample you need. Just as a right can be described in quite general terms, so can a rights-waiver. It is perfectly coherent to give permission for unknown researchers to carry out unknown cancer research on a tumor sample. Provided that the person using the sample is indeed a qualified scientist in a health-related field (we assume that the term "researcher" is mutually understood to mean something along these lines) and the research in question is indeed related to benefiting patients with or at risk for cancer (again, making assumptions about the meaning of "cancer research" in this context) it is clear that permission to their activities has been granted. It will also be clear that some activities fall outside the scope of this broad consent. For example, research on reproductive cloning is not within the scope of what "cancer research" would mean and so has been ruled out. There may also be some uncertainty about the boundaries of what is permitted; but that is no different than for cases of more narrow consent, if the words used to communicate admit of ambiguous interpretation.

Could a token of consent be as general as permitting the recipient to "do whatever you want"? For example, if someone agreed to being "surprised" by their wife would that permit absolutely any surprising actions?[28] Here we think there are always going to be limits on what is consented to. One limit, of course, is given by acts it is possible to give consent to, as discussed in chapter 2. But even among those acts to which it is possible, in principle, to give consent, the content of "whatever you want" will be drastically narrowed by the norms of communication that apply to that particular context. Much will depend on what is in the "common ground"—that is, the body of information that is, or is presumed to be, mutually understood by these conversational partners.[29] The spouse, we may assume, has not consented to being punched in the face, even though that would be very surprising to them.[30] A "surprise" in this context is implied to be something pleasant and to take the word literally would be to deliberately misunderstand what was agreed.

Sometimes an act clearly falls within or outside the scope of consent. Under normal circumstances, Faizan's consent to a surprise would permit Zoltán to invite a dear old friend over for their family dinner. It would do that even if Faizan does not, until he opens the door, understand that *this* specific act is what he has permitted. On the other hand, the very same surprise would be ruled out if Faizan had been begging Zoltán for a quiet night in. Finally, if Zoltán suspects that Faizan would be delighted if his old friend came to dinner, but is not sure if he has consented to have her over *tonight* because Faizan said he needs a quiet night in, then Zoltán should not proceed. At least, not without checking first. It is possible to give valid consent to a surprise, but proceeding when there are reasonable doubts about what has been authorized explains why the person surprised may have a legitimate grievance if the recipient is unlucky about what falls within the inferred scope—"Why on earth would you invite her over for dinner *tonight* when I have been telling you for weeks that I'm exhausted by all our socializing?!"

What if the consent giver does not know or is mistaken about some important fact?[31] The implications for the validity of consent will depend on whether the fact falls within the understanding requirement and, if not, why they are ignorant or in error.

First, no matter the source of the error, if the understanding requirement is not met then consent will be invalid. On our view, that means that the person giving consent must recognize that their communication signifies consent and what rights they are altering by giving it. On more maximalist views, that means that there will be additional facts, such as facts about important risks or the purposes of the consent receiver that must be understood if consent is to be valid. On such a view, for example, someone giving broad consent to future uses of her tumor sample would need to know if the sharing of samples entailed additional risks to her privacy.[32]

Second, the content and manner of disclosure can affect what someone understands (and do so in a predictable way). This means that disclosure can *control* someone's consent decision. For example, if a patient is told that they are likely to have a heart attack if they do not start taking anticoagulants, that might convince them to take the medicine. If the health professional making the recommendation has reason to think that the information will motivate them, their disclosure is controlling. On our view, this sort of control can invalidate consent when it is illegitimate. In the context of disclosure, such illegitimate control will arise when consent givers are deceived about something that matters to their decision. This deception could be a lie, but it could also be deception through omission—not telling someone a relevant fact that they would reasonably expect to be told.

Turn now to the recipient or requester of consent's ignorance. Imagine that there is an increased risk of cardiac depression in patients with chronic heart disease who undergo general anesthetic. Let us suppose that any surgeon practicing in accordance with their professional responsibilities would recognize that the surgery is contraindicated in this patient. However, suppose further that our surgeon is negligent, and her ignorance of these increased risks means that she has an erroneous belief about the surgery's safety. There is no doubt that she is blameworthy for her error.

In what ways can her error invalidate the patient's consent? Imagine that she does not disclose this increased risk because she did not keep up with the relevant literature and updated guidelines He consents to the surgery, even though he would not have done if he had known about these risks. On views of disclosure that are derived from a maximalist understanding requirement, her failure to disclose it would invalidate his consent to surgery *because* he needs to understand all the true facts about risks to give valid consent. On minimalist views of understanding like ours, however, that information is not required for a rights waiver. The question, then, is whether her withholding amounts to illegitimate control. We think not. The surgeon can only exercise *control* if she possesses the information, and she does not in this case. Hence, assuming other conditions for validity are met, the patient's consent is valid.

This conclusion does not imply that the surgeon is off the hook, ethically speaking. Consent might be valid, but the duty to obtain valid consent does not exhaust the surgeon's ethical obligations. On the story we have told, she has still violated a professional duty to keep herself up-to-date with her medical specialty. If her failure to do so leads to a harm to the patient, she will wrong him. Likewise, as a medical professional she has a duty to assist her patients to make good decisions about their health care (in the light of their values). This is a limited duty of beneficence—she does not have to ensure that they make the best decision, merely assist them insofar as time and other commitments allow. Her culpable ignorance might entail that she has violated this duty too.[33]

5. Conclusions

The informational requirements for valid consent—disclosure and understanding—are closely related. Consenters need to understand certain facts in order to exercise their rights, and the reason why the recipient of consent discloses information to them is to put them in a position to make an autonomous decision. However, as we have seen there is a lively debate about the nature and content of each requirement, as well as the relationship between them. We have outlined the major views of understanding and disclosure, and argued that we cannot derive the latter from the former. On our view, the disclosure and understanding requirements are conceptually distinct. They have different contents and separate normative grounds. Recipients of consent have a duty not to exercise illegitimate control over a consenter's decision. Not exercising illegitimate control often requires discharging substantial duties of disclosure. Consenters need to understand enough information to exercise their rights through consent. This does not require understanding everything that ought to be disclosed. It only requires that they understand that they are giving consent, how to give consent, and what they are giving the recipient permission to do.

Notes

1 Cf. *Montgomery v. Lanarkshire Health Board* [2015] UKSC 11. Nadine Montgomery, a primigravida patient with diabetes, agreed to a vaginal delivery, but was inadequately informed about the material risk of shoulder dystocia in her case, and the associated risks to her and the fetus. During labor and delivery, this risk manifested—the fetus's shoulder became lodged behind the patient's pelvic bone—and the resultant hypoxia meant that the child was born with cerebral palsy. Montgomery argued that if she had been properly informed, she would have opted for a caesarean section instead. For analysis, see Farrell, Anne Maree, and Margaret Brazier. "Not so new directions in the law of consent? Examining *Montgomery v. Lanarkshire Health Board*." *Journal of Medical Ethics* 42.2 (2016): 85–88.

2 For more in-depth versions of the arguments that follow, see Millum, Joseph, and Danielle Bromwich. "Understanding, communication, and consent." *Ergo* 5 (2018): 45–68 and Millum, Joseph, and Danielle Bromwich. "Informed consent: What must be disclosed and what must be understood?" *American Journal of Bioethics* 21.5 (2021): 46–58. To our knowledge, we are the only consent scholars who argue for a minimalist view of understanding simpliciter. See, Bromwich, Danielle, and Joseph Millum. "Response to open peer commentaries on 'Informed consent: What must be disclosed and what must be understood?'" *American Journal of Bioethics* 21.7 (2021): W1–W5. However, when additional conditions are met, other consent scholars have also endorsed minimalist conditions for valid consent. See, for example, Sreenivasan, Gopal. "Does informed consent to research require comprehension?" *The Lancet* 362.940 (2003): 2016–2018. For criticism of that view, see Bromwich, Danielle. "Understanding, interests and informed consent: A reply to Sreenivasan." *Journal of Medical Ethics* 41.4 (2015): 327–331; Walker, Tom. "Informed consent and the requirement to ensure understanding." *Journal of Applied Philosophy* 29.1 (2012): 50–62.

3 For a discussion about whether and when a recipient is justified on acting without valid consent, see Chapter 2, section 11.

4 Or, more precisely, they must understand that their act is one whose meaning is "I consent." This deals with potential counter-examples involving someone who tokens consent while erroneously believing that they cannot give consent (e.g., because they mistakenly think themselves too inebriated). See, e.g., Dougherty, Tom. *The scope of consent*. Oxford University Press, 2021: ch. 7.

5 Like us, other scholars have argued that in order to play its functional role, a token of consent must be observable. For an excellent and thorough analysis, see Bolinger, Renée Jorgensen. "Moral risk and communicating consent." *Philosophy & Public Affairs* 47.2 (2019): 179–207.

6 Unless he and Faizan had previously agreed on one of these as their special way of communicating agreement. Sometimes consenting parties have good reason to choose a word to communicate that they consent to or refuse the proposed act. For example, if a group of people enjoy role-playing sexual acts of domination and submission, the typical language and behavior that communicates willingness or unwillingness might be easily misread. To ensure that the acts are consensual, the parties might choose a "safe word" that unambiguously communicates that one party wants to stop or is refusing to consent, and will not implicate anything else in this context. For discussion of safe words in consent contexts, see "Non-binding bondage," *Harvard Law Review* 128.2 (2014): 713–734.

7 See Chapter 9 for a discussion of deception and consent to sex.

8 See Grice, H. Paul. "Meaning." *Philosophical Review* 65.3(1957). 377–388, Grice, H. Paul. *Studies in the ways of words*. Harvard University Press, 1989; and Saul, Jennifer M. "Speaker meaning, what is said, and what is implicated." *Noûs* 36.2 (2002): 228–248.

9 See Stalnaker, Robert. "Common ground." *Linguistics and Philosophy* 25.5 (2002): 701–721.

10 For example, all the major statements of research ethics articulate substantial understanding requirements. See World Medical Association. "Declaration of Helsinki: Medical research involving human participants." 2025. Available at: www.wma.net/what-we-do/medical-ethics/declaration-of-helsinki; Council for International Organizations of Medical Sciences. "International ethical guidelines for health-related research involving humans." 2016. Available at: www.cioms.ch/ethicalguidelines-2016; National Commission for the Protection of Human Subjects of Biomedical and Behavioral Research. *The Belmont report: Ethical principles and guidelines for the protection of human subjects of research*. US Department of Health, Education, and Welfare, 1978.

11 See, for example, Wendler, D., and C. Grady. "What should research participants understand to understand they are participants in research?" *Bioethics* 22.4 (2008): 203–208.

12 See, for example, Faden, R. R., T. L. Beauchamp, and N. M. P. King. *A history and theory of informed consent*. Oxford University Press, 1986.

13 See, for example, Dougherty, Tom. "Informed consent, disclosure, and understanding." *Philosophy & Public Affairs* 48.2 (2020): 119–150.

14 Dougherty, Tom. "Informed consent, disclosure, and understanding." *Philosophy & Public Affairs* 48.2 (2020): 139.

15 The analysis that follows is derived from Bromwich, Danielle, and Joseph Millum. "Disclosure and consent to medical research participation." *Journal of Moral Philosophy* 12.2 (2015): 195–219, Millum, Joseph, and Danielle Bromwich. "Informed consent: What must be disclosed and what must be understood?" *American Journal of Bioethics* 21.5 (2021): 46–58; and Bromwich, Danielle, and Joseph Millum. "Lies, control, and consent: a response to Dougherty and Manson." *Ethics* 128.2 (2018): 446–461.

16 As Alexander Capron and colleagues write: "[p]lainly, comprehension is essential for truly informed consent, for the act of disclosure would otherwise be pointless" Capron, A. M, et al. "Legal and regulatory standards of informed consent in research." In *The Oxford textbook of clinical research ethics*, ed. Ezekiel Emanuel. Oxford University Press, 2008.

17 See World Medical Association. "Declaration of Helsinki: Medical research involving human participants." 2025. Available at: www.wma.net/what-we-do/medical-ethics/declaration-of-helsinki; Council for International Organizations of Medical Sciences. "International ethical guidelines for health-related research involving humans." 2016. Available at: www.cioms.ch/ethicalguidelines-2016; National Commission for the Protection of Human Subjects of Biomedical and Behavioral Research. *The Belmont report: Ethical principles and guidelines for the protection of human subjects of research*. US Department of Health, Education, and Welfare, 1978.

18 Dougherty, Tom. "Informed consent, disclosure, and understanding." *Philosophy & Public Affairs* 48.2 (2020): 142.

19 Dougherty, Tom. "Informed consent, disclosure, and understanding." *Philosophy & Public Affairs* 48.2 (2020): 126.

20 Dougherty, Tom. "Informed consent, disclosure, and understanding." *Philosophy & Public Affairs* 48.2 (2020): 147.

21 Dougherty, Tom. "Informed consent, disclosure, and understanding." *Philosophy & Public Affairs* 48.2 (2020): 150.

22 Bromwich, Danielle, and Joseph Millum. "Disclosure and consent to medical research participation." *Journal of Moral Philosophy* 12.2 (2015): 195–219; Millum, Joseph, and Danielle Bromwich. "Informed consent: What must be disclosed and what must be understood?" *American Journal of Bioethics* 21.5 (2021): 46–58.

23 As one of us has argued, the recipient of consent might be innocent or even unaware of that interference. It might be exercised by a third party. See Millum, Joseph. "Consent under pressure: The puzzle of third party coercion." *Ethical Theory and Moral Practice* 17 (2014): 113–127.

24 It is worth pointing out that we accept that the disclosure process can serve other functions. However, this chapter is an analysis of its relationship to validity. For criticism of our view on this point, see Sreenivasan, Gopal. "Varieties of minimalism about informed consent." *American Journal of Bioethics* 21.5 (2021): 66–68. For response, see Bromwich, Danielle, and Joseph Millum. "Response to open peer commentaries on 'Informed consent: What must be disclosed and what must be understood?'" *American Journal of Bioethics* 21.7 (2021): W1–W5.

25 Of course, the recipient can be wrongfully ignorant. They may breach professional duties to know, or be otherwise negligently ignorant, or even willfully ignorant. This behavior will often be disrespectful of the consenter's autonomy or fail to treat them with due care. However, when the recipient is ignorant, they cannot exercise wrongful control over the consent decision.

26 See Villiger, Daniel. "Informed consent under ignorance." *American Journal of Bioethics* (2024): 1–13.

27 See, for example, Sheehan, Mark. "Can broad consent be informed consent?" *Public Health Ethics* 4.3 (2011): 226–235.

28 See Dougherty, Tom. "Informed consent, disclosure, and understanding." *Philosophy & Public Affairs* 48.2 (2020): 119–150.

29 See Stalnaker, Robert. "Common ground." *Linguistics and Philosophy* 25.5 (2002): 701–721.

30 Dougherty, Tom. "Informed consent, disclosure, and understanding." *Philosophy & Public Affairs* 48.2 (2020): 135–136.

31 For a discussion of the potential significance between being in error and simply being ignorant about a relevant fact, see Keren, Arnon, and Ori Lev. "Informed consent, error and suspending ignorance: Providing knowledge or preventing error?" *Ethical Theory and Moral Practice* 25.2 (2022): 351–368.

32 Beskow, Laura M., and Kevin P. Weinfurt. "Exploring understanding of 'understanding': The paradigm case of biobank consent comprehension." *American Journal of Bioethics* 19.5 (2019): 6–18.

33 Elsewhere, we distinguish two goals of the informed consent process—to obtain valid consent and to facilitate good decision making—and explain why respect for a consenter's decision entails a duty *not* to require that all the information that ought to be disclosed must also be understood. See Bromwich, Danielle, and Joseph R. Millum. "Informed consent to HIV cure research." *Journal of Medical Ethics* 43.2 (2017): 108–113.

5 Voluntariness

Coercion, manipulation, and deception

1. Introduction

In order for someone's token of consent to be valid, the consent giver must be competent, they must have sufficient understanding of what they are giving consent to, and their consent must be voluntary. Previous chapters have established that the token of consent must be a speech act, considered the criteria for competency, and examined different views of the understanding requirement and its relationship to disclosure. In this chapter, we turn to the concept of *voluntariness*.

Voluntariness matters because it is closely connected with important features of interpersonal morality. It is relevant to whether someone is responsible for their action and whether they should make amends, as well as to whether they can exercise their rights. To illustrate, the other day, Joe gave £10 to a volunteer requesting donations to a water charity. The volunteer was standing there with his bucket, as people passed by, and Joe deliberately walked up to him and dropped the money in. No one forced Joe to donate: he exercised his rights voluntarily. But imagine that Danielle had given Joe this money to buy them both coffee. Joe would be responsible for not using the money as he should have. Voluntariness is also connected to well-being: it is bad for persons if they are unable to act voluntarily and if important aspects of their lives are controlled by others. Had a tough frog-marched Joe to the bucket and forced his hand into his wallet, the "donation" would not have been voluntary. Not only would this not constitute an exercise of his rights (he would have been justified in asking for his money back), he would not be responsible, *and* domination by the tough would be a harm to him.

Paradigm cases of apparently voluntary and involuntary acts are easy to describe. But what if the tough had only threatened to throw water on Joe if he did not donate? What if the charity volunteer had lied to get the money—claiming that they represented a water charity when really the funds went to a political campaign? What if they were honest, but they got Joe to give by showing him pictures of adorable, desperate children whose plight made him feel guilty? Minor threats, deception, and manipulation are all common techniques for obtaining consent, especially in sexual and business contexts. Do they invalidate consent? A systematic way to think about voluntariness is clearly needed in order to address these sorts of cases.

DOI: 10.4324/9781003287391-6

The chapter begins by asking what it means for an action to be voluntary in general. This involves distinguishing voluntary actions from reflexive, accidental, and forced motions. We then move onto voluntariness in the specific context of consent. Non-voluntary motions do not count as tokens of consent and so cannot be morally transformative. For other acts, whether or not they count as voluntary depends on who ultimately controls the act and how. Consent proffered as the result of *illegitimate control* will be involuntary in this sense and so invalid. The remaining sections address coercion, deception, and manipulation—the major ways in which others can illegitimately influence us.[1] In each case, we provide an overview of how philosophers think about the concept and consider whether and when it involves illegitimate control.

2. Is voluntariness possible?

Before exploring what voluntariness is and the specific ways in which other people can undermine it, we should acknowledge a question that may be on the reader's mind: does causal determinism render the discussion of this chapter pointless? *Causal determinism* is, roughly, the view that all physical events, including all human actions, are fixed by the state of the world at some point in time and the laws of nature. Even though we do not know those laws of nature—and, indeed, even if they involve some randomness—what each of us does is caused by a very complex process that was set in motion a long time before we were born.[2] Some worry that if causal determinism is true, then it undermines individual agency, since it would imply that all acts are involuntary and so no one is responsible for their actions.[3]

There is considerable philosophical debate over the truth of determinism and its implications. Yet, we doubt that, in the end, this debate will have significant consequences for theorizing about consent. After all, we care about whether others respect our decisions no matter what causes them to do so. It is bad for us to be controlled by others, whether or not they could—in some metaphysical sense—help themselves. Thus, the sense in which a token of consent can be rendered *involuntary* is importantly different than the sense in which causal determinism might render all actions *involuntary*. Even if all actions were involuntary in the latter sense, some would be voluntary and some involuntary in the former sense; and, we care a great deal about which is which. We therefore set aside concerns about determinism for the purposes of thinking about voluntary consent.[4]

3. What is voluntariness?

Frankie kicked Noah. Did she do it voluntarily?

Suppose Frankie and Noah were sleeping in the same bed and Frankie kicked out when twitching in her dreams. Clearly that was not voluntary. Or, suppose Noah had just tapped her knee with a tiny hammer. Then the resulting reflex was involuntary. The same would apply if Frankie was fully conscious but a neighbor grabbed her foot and shoved it into Noah's shin while she lacked the strength to resist. These are uncontroversial cases.

We might think that Frankie's action is voluntary only if she meant to do it. However, what if Frankie kicked Noah deliberately, but only because that was the only way to avoid standing on a venomous snake? It seems that she could say, reasonably, that she had no choice. "No choice," here would mean "no other good choice." Was her action therefore involuntary? Actions like this are clearly different than those that are unconscious, reflexive, or physically forced. In this case, but not the others, we could ask Frankie why she kicked Noah and she could give us her reasons for acting, not just a causal explanation of what happened. One way to describe this would be to say that we can *attribute* the action to Frankie—it was *her action*. Another is to say that this action, unlike the others, was *intentional*—Frankie meant to do it.

This analysis does not yet solve the problem of whether Frankie acted voluntarily when she only had one good choice available to her. To describe an act as intentional is not the same as describing it as voluntary. Confronted by a robber with a gun, I might give him my wallet intentionally. But I would not describe my action as voluntary—quite the opposite! Another way in which the concepts of *voluntariness* and *intentionality* come apart can be seen by looking at different ways that the same action can be described. We can intend to perform an action under one description, while voluntarily performing another. For example, Frankie might *intend* to step over a puddle. She might also know that in doing so, she would tread on Noah's foot. Then it is true that she treads on Noah voluntarily, even though that was not her intention—it is not *why* she placed her foot where she did.[5]

We might think, then, that Frankie's action is voluntary only if she had a meaningful choice. After all, reflecting on the armed robber case might make us think that if someone only has one good option then they do not act voluntarily by taking it. Consequently, consent given under such circumstances must be invalid.

This would be too quick. Consider a patient who needs lifesaving surgery for a traumatic injury incurred at work and a surgeon who is the only person available to provide it. "Without this surgery, you will die," she might tell him. Of course, the surgeon needs the patient's consent before she can operate. But if having only one good option meant that his consent was invalid, it would be impossible for him to agree to the surgery.

There is an important difference between the robbery and surgery cases—a difference that helps us get clear on how voluntariness can be undermined so as to invalidate consent. In the first case, there is another agent (the robber) who has engineered a situation in which their victim has only one good option. They thereby *control* the victim's decision by credibly threatening them with serious harm unless they hand over their wallet. We all have a claim against interference of this sort, so the robber is threatening a rights violation when they pull the gun on their victim. They exercise control in a way that they have no right to—that is, they act *illegitimately*. It is this *illegitimate control* that renders the action of handing over the wallet involuntary and makes the consent invalid. However, in the second case, the recipient of consent is not responsible for the choice situation of her patient. She did not cause the traumatic injury for which he now needs a life-saving surgery. She, might be controlling his decision by offering the lifesaving alternative, but, unlike the robber, she does not exercise *illegitimate* control.

This analysis is not exhaustive of what voluntariness is. However, it is sufficient to guide our thinking about voluntariness as a necessary condition of valid consent. We have learned that some acts are involuntary because they are not intentional actions at all. These include unconscious behaviors, reflexes, and physically forced motions. They cannot really be attributed to the agent as *the agent's actions*. Consequently, they cannot count as tokens of consent. The question of validity simply does not come up. Other acts are intentional, but can still be involuntary—like handing over one's wallet to the armed robber. To undermine consent, another agent must be involved. If another agent *illegitimately controls* whether someone gives them consent, that will render the token of consent invalid. The force of nature is insufficient to have this normative effect.[6]

4. Coercion

Intuitively, coercion undermines voluntariness. But what is coercion and how does it have this normative effect?

At its most basic, coercion involves one party forcing another to do what they want. One way to do this is to actually use physical force. For example, a patient experiencing psychosis might be held down by nurses and then injected with haloperidol. This form of coercion may be labeled *occurrent coercion* or *compulsion*.[7] Alternatively, compliance may be achieved by simply threatening to use force (so-called *dispositional coercion*). For example, a patient in a long-term care facility might be threatened with the withdrawal of their privileges if they do not take their Parkinson's medication. As these examples suggest, both occurrent and dispositional coercion are ethically fraught.

With respect to consent, the verdict on occurrent coercion is straightforward. If someone is forced, so that they physically could not do otherwise, then they are not performing an action themselves. There is no token of consent, so there is no question of whether consent is valid. Occurrent coercion entails that no right is waived.

Dispositional coercion, which is the topic of most recent philosophical writing on coercion, is more complicated. Take the patient who refuses to take their medication. They are told that if they do not comply then they will not be given a day pass to go into town with the other residents. If they now agree to take their drugs, have they been coerced into treatment?[8]

To answer this question, we need to distinguish between threats and offers. Recall the earlier cases of the armed robber and the surgeon. The armed robber has made it such that her victim has no option but to comply. She has done this by issuing a *threat*. This means that she is proposing to make her victim worse off (dead) if he does not comply (give over his wallet). By contrast, the surgeon makes her patient an *offer*. She proposes to make him better off (alive) if he complies (consents). Only threats coerce, it is argued, and so only threats invalidate consent.

The idea that only threats can be coercive is intuitively appealing. In addition, there are plausible explanations of why this distinction would matter morally. When someone makes an offer, they generally add to the options available to the other party.[9] An offer makes one course of action more attractive but does not make any other course of action worse. The surgeon, for example, makes giving consent very attractive, but her patient still has whatever other options were open to him before she made her proposal.[10] He appears to have just as much freedom, if not more. But a threat reduces one's options: before the robber acted, her victim could keep her money and her life, now she must choose between them. In brief, offers make one better off and threats make one worse off with respect to freedom.

Coercive offers

The view that only threats coerce is probably the received wisdom in philosophy, but the question of whether coercive offers are possible has been much discussed.[11] A recent analysis of this question suggests that there are actually two concepts of coercion at play here, corresponding to two ways in which coercion can be problematic.[12] The first is a "deontic" concept which is relevant to whether consent is undermined. The second is a "eudaimonic" concept which is relevant to whether being coerced is bad for the victim: in addition to its effects, it is plausible that it is bad for someone to be coerced, since it involves being subject to another's will.[13] Most of the time these two forms of coercion coincide—the robber who issues a threat of death undermines her victim's consent *and* subjects her victim to her will (that is, makes him do what she wants him to do). Sometimes, however, they come apart. This explains the sense in which the law can be described as coercive, even when it is legitimate: effective law enforcement makes us subject to the law and thereby subject to the will of others. This is bad for us, even though it does not violate our rights. In this chapter we are focused only on the deontic concept—the one that is essentially concerned with threats and can undermine the validity of consent. However, the latter concept can be valuable in thinking about what might be problematic about certain forms of control that do not undermine the validity of consent. For example, in Chapter 7 we discuss the potential effects of paying people to undergo risky research, which might be fruitfully understood in terms of eudaimonic coercion (that is, in terms of how being subject to another's will is bad for a person). Under certain rare circumstances, this could constitute a coercive offer, though not one that invalidates consent.

Baselines

Most of the time, it is clear whether a proposal constitutes a threat or an offer. But not always. Suppose a prosecutor is considering whether to take a case to trial. She may propose a "plea bargain"—in exchange for not being charged with one crime the defendant will plead guilty to a lesser crime. Is this a threat because it renders the defendant worse off than they would be without any charge at all, or an offer because it permits them to choose a lesser penalty? Or consider the surgeon who proposes a life-saving operation but insists on payment from the patient. Does she offer to save the patient's life—since he would definitely rather pay the fee—or does she threaten not to save him? Distinguishing threats from offers requires that we identify a *baseline* against which to compare proposals.

The baseline could be conceptualized in either *descriptive* or *normative* terms. For example, one version of a descriptive baseline distinguishes threats from offers based on what would be predicted to happen otherwise.[14] Without the robber, her victim would retain his money and his life, so the robber's proposal is a threat. Alternatively, a normative baseline might compare the pre- and post-proposal situations according to how the person making the proposal *ought* to behave. The robber ought not to shoot her victim, so her proposal is a threat.

The verdicts that result from using descriptive and normative baselines will often coincide, as they do in the robber case. Where they do not, we favor the normative. This is because descriptive baselines seem to give mistaken verdicts when the status quo involves wrongful treatment. Consider a playground bully who punches his victim every day. One day, he offers to refrain from hitting them, in exchange for a dollar. Since the predicted course of events is getting punched, compared to a descriptive baseline this looks like the bully is making an offer.[15] Yet, surely this verdict is mistaken—the dollar is coerced from his victim just like the "protection money" extorted by a gangster is coerced from a storekeeper.[16] The reason is that the correct baseline is one in which the bully does not hit anyone.[17]

Armed with a normative baseline, we can return to some of the prior cases. Assume that the prosecutor is within her rights to take the case to trial or to prosecute a lesser charge. Then proposing the plea bargain constitutes an offer, not a threat. Assume that the surgeon who demands a fee is working within a public health system that grants residents the right to receive surgery free of charge. Then making treatment conditional on additional payment from the patient (effectively a bribe or kickback) is coercive. Finally, return to our original puzzle of the patient who refuses to take their medication. Whether restricting his freedom to leave the facility for the day is coercive depends on whether he has a right to leave or if the day pass is rightly treated as a "privilege" by the staff that they are permitted to withhold. Such a case would require some further ethical analysis. We suspect that it will normally be wrong to restrict residents' freedom—provided that they are competent and not posing a serious risk to others—and so this attempt to make the patient take his medication would be coercive.

Coercion and the validity of consent

Turn now to the effects of coercion on the validity of consent. Whether a proposal renders a token of consent to that proposal invalid depends on two factors: whether the proposal is wrongful and whether it is controlling.[18] The discussion so far has focused on the first of these factors. But a threat can motivate someone without controlling them. If a kid points a water pistol at you and says, "Let me in the shed or I'll spray you!" then you might agree to let them in, but you could definitely say no and take the consequences. The threat is too weak to control you and so too weak to invalidate consent. But how do we draw the line between a real gun and the water pistol—between threats that control and those that do not?

This question has a parallel in discussions of the broader concept of *duress*. When someone commits a crime and claims to have acted under duress, they are claiming that they had no (acceptable) choice under the circumstances and so should not be held responsible for their actions.[19] Likewise, if someone signs a contract but only under duress, the agreement they entered into will lack force—effectively they did not exercise their rights by signing the contract and so should not be held to its terms. Similarly, consent obtained under duress will not have its morally transformative effect in virtue of the pressure put on the person giving consent. They should not be held responsible for their action in giving consent.

A claim of duress has two parts.[20] First, that the agent putting someone under duress acts wrongly in so doing, as we have already discussed. Second, that their victim was justified in carrying out the action, given the alternatives. Duress, then, is a thoroughly normative notion.[21] As Alan Wertheimer puts it: "we are measuring not the amount of pressure which A's proposal imposes on B, but whether B is entitled to succumb to A's proposal."[22] As well as implying that claims of duress can only be evaluated by engaging in ethical analysis, this means that how bad a threat must be to constitute control may vary depending on the context. For example, Simon might be excused for punching Saskia's arm, if Theodore threatened to break Simon's arm otherwise. But he would not be excused for killing her in response to the same threat.[23] Unfortunately, this leaves us without a straightforward account of when someone has been controlled to a degree that their token of consent can be rendered invalid. For the moment, we can say only that the conditions under which a threat invalidates consent are the same as those under which someone could cite a threat as a justification or excuse for their actions or, equivalently, under which we would not hold them responsible.[24]

Return again to our stubborn patient. Assume that we have agreed that the residents of his care facility should be permitted to leave (where safe to do so, during the daytime, etc.). Thus, the proposal to withhold this right is indeed a coercive threat. Still, if he protests that he was forced to take his medication, we might question whether the withholding of his day pass met the standard for duress. After all, it is not as if he had no acceptable alternative—he could have stayed home! The resident in this case might well have been coerced but not controlled.[25]

The possibility of a wrongful threat that falls short of control allows for nuanced analyses of cases like these. Since the threat is not controlling, consent given as a result can still be valid, so proceeding would not involve a rights violation. However, there is a plausible moral (and legal) principle that says that it is wrong to profit from one's wrongdoing.[26] This was famously cited in a New York court case considering whether someone should inherit property, when he had murdered his grandfather in order to prevent him from changing his will to disinherit him.[27] Likewise, someone who secures valid consent via wrongful means should not benefit from proceeding on the consent. If I agree to give you £10 in order to avoid you soaking me with a water gun, the transfer might be valid, but you ought not to take the money.

To threaten someone is normally *pro tanto* wrongful—this means that it should not be done unless there are justifying reasons that outweigh the wrong.[28] In some cases, there can be good reasons to proceed on a valid token of consent that resulted from a non-controlling threat. Such reasons might include important benefits to that individual or to third parties that could not be obtained otherwise. Whether the threat to the resident is justified or not will depend on why it is being done. If taking the medication is very important for the resident's health and he risks an accident while out for the day, then the threat might be justified.[29] On the other hand, if the risk of skipping a dose is low, and the threat is being made just to save the staff some extra paperwork, then it should probably not be made.

5. Deception

As we saw in the last chapter, coercion is not the only way in which someone can act so as to undermine the voluntariness of consent. Consider the following examples.

Clo, an experienced cyclist, tells Mo that her bicycle is in "excellent condition." He buys it from her for £200. The next day, he discovers that the brakes do not work and the frame is bent.

Dr. Brown's patient has severe lower back pain that has not been relieved by over-the-counter oral medications. Because this patient has a history of substance misuse, she would rather not prescribe stronger painkillers unless it is really necessary. "Let's try weekly injections of this new extra-strong medicine," she suggests. He agrees and she injects him with a saline solution hoping that the placebo effect will relieve his pain.

Barry Tyles has an uncanny resemblance to a famous pop star. He introduces himself to a woman as that celebrity and they get chatting. "I've never kissed someone famous before," she says, and they snog.

All these cases involve deception. Do they all involve invalid consent? Intuitive verdicts may differ. Some endorse *caveat emptor* ("let the buyer beware") in commerce and so will claim that Mo ought to have checked the bike. Some might think that Dr. Brown acts rightly in trying a placebo treatment first and so while the consent may not be ideal, it is sufficient. Deceiving someone into sex—let alone just a kiss—is often treated very leniently and so many may be inclined to think that Barry has obtained valid consent from his would-be groupie. Contrary to all these verdicts, we will argue that consent is invalid anytime it is obtained through deception that is wrongful and controlling.

Forms of deception

Start with the nature of deception. One person *deceives* another when the deceiver intentionally causes the other party to believe something that the deceiver correctly believes is untrue. This rough definition will be precise enough for our purposes here.[30]

There are different forms of deception. Lying is one. Another, as discussed in Chapter 4, is false *implicature*. False implicature involves the deceiver making use of norms of communication to deceive without literally saying anything untrue. For example, if Dr. Brown were to say to her patient, "I've found injections with this solution very helpful in the past," she could reasonably expect him to infer that the solution was a medicine—not saline—but she would not be speaking any literal untruths. A further category of deception does not involve communication at all. This *covert deceit* is exemplified by someone who wears a wig with the intention of pretending that it is their own hair or someone who puts on a police officer's uniform when they are not in the police.[31] If Barry said nothing but dressed and did his makeup like the pop star then he would be engaged in this sort of deception (provided that he did so in order to make people think he was the pop star, not simply as a form of fan homage).

A great deal of ink has been spilled on the question of whether there are ethical differences between these types of deception. Philosophers have principally focused on the question of whether lying is in some way worse than other forms of deception.[32] In the present context, we are skeptical that there is any important difference between them: we see no reason why successful deception would have a different effect on the validity of consent if it resulted from lying than if it resulted from misleading implicature. We leave it up to the reader to consider if they agree with us on this point.

Deception and the validity of consent

Turn now to how deception affects consent. Someone can be deceived into giving assent in several different ways. One is when they are deceived about the act itself. For example, suppose someone comes to the door, gives you a parcel, and asks for your signature to acknowledge receipt. Unbeknown to you, the signature box is actually attached to a contract for plumbing work. Here, you do not think that what you are doing signifies consent. This is therefore not even a token of consent. The contract is invalid.[33]

In other cases, someone gives consent to *something*, but the deception means that what they consent to is not what is done. Suppose Dr. Brown says that the syringe contains a powerful opiate, but it really is just saline. If her patient agrees to "an injection of opiates," then the *scope* of his consent will be limited. He might have given valid consent, but only to an injection of opiates, not saline. The injection violates his rights because he has not given valid consent to that act.[34]

Finally, the act performed and the act consented to might be the same, but the consent giver is deceived about some other fact. For example, a hair stylist tells Lin Lin that he has ten years' experience cutting hair, but actually this is his first time. Here, she may token consent to having her hair cut by him—i.e., that's the right that she attempts to waive—and the question becomes whether that consent is *valid*.[35]

For these deception cases the scope of consent is agreed on. As with coercion cases, we think the question of validity can be answered by assessing whether the deceiver *illegitimately controls* the consent decision. We should look, then, to whether the deception is *wrongful* and whether it is *controlling*.[36] Only if both conditions are met will consent tokened as a result be invalid.

Most philosophers who have written about deception have concluded that it is usually wrong to deceive. In addition to its negative consequences, deception breaches the victim's trust and interferes with their autonomy.[37] However, there are situations in which deception is permissible. For example, someone may give permission to be deceived and so not have their trust breached or their autonomy (wrongly) interfered with. The "authorized deception" of research participants falls into this category.[38] To give another example, we have privacy rights with respect to many types of information about ourselves. In most cases, when asked about information that we do not wish to reveal, we should simply refuse to answer, so as not to mislead. But sometimes refusing to answer itself communicates an answer, in which case lying may be permissible. Suppose that Betty does not want to have sex with anyone who has had sex with men. She asks Luigi if he has ever slept with a guy (he has). Saying "It's none of your business" in these circumstances might imply "Yes." Then, we judge, it would be permissible for Luigi to lie on the grounds that this is the only way to keep private information private. In such a case, even if Luigi knew that this was a dealbreaker for Betty, it would not constitute illegitimate control. However, it might still be ethically problematic for Luigi to act on Betty's consent.[39] As we argue in Chapter 9, valid consent is not all there is to permissible sex.

Turn now to the control condition. Deception will control someone's consent decision just in case it leads to a different decision than the one they would make if they were told the truth *and* the decision is the one the deceiver aims to have them make. The key difference from other forms of control lies in the first of these conditions. We may say that *deception* is controlling only if it concerns a "dealbreaker."[40] Thus deception about matters that are immaterial to a consent decision might be wrongful, but they will not be controlling and so will not invalidate consent.[41]

What should we make of Lin Lin's hair cut? Here, it seems clear that the deception is wrongful, since it breaches her trust and it interferes with a decision that she has the right to control. Assuming that Lin Lin would not agree to have her hair cut at this price by a novice, it is also controlling, since it concerns a dealbreaker. It constitutes illegitimate control, and so we would say that Lin Lin's token of consent is invalid.[42]

6. Persuasion and manipulation

Suppose that Clo truthfully tells Mo that her bicycle is in good condition and will last a couple of years. She notes that her price is lower than he would get it for in a bike shop, that the cycle paths through the city are easy to navigate, and that in rush hour biking is faster than taking the bus, though outside of rush hour it depends on the individual. All these claims are accurate. Convinced, Mo buys the bicycle. Here, Clo has *persuaded* Mo to buy the bicycle. Assuming that she has not omitted any obvious important details, doing so seems morally innocuous. She has told him what she thinks are the relevant facts and shown how those facts relate to his reasons for action.[43] This respects his autonomy.

Here is an alternative scenario. Mo is leaning towards not buying the bicycle, skeptical that he will actually use it during the winter. Clo starts to explain how urgently she needs the money and how she could have sold the bike last week but wanted to give him—her good friend—the first chance to buy. Tough men bike in all weather, she tells him. Feeling guilty and a little emasculated, Mo buys it. This exchange involves no deception and no threats, yet it may strike us as problematic. If so, it is because it involves *manipulation.*

Persuasion and manipulation both leave the agent's options unaltered—this sets them apart from threats and offers. The difference between persuasion and manipulation lies in how they treat a person's decision-making processes. While persuasion engages with the agent's ability to make decisions on the basis of reasons, manipulation aims to bypass rational decision-making. As Joseph Raz puts it: "manipulation … perverts the way that person reaches decisions, forms preferences, or adopts goals."[44] Now, stated this broadly, deception counts as a form of manipulation.[45] We can be a little more specific here in order to carve out the set of non-deceptive manipulative acts for separate ethical analysis. For our purposes, we will say that one agent *manipulates* another when he causes the other to act on desires that she would reject as reasons to carry out that act.[46] If Mo, on reflection, thought that he really ought to feel guilty about not buying the bike, Clo would not be manipulating him.[47]

This conception of manipulation makes the potential wrong of manipulating someone clear: it is wrong insofar as it disrespects autonomy. It will not disrespect autonomy if it provokes action on grounds that the agent really would accept—as in the warranted guilt case. Further, it will not disrespect autonomy if the agent freely endorses the manipulation. Someone may know that they are being seduced, for example, yet decide that they do not mind just following their desires. Outside of these cases manipulation constitutes a form of illegitimate influence and is pro tanto wrongful.

Manipulation and the validity of consent

Does wrongful manipulation invalidate consent? Since it is, by definition, wrongful, this question boils down to whether manipulating someone into giving consent is controlling. A range of views are plausible on this question. Some may think that any successful manipulation will compromise consent, others that it will depend on how difficult it would be to resist the manipulation. As we now explain, we are skeptical that the level of influence involved in motivational manipulation often, if ever, reaches the point of control.

One reason for skepticism is theoretical. Assume that the other conditions for valid consent are met—the individual understands what they are consenting to, they are competent, and so on. Manipulation does not change the options open to the person, so the costs of refusing consent are not increased. On what grounds could the individual say that they could not (reasonably) have done otherwise? Only, we think, if the desire on which they were caused to act was so powerful that they were effectively rendered incompetent—unable to bring reason to bear on the question. This will be a very small fraction of cases at best.

The other reason for skepticism comes from comparing the force of motivational manipulation to the force of desires that are not produced or played on by another agent. In our discussion of coercion above, we argued that a threat will be *controlling* enough to invalidate consent just in case it would be bad enough for the victim to cite it as a justification or excuse for their actions. Importantly, to justify or excuse an act, the threat need not originate from another agent—it can equally have natural causes. By analogy, if manipulating someone's desires could control them sufficiently to invalidate their consent, then a naturally occurring desire of similar strength should excuse someone's behavior. Intuitively, this is not the case. Someone who felt guilty or horny or impetuous without the intervention of any agent could not cite that desire as an excuse for their action. This suggests that manipulation does not invalidate consent.

We think that manipulation is pro tanto wrongful and yet does not invalidate consent proffered as a result. This suggests that there may be cases in which manipulating someone into giving consent is justified, even if they have not already endorsed the manipulation. It will be justified when obtaining that consent is the least bad means to achieving an outcome that is morally important enough to outweigh the pro tanto wrong. For example, take a patient who is refusing to seek care despite experiencing shortness of breath and chest pains. If simple reasoning does not persuade them, we think that guilt-tripping, nagging, and other manipulative strategies would be permissible (and, indeed, an expression of care). We suspect that most cases in which manipulating someone into giving consent is justified will involve paternalistic reasoning like this. There may also be cases in which third party interests play a justifying role—such as for reasons of public health or for vitally important medical research.[48]

Note that this sort of analysis allows for a suitably nuanced assessment of manipulation in close personal relationships. Romantic partners will sometimes manipulate each other in ways that the other person endorses—for example, by wearing those sexy tight-fitting trousers when suggesting a make-out session. They may also manipulate each other in ways that are not endorsed, but are nevertheless justified, as with guilting the other person into agreeing to medical care. In still other cases, one partner may justifiably be angry with the other for manipulating them in a way that is neither endorsed nor morally justified. The person who knows all the right buttons to press to play on his partner's insecurities and get his own way, will, if he's doing it for selfish reasons, not be violating his partner's rights but nevertheless acting wrongly.

7. Conclusions

We began this chapter by distinguishing behaviors that can be attributed to agents as their actions from those that cannot. The latter—unconscious behaviors, reflexes, and forced motions—cannot constitute tokens of consent. For actions that do token consent, we analyzed what can render them involuntary. We noted a difference between the involuntariness that excuses actions and the involuntariness that invalidates consent: the latter, but not the former, has to involve another party. We then examined four ways in which one agent can influence another's consent decision: coercion, deception, manipulation, and persuasion. For each, we considered whether and when the use of this technique invalidates consent tokened as a result by assessing when it constitutes illegitimate control.

Notes

1 Some writers think that internal influences can also affect voluntariness (e.g., Beauchamp, Tom. "Autonomy and Consent." In Frank Miller and Alan Wertheimer (eds.), *The ethics of consent: Theory and practice*. Oxford University Press, 2010: 70). Our view is that insofar as they relate to the validity of consent, such influences are better thought of as affecting competence (Chapter 3).
2 For an overview of the state of the science, see Hoefer, Carl, "Causal determinism." *The Stanford Encyclopedia of Philosophy* (Summer 2024 edition), ed. Edward N. Zalta and Uri Nodelman.
3 Pereboom, Derk. *Living without free will*. Cambridge University Press, 2001.
4 Some readers might wonder what the implications are for our specific view of competence, which ties the claim against paternalistic interference to the capacity to be responsible for one's actions. We are also curious about this issue. Responsibility seems more vulnerable to worries about free will and determinism than the other ethical concepts we discuss.
5 This distinction will prove important later on, when we look at cases in which it seems to matter how the act consented to is described.
6 Note that the implications for consent of having only one good option are different than for other normative phenomena, such as responsibility. Avoiding stepping on a venomous snake is a perfectly good excuse for kicking someone. Avoiding being shot is a perfectly good excuse for handing over one's wallet. That one lack of choice stems from nature and the other from an agent seems irrelevant here. This suggests that voluntariness is not a unitary concept. What makes consent involuntary *in the sense that the consent is rendered invalid* is not the same as what makes a harmful action involuntary *in the sense that the individual is not blameworthy for the harmful action*. In his analysis of coercion, Michael Berman distinguishes two concepts: coercion_W and coercion_E. Coercion_W refers to a way of causing someone to act that is wrongful; coercion_E refers to an excuse for one's conduct in the light of being compelled to act. He argues that coercion_E does not require another agent to be the source of the pressure that compelled the individual to act. See Berman, Mitchell N. "The normative functions of coercion claims." *Legal Theory* 8.1 (2002): 45–89.
7 Bayles, Michael D. "A concept of coercion." In J. R. Pennock and J. W. Chapman (eds.), *Coercion: Nomos XIV*. Aldine-Atherton, 1972: 17; Ferzan, Kimberly Kessler. "Consent and Coercion." *Arizona State Law Journal* 50 (2018): 959–960, n35. Wertheimer labels this "nonvolitional coercion." Wertheimer, Alan. *Coercion*. Princeton University Press, 1987: 22.

8 Note that throughout this chapter we consider only cases of coercion in which the recipient of consent is also the coercer. There can also be cases in which the recipient of consent is not responsible for the threat that motivates it. We discuss the phenomenon of third party coercion further in Chapter 6.

9 Wertheimer, Alan, and Franklin G. Miller. "Payment for research participation: A coercive offer?" *Journal of Medical Ethics* 34.5 (2008): 390.

10 We are setting aside more complicated and unusual cases here, such as throffers—proposals to make someone better off if they comply and worse off if they do not. Steiner, Hillel. "Individual liberty." *Proceedings of the Aristotelian Society*, new series, 75 (1974–1975): 39.

11 See, e.g., Feinberg, Joel. *The moral limits of the criminal law, volume 3: Harm to self.* Oxford University Press, 1986: 216f; Zimmerman, David. "Coercive wage offers." *Philosophy & Public Affairs* (1981): 121–145; Wertheimer, Alan, and Franklin G. Miller. "There are (STILL) no coercive offers." *Journal of Medical Ethics* 40.9 (2014): 592–593.

12 Garnett, Michael. "Coercion: The wrong and the bad." *Ethics* 128.3 (2018): 545–573; Millum, Joseph, and Michael Garnett. "How payment for research participation can be coercive." *American Journal of Bioethics* 19.9 (2019): 21–31.

13 Garnett, Michael. "Coercion: The wrong and the bad." *Ethics* 128.3 (2018): 550–554.

14 For more discussion of alternative baselines, see Anderson, Scott, "Coercion." *The Stanford Encyclopedia of Philosophy* (Spring 2023 edition), ed. Edward N. Zalta and Uri Nodelman.

15 Compare Nozick, Robert. "Coercion." In Sidney Morgenbesser, Patrick Suppes, and Morton White (eds.), *Philosophy, science, and method: Essays in honor of Ernest Nagel.* St. Martin's Press, 1969: 450–451.

16 For extensive discussion, see Wertheimer, Alan. *Coercion.* Princeton University Press, 1987: 204–217.

17 One key challenge for proponents of normative baselines is what to say about *legitimate coercion*. It is widely thought that the state coerces via the criminal law. This is why there is a special burden of justification for enforcing some behavior through criminal sanctions. But if a proposal is only a threat when it is wrongful, then any *justified* criminal sanction will not constitute coercion. For an argument that the law does not coerce, see Edmundson, William A. *Three anarchical fallacies: An essay on political authority.* Cambridge University Press, 1998: 73–124. An alternative way to understand how the law can be coercive can be found in Garnett, Michael. "Coercion: The wrong and the bad." *Ethics* 128.3 (2018): 550–554.

18 Cf. The "two-pronged theory of coercion" (Wertheimer, Alan. *Coercion.* Princeton University Press, 1987: 172). Some think that this is not true in cases of third-party coercion, as we discuss in the context of involuntary treatment of patients who refuse care in Chapter 6.

19 This may be a *justification* (given the circumstances, the action was the right thing to do) or an *excuse* (given the circumstances, the action was wrongful but the person should not be held responsible).

20 Wertheimer, Alan. *Coercion.* Princeton University Press, 1987: 53.

21 Compare Wertheimer: "For the sense of having 'no acceptable alternative' that is relevant here is not that B finds the other alternatives unacceptable or that it would be irrational or unreasonable for B not to accept A's proposal, but that B has no obligation to accept the other alternatives, or, what is sometimes more accurate, that B is entitled to yield to A's proposal and then be released from the normal moral and legal consequences of his act." Wertheimer, Alan. *Coercion.* Princeton University Press, 1987: 267.

22 Wertheimer, Alan. *Coercion.* Princeton University Press, 1987: 273.

23 The threshold for duress therefore varies depending on what the person is being pressured into doing. For discussion in the context of consent, see Ferzan, Kimberly Kessler. "Consent and Coercion." Arizona State Law Journal 50 (2018): 972–976.

24 Tom Dougherty argues that we should not treat threats that exculpate wrongdoing in the same way as we treat threats that undermine consent. Instead, they think that any "unacceptable threat" that motivates someone to consent is sufficient to invalidate that consent. Dougherty, Tom. *Consent under duress.* Oxford University Press, 2024: 80. Dougherty argues against this view by giving an example in which someone is indifferent between a threat being carried out and the harm to them of complying with the threat (p. 79). Since either is a "reasonable" choice, it is not

true that the victim in this case has no reasonable choice but to comply; nevertheless, Dougherty argues, the consent is invalid. This suggests to us that the standard used for judging when someone exercised their agency under duress cannot be as simple as whether the coerced option was the only reasonable one. However, this does not tempt us to accept Dougherty's conclusion. The fact that we lack a straightforward standard for when a threat is controlling does not mean that any threat that motivates is controlling. As we will see later in this chapter, there can be cases in which mild threats or manipulation that lead someone to consent can be justified—either for the person's own good or for the sake of third parties.

25 As Berman would put it, he experiences coercion$_W$ but not coercion$_E$.

26 Hyams, Keith. "When consent doesn't work: A rights-based case for limits to consent's capacity to legitimise." *Journal of Moral Philosophy* 8.1 (2011): 110–138; Ferzan, Kimberly Kessler. "Consent and Coercion." Arizona State Law Journal 50 (2018): 983–988.

27 Described in Dworkin, Ronald. *Taking rights seriously*. A&C Black, 2013: 39.

28 If an action is *pro tanto* wrong then that is a moral reason that counts against the action. This wrong could still be outweighed by other moral reasons that support it.

29 For those who think that paternalistic reasons should not count here, it might even be justified in terms of the burden on third parties who care about the patient and those who would have to look after him in the case of an accident.

30 Getting a perfect definition of deception is tricky. See Mahon, James Edwin. "The definition of lying and deception." *The Stanford Encyclopedia of Philosophy* (Winter 2016 edition), Edward N. Zalta (ed.).

31 "Covert deceit" is Collin O'Neil's label. O'Neil, Collin. "Lying, trust, and gratitude." *Philosophy & Public Affairs* 40.4 (2012): 327–329.

32 For a spectrum of views, see Rees, Clea. "Better lie!" *Analysis* 74.1 (2014): 59–64; Saul, Jennifer. "Just go ahead and lie." *Analysis* 72.1 (2012): 3–9; Strudler, Alan. "The distinctive wrong in lying." *Ethical Theory and Moral Practice* 13.2 (2010): 171–179; Webber, Jonathan. "Liar!" *Analysis* 73.4 (2013): 651–659.

33 Legally speaking, it is *void*, since no consent was given.

34 As discussed in Chapter 4, it *is* possible to give consent to being injected with an unknown substance (the patient could give consent to being injected with whatever his doctor recommends). In the case described he does not give valid consent to the saline injection because his consent is explicitly limited to opiates. Consent frequently involves waiving a right in a narrowly defined way—with regard to a specific individual, a specific body part, or a specific intervention.

35 One might be tempted to analyze this case along the same lines as the previous one—that is, to say that Lin Lin gave consent to *having her hair cut by a stylist with ten years' experience*, and since the hair stylist does not fit this description, he does not have her valid consent. The problem with this strategy is that it does not distinguish cases where the deception is relevant to consent from those where it is not. Intuitively, it is relevant whether Lin Lin cares about how experienced her hair stylist is. Suppose that she would never agree to have her hair cut by a complete novice, but is indifferent between someone with nine and someone with ten years' experience. The novice is accurately described as deceiving Lin Lin *into* giving consent; the experienced stylist who deceitfully adds a year deceives her but does not thereby affect her decision.

36 Readers may disagree with us on what makes deception permissible, if anything, and, indeed, on when it is controlling. We nevertheless invite you to analyze cases of deception and consent in these terms, substituting in your own views on the ethics of deception and the nature of control.

37 See, e.g., Pugh, Jonathan. "Ravines and sugar pills: Defending deceptive placebo use." *The Journal of Medicine and Philosophy: A Forum for Bioethics and Philosophy of Medicine* 40.1 (2014); Simpson, D. I. "Lying, liars and language." *Philosophy and Phenomenological Research* 52.3 (1992): 623–639; Williams, Bernard. *Truth and truthfulness*. Princeton University Press, 2004.

38 Wendler, David, and Franklin G. Miller. "Deception in the pursuit of science." *Archives of Internal Medicine* 164.6 (2004): 597–600.

39 For a contrary view, see Lazenby, Hugh, and Iason Gabriel. "Permissible secrets." *The Philosophical Quarterly* 68.271 (2018): 265–285.

40 We take this terminology from Dougherty, Tom. "Sex, lies, and consent." *Ethics* 123.4 (2013): 717–744.

41 Note that someone may not know whether consent was invalid because they may not know whether they in fact affected their victim's decision. Nevertheless, they should normally not proceed, since, first, deception is wrongful anyway, and second, they are risking proceeding on an invalid consent token. This is one justification for extensive disclosure requirements in clinical contexts.

42 There is a well-known distinction in the law between *fraud in the factum* and *fraud in the inducement*. Fraud in the factum occurs when someone is deceived about what they consent to (e.g., they sign a contract believing it is about the sale of a car but it is about the sale of a bike). Fraud in the inducement occurs when someone is aware of what they are consenting to but are deceived about something else material to their consent decision (e.g., they sign a contract because they are told that this company pays its workers a living wage, when this is a lie). Not only is this distinction found in the law in several countries, it also appears to map onto the way that many people judge cases of deception and consent. See Sommers, Roseanna. "Commonsense consent." *Yale Law Journal* 129 (2019): 2232. The difficulty with making ethical sense of the distinction is that it is often possible to redescribe cases of *fraud in the factum* as *fraud in the inducement* and vice versa. For instance, Wertheimer describes a case in which someone sets back the odometer of a car before selling it (Wertheimer, Alan. *Coercion*. Princeton University Press, 1987: 197). Is this *fraud in the inducement* because the buyer knows which car they are buying? Or *fraud in the factum* because they think they are buying a car with one mileage but in fact they are buying one with another? Moreover, even if the distinction could be drawn in a principled way, it is not clear why it should matter morally (pp. 206–209). At first glance, one might think that the *factum/inducement* distinction maps onto the distinction we draw between deception regarding scope—what is consented to—and deception regarding dealbreakers. The distinctions are quite similar. However, we think that what one has consented to depends on norms of communication regarding what rights have been waived. This means that there is not a fact about the *factum* independent of the specific consent interaction. Consequently, the worry about redescription does not apply.

43 Cf. Faden, R. R., and T. L. Beauchamp. *A history and theory of informed consent*. Oxford University Press, 1986: 261.

44 Raz, Joseph. *The morality of freedom*. Oxford University Press, 1988: 377.

45 We think that *deceptive* manipulation invalidates consent when it exercises illegitimate control. Similarly, Sophie Gibert argues that acts of wrongful manipulation are wrong "in virtue of some *other* wrong they involve—namely, a rights-infringement." Gibert, Sophie. "The wrong of wrongful manipulation." *Philosophy & Public Affairs* 51.4 (2023): 335.

46 This is "motivational manipulation," in the terminology of Mandava and Millum. See Mandava, Amulya, and Joseph Millum. "Manipulation in the enrollment of research participants." *Hastings Center Report* 43.2 (2013): 40. They distinguish this concept from "deceptive manipulation" and "circumstantial manipulation." We do not address the latter here. For discussion of alternative definitions, see Noggle, Robert. "The ethics of manipulation." *The Stanford Encyclopedia of Philosophy* (Summer 2022 edition), ed. Edward N. Zalta.

47 Compare Thomas Hill: "Manipulation, broadly conceived, can perhaps be understood as intentionally causing or encouraging people to make the decisions one wants them to make by actively promoting their making the decisions in ways that rational persons would not want to make their decisions." Hill, Thomas. *Autonomy and self-respect*. Cambridge University Press, 1991: 33.

48 For discussion in the context of clinical research, see Mandava, Amulya, and Joseph Millum. "Manipulation in the enrollment of research participants." *Hastings Center Report* 43.2 (2013). Note that in *most* cases, the interests of the manipulator will be irrelevant to the permissibility of manipulation on the basis of the previously mentioned principle that someone should not benefit from their own wrongdoing.

Part II Consent in practice

6 Consent to medical care

1. Introduction

Most people receive medical care at multiple times in their lives. Many common medical procedures—like a blood pressure test, a vaccination, or sutures—involve a medical professional touching the patient's body. This chapter examines the question: what gives a clinician permission to treat a patient?

The answer might seem obvious: the patient agrees to be treated. If they have the capacity to make their own decisions, then this decision is theirs to make. The clinician's authority to treat them can be derived from their agreement. Or, to put it another way, their consent gives the clinician permission to treat them.

While some version of this answer is correct most of the time, the devil is in the details. Their agreement only releases the clinician from the duty not to treat them if their consent is valid. As the previous theory chapters make clear, this means that they must be *competent* to make their own medical decisions, they must decide *voluntarily*, and they must *communicate* their consent to their clinician. Two informational conditions must also be met: the clinician needs to *disclose* certain facts about the patient's options for care and the patient needs to *understand* some of this information.

We begin this chapter with the history of consent requirements in medicine. We then describe current practice in Western countries, where it is now expected that clinicians will obtain the informed consent of their patients. We address several open questions concerning the informational and competence requirements. After considering how clinicians ought to obtain valid consent to treatment from willing competent adults, we turn to the question of how treatment decisions should be made for incapacitated adults. We then consider two hard cases. The first is a perennial problem in medicine: the presentation of information to patients who face difficult treatment decisions. Clinicians have a professional duty to promote their patient's interests and the consent process represents an opportunity to help a patient make a good decision. To what extent are clinicians permitted to persuade, manipulate, or deceive in order to improve their patient's choice? The second hard case considers the treatment of patients who refuse to consent to treatment. Many jurisdictions permit the involuntary detention and treatment of patients who are thought to pose a risk to themselves or others. When is this ethically justified?

DOI: 10.4324/9781003287391-8

In our discussions in this and the following chapter it is particularly important to keep in mind the distinction between what is ethically required and what is required by law or policy. Because the practice of obtaining consent has been so thoroughly institutionalized in health care and clinical research, it can be easy to conflate the two. But what is legal is not identical with what is ethical. In addition, even just ethically speaking, there are two different types of question we can ask about obtaining consent. The first covers questions about what is required for valid consent, what decides its scope, and so on—that is, the questions that have concerned us for most of the first half of this book. The second covers questions about what laws or policies governing consent would be ethically justified. For example, in section 4, we discuss different laws that govern medical decision-making by adolescents. Such laws have to draw a line that strikes the right balance between protecting persons who should not be making their own decisions and empowering those who should.

Before proceeding further, a point about terminology is in order. In integrated healthcare systems, patients are treated by a vast array of healthcare professionals, not just medical doctors. We use "clinician" to refer to all those who are qualified and trained to provide care. It is true that the history of the informed consent process in medicine is closely tied to the evolution of the *doctor*–patient relationship, and the majority of discussions about role morality in medicine concern that relationship. Nonetheless, provided that they are qualified and trained to provide treatment, consent theory does not imply that the duties of a nurse, psychologist, or any other clinician are different from a doctor's.

2. A brief history of informed consent in medicine

Before the advent of modern bioethics, consent was rarely emphasized in discussions of the ethics of medical practice.[1] Prior to the civil rights movements of the mid-twentieth century, clinicians trained in the Hippocratic tradition were taught to "make a habit of two things—to help, or at least do not harm."[2] Across medical traditions, clinicians understood that their primary and overriding duty was to promote and preserve their patient's best medical interests, and the most efficient way to do this was to involve patients in medical decision-making as little as possible.[3] In other words, traditional medical practice was deeply paternalistic.

To determine what was in a patient's best medical interests, clinicians were taught to start with their own expertise, perform diagnostic tests and clinical examinations, and draw on the collective knowledge of their colleagues if necessary.[4] Patients were not included in this medical decision-making—in fact, the principle of beneficence implied that they often ought to be *excluded*, both because knowing the truth might cause unnecessary anxiety and because patients could not be trusted to comply with medically indicated care. Manipulation, deception, and coercion were used to keep them in line and on track.[5] Deviation from this "Hippocratic beneficence" could bring professional condemnation.[6]

All this started to change in the mid-twentieth century. After the second world war, the Nuremburg Trials exposed the horrors of the Nazi medical experiments.[7]

These, together with the nuclear destruction wrought on Hiroshima and Nagasaki, led to public mistrust, anger, and anxiety towards science, including medicine.[8] In the 1950s, thalidomide was widely used to treat morning sickness in pregnancy. A global epidemic of birth defects followed. While some of the affected infants survived, many died within their first year of life. In different parts of the world, clinicians started to suspect, and then warn the public, that these birth defects and deaths were caused by thalidomide itself—a drug that patients had been assured was safe.[9] Around the same time, technological innovations in healthcare gave rise to public doubts about whether clinicians *alone* ought to decide whether a patient in a persistent vegetative state should remain on life-support indefinitely.[10]

Growing public mistrust, coupled with social movements championing the civil rights of racial minorities, women, and persons with mental and physical disabilities, forced medicine to reckon with its paternalism.[11] A slew of lawsuits alleged medical negligence and demanded a recognition of patients' rights.[12] By the 1980s, various court rulings implied that *simple* consent—just agreeing to what the clinician proposed—was insufficient to protect patients' autonomy rights.[13] What emerged instead was a legal recognition of a patient's right to make their own medical decisions along with a right to receive material information related to those decisions.[14]

As the law evolved, so too did clinical ethics. First, best interests were reimagined. A narrow medical conception was replaced by a patient-centered view of well-being that included the patient's non-medical interests.[15] The clinician's unilateral authority was replaced by the ideal of *shared* medical decision-making—the clinician and patient were encouraged to work together to help the patient make the subjectively correct decision about their care.[16] Second, the legal recognition of patient autonomy also gained professional recognition in various codes, guidelines, and regulations of best medical practice. While there is variation across the world, there is now widespread recognition of a competent patient's right to make their own medical decisions, and a clinician's duty to obtain their patient's voluntary informed consent to treatment.[17] While beneficence (and non-maleficence) are still core principles that underlie the clinician–patient relationship, they have now been joined by respect for patient autonomy.

These core principles also ground the goals of the informed consent process.[18] The primary goal of the process is to obtain valid consent to treatment. The principle of respect for patient autonomy requires that clinicians obtain a valid rights waiver for actions that require the patient's permission.[19] An important secondary goal of the process is to facilitate good medical decision-making. The principle of beneficence encourages clinicians to help their patients make subjectively good medical decisions—that is, decisions that align with their interests and values. However, unlike obtaining valid consent, ensuring that the final decision made is in fact the best decision cannot be a legal or ethical requirement. This is because, first, competent patients have the right to make unwise decisions, and respect for autonomy means that clinicians cannot insist that they be prudent or virtuous.[20] Second, given scarce time, there are limits to how much effort could be required of clinicians to improve patient decision-making.

3. Standards of disclosure

As our brief history indicates, the doctrine of informed consent in medicine largely emerged from malpractice lawsuits. What followed—swiftly in some places, gradually in others—were laws, professional regulations, and medical ethics guidelines that codified what came to be known as "informed consent."[21] It is now widely accepted that a simple token of assent is not enough to render invasive medical treatment permissible. Valid consent requires that a clinician disclose relevant facts to their patients about their treatment and treatment options (including their right to refuse treatment).[22]

Note that though the term "informed consent" is widely used in the context of clinical care and clinical research, it does not in fact label a different type of consent: duties of disclosure are not limited to clinicians. As we saw in Chapter 4, the requestor of consent in *non-medical* cases risks exercising illegitimate control if they withhold or misrepresent a fact that they have reason to think is relevant to the consenter's decision and which they judge the consenter would expect to be told. It would be a mistake, then, to think of disclosure as a *professional* or *role-based* duty special to the clinical context. It is a requirement of all valid consent.

That said, the disclosure requirement has been extensively analyzed in medical ethics in large part because of the legal evolution of informed consent. There are still lively debates about what ought to be disclosed to patients and why.[23] While various court cases established a clinician's legal duty to disclose, those rulings did not settle precisely what facts ought to be disclosed or how decisions about them ought to be made. As a result, early legal judgements about informed consent were interpreted paternalistically—either by the medical community or in subsequent court decisions.[24]

The legal evolution of the disclosure requirement in the United Kingdom represents a particularly stark example. In *Bolam v. Friern Hospital Management Committee* (1957), the House of Lords ruled that a clinician was not negligent if "he has acted in accordance with a practice accepted as proper by a responsible body of medical men skilled in that particular art."[25] This standard—the *Bolam* test—was subsequently used to determine the appropriateness of disclosures to patients. For example, in 1985, Amy Sidaway underwent an operation to relieve pressure on her cervical spine—a surgery that was known to carry a 1–2% risk of severe spinal cord damage.[26] The surgery was unsuccessful and left her severely disabled. At no point prior to the procedure had she been informed of the risk of paralysis. The House of Lords applied the *Bolam* test. Against a background of paternalistic disclosure practices, the surgeon was not found negligent for failing to disclose this risk, and Sidaway's consent was not judged to be invalidated by this disclosure.

The *Bolam* test described a *professional practice* standard of disclosure: a clinician only has a duty to disclose what other responsible clinicians would judge relevant to ensuring that the patient acts in their own best medical interests. This standard was roundly rejected in the bioethics literature, even at the time.[27] By the time the UK Supreme Court rejected it in favor of a reasonable person standard in *Montgomery v. Lanarkshire Health Board* (2015), professional guidelines in the region already required patient-centered disclosure,[28] and legal rulings across the world had rejected a paternalistic standard of disclosure.[29]

Patient-centered standards of disclosure can be divided into *reasonable person* standards and *subjective* standards. The reasonable person standard requires that a clinician disclose only those facts a reasonable patient would want to know about the treatment decision. The subjective standard, by contrast, requires disclosure of the information that is material to the individual patient's treatment decision.[30]

To see how the two might differ, consider an informed consent process for a family with a premature baby with respiratory distress syndrome who can be treated with animal-derived surfactants. Facts about what kind of animal the surfactant is derived from would be immaterial to many decision-makers in this context, which might lead clinicians to consider disclosing it unnecessary on the reasonable person standard. But suppose that there are many Hindu and Muslim families in the area and the infant could either be treated with a bovine or porcine derived surfactant. This clinician now has good reason to believe that the animal the surfactant is derived from is likely to be relevant to some of these decision-makers. On a reasonable person standard it is debatable whether this information should be disclosed—i.e., which population of patients sets the standard. Indeed, neonatologists guided by this standard vary in their practice.[31] The subjective standard of disclosure is clear on this point: the clinician is directed to tailor information to the *actual* decision-maker. What matters is not what would be material to some reasonable patient, whoever that might be, but what is material to the individual whose consent decision this is.

In Chapter 4, we argued that the understanding requirement is relatively minimal, but that there may still be a substantial disclosure requirement. This is because by withholding information or presenting it in a misleading way, someone requesting consent may control the consent giver's decision. This sort of control is only possible, of course, if the information is in fact relevant to the decision. Our analysis therefore entails a subjective standard of disclosure: the clinician ought to disclose what she knows, believes to be relevant to this person's consent decision, and judges that they would expect to be told. She should encourage the person making this treatment decision to ask questions and she should answer these honestly. By doing so she avoids illegitimately controlling the consent decision.

Note that, in practice, the two standards will be quite close to each other. What counts as reasonable will likely be judged by the yardstick of what patients tend to care about and what tends to affect their interests. And on the subjective standard, clinicians are not expected to investigate whether their patients have idiosyncratic preferences, but will generally start by presenting the sorts of facts that are relevant to most patients (before adding information that they think this individual will care about and asking them what else they want to know).

4. Children and medical decision-making

Another distinctive feature of consent to clinical care is the gradual involvement of children and young persons in medical decision-making. The UN Convention on the Rights of the Child (CRC) states that:

> Parties shall assure to the child who is capable of forming his or her own views the right to express those views freely in all matters affecting the child, the views of the child being given due weight in accordance with the age and maturity of the child.[32]

A child's developing autonomy is also recognized in many legal systems. Some countries, like Canada, the United States, and Australia, adopt a "mature minor doctrine"—regardless of age, a minor who possesses sufficient maturity and capacities of understanding, appreciation, and reasoning, is capable of giving consent to medical treatment.[33] However, there is wide variation in how this doctrine is incorporated into law. Take Canada. In some provinces and territories, there is a presumption that a patient has capacity "until the contrary is demonstrated."[34] This applies equally to children and adults. In others, a child is *presumed* to have capacity to consent to treatment at 16, but for younger patients evidence of capacity would need to be established.[35] In others still, a competent minor is any child who can understand the nature and consequences of a medical treatment, and yet their capacity is not sufficient for a valid rights waiver. The care must also be in their best interests.[36] Setting a legal threshold for independent decision-making must strike a delicate balance. If it is set too low, a child without decision-making capacity is left vulnerable to harm; but, set too high, and a child with it is wrongfully denied their right to consent to or refuse care. These mature minor doctrines illustrate different ways to strike that balance.

Some jurisdictions, like England and Wales, choose to balance these trade-offs by treating competence to give and refuse consent asymmetrically. A patient is presumed to have full capacity at 18—meaning that they have the legal right to consent to or refuse medical care. At 16, they are presumed to have the capacity to *consent* to treatment, but, unlike their adult counterparts, they are not presumed to have the capacity to refuse treatment.[37] The refusals of 16- and 17-year-olds can be overruled by the Court of Protection.

Many find this asymmetry baffling. Rosy Thornton expresses the puzzlement well:

> if a child of sufficient maturity is to have the right to consent to a desired course of treatment, it is difficult to comprehend why he or she should be denied the right to refuse unwanted medication.[38]

The asymmetry is more comprehensible if one adopts a separate grounds view of competence, like the one that we defended in chapter 3. According to that view, there are *two* separate rights implicated in medical decisions. The first is the power to waive one's rights and thereby permit treatment. This only requires minimal cognitive capacities: the capacity to value and the capacity to understand certain facts about the proposed treatment. The second is the right against others interfering with one's decisions on paternalistic grounds. This requires the possession of more substantial capacities to be responsible for your own actions. It is therefore perfectly possible that a 16-year-old could understand what his oncologists are proposing to do to treat his aggressive cancer. He might also be capable of deciding to accept this proposed care based on his values. However, this 16-year-old *might* lack the capacities required to be held responsible for his own decisions. This would explain why, if he chose to refuse the treatment, others could override his refusal on the grounds that he is choosing contrary to his interests.[39]

The separate grounds analysis of competence explains why laws like these are correct *not to assume* that the possession of capacities that ground the right to consent straightforwardly entail a claim against others—parents, clinicians, or the courts—interfering with risky or poor treatment decisions on paternalistic grounds. It does not imply that they draw the line in the right place. It is an empirical question whether most 16-year-olds have the capacities needed to take responsibility for their own decisions and so should be permitted to refuse life-saving treatment.

5. Treatment decisions for incapacitated adults

Polina suffered a severe traumatic brain injury in a car accident six months ago. She was in a medically induced coma for a month, and her recovery has been slow. She experiences profound confusion, difficulties with speech and communication, and bouts of extreme agitation. Due to the complexity of her needs, she now lives at a private long-term care facility. Last week, she was admitted to an acute medical unit with aspiration pneumonia. Although she is found unable to make her own treatment decisions, the medical team involve her, and she initially agrees to antibiotic treatment. Later, she gets agitated when a nurse tries to take her blood and says she wants to "go home." It takes considerable persuasion to calm her enough so that the team can continue treatment.

How should decisions be made for patients like Polina? Who should decide whether she stays in hospital and what treatment she receives?

Whoever the proxy decision-maker is, the conditions for valid consent will apply to that person's decision. In other words, the proxy decision-maker should be competent, they should be given the relevant information, and their decision should be voluntary. But who should make the decisions and the standard by which they should make them depends on the details of the case. Consider three variations. In the first, Polina has expressed no prior wishes for her care were she to become incapacitated. In the second, she has completed an advance directive. In the third, she appointed her sister, Yulia, to be her healthcare proxy decision-maker prior to undergoing major surgery a couple of years earlier.

In the first version of the case, where Polina has made no prior decisions, consent theory has little to say about how decisions should be made for her. Her situation is no different than that of someone who has never had decision-making capacity. Even in the best-case scenario—one in which friends or family are well informed about her interests, preferences, and values—they only possess evidence of what Polina might consent to or refuse. They do not possess the normative authority to waive her rights for her. The correct standard for how decisions should be made for Polina will depend on judgments about what would be in her interests (*best interests standard*), what she would have decided (*substituted judgment standard*), or what would have been reasonable for her to decide (*reasonable subject standard*).[40] It will not depend on any actual decision by her.

Consent theory has more to say about the scenario in which Polina has an advance directive—a legal document in which a patient sets out instructions for their care if they were to become incapacitated.[41] The legal authority of advance directives varies. In most jurisdictions, advance decisions to *refuse* specific treatments—such as, do not attempt cardiopulmonary resuscitation—are legally binding. Advanced decisions to consent to specific treatments are not always legally recognized.[42]

Unless Polina revoked her advance directive before her accident, ethically it ought to be followed if it is relevant to her care now. As a competent adult at the time of choosing to complete an advance directive, Polina had the right to make these decisions about her future care for herself. An advance refusal of a specific treatment—like, say, curative antibiotics—leaves her right against this treatment unwaived and prohibits proxy decision-makers from insisting on the treatment. An advance consent to a specific treatment waives the relevant right once the conditions for needing the treatment are met. Provided that the conditions for valid consent were met when she completed her advance directive, her prior autonomous decision authorizes her clinicians to treat her now even if her currently incapacitated self objects.

This might seem odd. Advance consent might seem normatively different from what we have been discussing so far. Many patients who make advance decisions have not, and often could not, fully appreciate the condition of their future incapacitated self.[43] Why not think that this lack of understanding undermines the validity of advance decisions about whether to accept or refuse treatments?

The analysis in Chapter 4 provides the answer: it must be possible to give valid consent to acts we have not experienced before, otherwise consent to almost any (first-time) medical procedure would be impossible. On the specific view of understanding we defended, provided that Polina understood *that* she was giving or refusing consent, that this advance directive was *how* she was doing it, and *what* she was giving or refusing her clinician permission to do, then her advance directive has normative authority (assuming that the other conditions for valid consent were met, of course). Polina can meet these requirements while being completely ignorant of many facts about her future incapacitated self. She can also meet these requirements while making an ill-informed, imprudent, or risky decision.

There is another problem with advance directives, however. While competent patients can retract their consent to treatment, non-competent patients cannot.

Patients like Polina are hostages to their acts of precedent autonomy. Their treatment and care are determined by decisions that they may not be able to recall or understand. They might now be actively dissenting against these decisions, as Polina would be if her advance directive requested all possible measures be taken to extend her life while she tried to leave the hospital.

It is very challenging for family members and clinicians to follow advance directives when they do not appear to be in the patient's best interests or when the now incapacitated patient dissents. However, there is nothing wrong in principle with someone giving or refusing consent to an act that cannot be immediately stopped or reversed. As discussed in Chapter 2, this is a common occurrence and so advance directives pose no special problem for the validity of consent in this respect.

The central question here is: why does the advance directive have normative authority? The answer is that the decision recorded in it, just like other decisions made when the person was competent, has normative authority. Before her accident, Polina was autonomous; she had authority over her own life. By giving and refusing consent, she could direct her life in accordance with her interests, preferences, and values. Completing an advance directive allowed her to extend this self-governance into the future. It allowed her to direct her own care in accordance with her values at a time at which she would not be able to do that for herself. While competent, Polina had the exclusive authority to shape her future in accordance with her values. That authority cannot be revoked by her now incapacitated self, her family, or her clinicians.[44]

Consider, finally, the third scenario in which Polina has assigned Yulia to make decisions on her behalf. In many jurisdictions, a competent adult can appoint a healthcare proxy decision-maker who has the legal authority to make any treatment decisions the patient could have when they were competent.[45] This is a form of broad consent. Polina has given consent for her sister to make medical decisions for her. Provided those decisions fall within the scope of Polina's consent—that is, they are healthcare decisions, that they are consistent with her advance directive, and so on—Yulia has the ethical and legal authority to make them as though she were Polina.

Sometimes proxy decision-makers face clinical scenarios in which, despite having the legal authority to make the medical decisions, they are not sure how the patient would have decided. Imagine that Yulia is in that situation now while Polina is refusing care. Should she respect Polina's dissent when she does not know what Polina would do? In such a situation it may be reasonable to take Polina's dissent into account. However, just as with a young child, Yulia should not treat the dissent as an expression of Polina's autonomous refusal. Rather, reasons of beneficence might explain why it would be appropriate to redesign her treatment and care plan in the light of her dissent. Dissent indicates distress. If the treatment plan is only marginally in her medical interests, evidence of high or prolonged distress would give Yulia some reason to think that this treatment may not be in Polina's *overall* interests.

6. Case: helping patients make difficult decisions

Sometimes patients face difficult decisions. Consider Halil, who has advanced bowel cancer. Since being diagnosed, he has had three surgeries, each followed by a round of chemotherapy. During the last round, his clinicians noticed an uncharacteristically low mood. Halil is a quiet and reserved man. His wife, Iqra, has noticed his difficulty tolerating the chemotherapy's toxic side-effects, but he insists they should be grateful for the care he has received. She worries that he is putting himself through all this so as not to let his family or doctors down.

Dr. Okoro, the medical oncologist on Halil's care team, is preparing for their next appointment. Halil's test results confirm the cancer has now spread to his lungs, and there are no curative treatment options for this secondary cancer. The options are either comfort care or palliative chemotherapy. The latter will not cure his cancer, but it could extend his life by a few months. The precise survival gain for an individual patient is almost impossible to gauge, however. She knows that some patients overestimate the benefits of palliative chemotherapy, and some even fail to grasp that it will not cure their cancer. Knowing Halil, she suspects he will suffer with another round of chemotherapy. She worries that hearing about the life extending benefits will make him choose chemotherapy even if comfort care would really be better for him on balance. She is unsure how to help him make a good decision.

Dr. Okoro recognizes something important: a well-crafted informed consent process can help a patient make a good decision. When the patient is receptive to a frank, open, and reflective conversation, a clinician can facilitate good decision-making by adopting an empathetic teaching style, presenting relevant information in an understandable way, and asking questions that encourage and challenge the patient to move beyond their immediate responses.[46] If the clinician outlines everything that ought to be disclosed in a clear and accessible manner, they can achieve this goal without undermining either the voluntariness or understanding conditions for valid consent. In these circumstances, the goals of the informed consent process—to obtain valid consent and to facilitate good decision-making—are complementary.

But these are not the circumstances in which Dr. Okoro finds herself. Halil is reserved, disinclined towards open reflection, and reticent to the extent that it is hard to get a handle on his decision-making tendencies. There is *some* evidence that he is moved by a sense of gratitude, has not reflected on what matters to him most at the end of life, and leans towards life prolonging clinical options. There is also some evidence that when patients are faced with complex or momentous decisions—as Halil is here—fear, uncertainty, and other common deliberative frailties are impediments to good decision-making.[47] These barriers are rarely surmounted by a standard informed consent process that just amounts to presenting information and answering questions.[48] If Dr. Okoro proceeds with this standard of disclosure, she may well obtain his valid consent to treatment, but she is unlikely to help him make a good decision about his future care.

How, then, should she present his options? She might speculate about engaging in benevolent deception. Halil cannot make a bad treatment decision if he is unaware of the "bad" option. Perhaps she should not tell him about palliative chemotherapy or should deceptively manipulate his perception of it by withholding or downplaying the benefits and exaggerating the risks and burdens? However, this form of influence is wrongful *even if* she means well. Good motives do not change the fact that deceptive disclosure risks invalidating Halil's consent.

Dr. Okoro might consider another tack. Deception usurps a patient's agency, but rational persuasion engages it. A clinician can use reason, evidence, and argument to persuade a patient to reflect for themselves, seriously consider an alternative, or even select a particular course of care.[49] In this case, Dr. Okoro is worried Halil will overestimate the benefits of palliative chemotherapy, so after disclosing its potential life-extending benefits, she could say: "The *average* survival gain of this treatment might be a few months, but let's be clear about what that means. Very few people are statistically average—so, in practice, *many* patients only get a few more weeks of life, and some get no life-prolonging benefits at all. I know it is hard to hear this. But I'm emphasizing it because, as you know first-hand, chemotherapy is hard. And, unlike the chemotherapy you've had before, there is no possibility that this round will cure your cancer. Given that you might not benefit at all, and given how hard you have found this form of treatment in the past, I don't think it is right for you. But this is not my decision—it is yours. It is important that you spend some time thinking about what matters to you most now."

This form of influence is not wrongful. By explaining commonly misunderstood material, making a clinical recommendation, and encouraging Halil to make a reflective treatment decision, Dr. Okoro does not exert any *illegitimate* control over him. In fact, far from undermining his autonomy rights, she enhances them by attempting to engage his reflective agency. By translating statistical averages, she helps him understand the uncertain benefits of palliative chemotherapy. By making it clear that she does not recommend this treatment, she helps him grasp that even clinicians do not always favor the most aggressive options. By encouraging him to think about what matters to him most, she guides and supports him in making a decision that is right for him at the end of his life. Of course, rational persuasion can be clumsy, but when it is done well it meets both goals of the informed consent process: it respects patient autonomy, and it facilitates good decision-making.

However, given Halil's deliberative dispositions, Dr. Okoro might wonder how effective rational persuasion would be at facilitating good decision-making. Far from empowering him, she might worry that asking him to think about what matters to him most at the end of his life could leave him dejected, anxious, and uncertain. Perhaps she should use a manipulative but non-deceptive form of influence.[50] For example, instead of framing life-expectancy in terms of survival rates (e.g., 30% of patients are still alive 2 months after completing palliative chemotherapy), she could use the mortality frame (70% of patients are dead 2 months after completing palliative chemotherapy).[51] She could use the same loss frame to discuss the risks of this intervention. However, when it comes to comfort care, she could switch the frame. Without engaging in any deception, she could give palliative chemotherapy a negative presentation, and comfort care a positive one.

Of course, Dr. Okoro could use framing effects to *supplement* rational persuasion. For example, she could warn Halil about how meagre the benefits of palliative chemotherapy are, and how pronounced the risks, and she could use these frames to illustrate the point. But when she uses them *instead* of rational persuasion, she circumvents his rational capacities.

We argued in Chapter 5 that this form of influence is inherently disrespectful of a competent patient's autonomy. However, it does not exercise the kind of illegitimate control that invalidates consent either. First, the patient's options are not altered: Halil still can choose between palliative chemotherapy and comfort care. Second, no information is withheld from the patient: the information presented is accurate and Halil could always flip the frame. It therefore does not control Halil's decision. When manipulation of this sort is divorced from rational persuasion, it should not be a clinician's first line of disclosure because it is disrespectful of the patient's autonomy. However, in this instance, it might be justified if there is good reason to think that Halil will otherwise make a very poor decision by his own lights. If, on the other hand, Dr. Okoro is not very confident what the right decision would be, given Halil's values and preferences, she should avoid the pro tanto wrong of manipulation.

7. Case: involuntary detention and treatment

Malik rents his sister's basement apartment. He has schizophrenia and he occasionally self-medicates with cocaine. After a recent drug-induced psychosis, his sister threatens to evict him immediately unless he enters rehab. With nowhere else to go, he agrees to treatment. During the first week at the facility, Malik attempts to take his own life. As is standard practice, his clinicians detain him to assess the level of risk he poses to himself. During this involuntary commitment, Malik becomes violent. Despite his resistance, his clinicians sedate him with a shot of haloperidol.

Malik is subject to three forms of interference that would usually be permissible only if he had given his valid consent. First, he enters treatment rehab. Second, he stays at the rehab facility for assessment. And, finally, he is injected with a powerful antipsychotic medication. The use of coercive measures to treat certain patients with severe mental illness is widespread, though it is controversial.[52] Sometimes these patients appear to pose a serious threat of harm to themselves or others.[53] Yet outside of psychotic episodes, Malik may retain the capacity to make his own decisions. Under what conditions is it permissible to force him to receive treatment?[54]

First, consider Malik's decision to enter rehab. Assume that he had decision-making capacity when he signed himself in. His decision is controlled by his sister's threat to evict him. Assume further that she has no right to throw him out but knows that he will not be able to effectively contest the eviction. Her controlling threat is then also illegitimate. The normative effect on validity seems clear:

as we argued in Chapter 5, an illegitimate and controlling threat undermines the voluntariness condition for valid consent. However, unlike most cases, the coercer (Malik's sister) is not the recipient of his coerced consent to treatment (his clinician). We might wonder whether it makes a difference if coercion comes from a third party rather than the recipient of consent itself.

In terms of the validity of his consent, we think it does not make a difference. Malik has a right to make decisions for himself about his body, yet someone else is making those decisions—by coercing him. Whether he gives consent to his coercer or to a third party, he does not autonomously authorize the recipient of consent's action and so he does not waive his rights.[55] His sister wrongs Malik by having other people treat him without his valid consent.

However, even if Malik's consent is invalid, his clinicians might be ethically permitted to treat him. First, they would be permitted to proceed on his invalid consent if they were ignorant of this coercion. Upon entry, suppose that Malik reads and signs a consent form that states, "No one has exerted pressure on me to select McDonald Lodge Drug Rehabilitation Centre." The person admitting him sees no signs that Malik is unwilling. Given that we can never be certain that another person's consent is valid, we can only go on what evidence we have. This evidence, as we argued in Chapter 2, determines the permissibility of proceeding on a token of consent.

Imagine, instead, that Malik pauses when he gets to this section of the consent form. He shrugs, and says, "Well, my sister will make me homeless unless I give this a try. I guess that's pressure, right?" Now the clinician knows that Malik has consented under duress. But this revelation does not automatically mean that Malik should be turned away, though it certainly complicates matters.

Both the principle of beneficence and respect for autonomy suggest an alternative: the clinician should ask what Malik would prefer to do given he now faces homelessness without rehab or housing with it. Given that the clinician cannot change these controlling background conditions, but only whether Malik enters rehab or not, it would be appropriate for them to attempt to come to a shared decision with him about whether they should proceed on his invalid token of consent.[56] This would be a shared decision that respects the remaining autonomy he has in this situation and attempts to find out what would be in his overall best interests to do now.

Turn now from the third party coercion case to the question of whether Malik's clinicians are permitted to detain him against his will after his suicide attempt? If Malik was competent, this detention would be a clear rights violation. However, his competence is precisely what is at issue here[57]—does Malik have a disturbance or impairment that compromises his ability to make an autonomous decision? This question can only be answered by assessing his mental capacity, and so his clinicians are justified in temporarily detaining him to complete that assessment. If he were then found competent, continued detention would be wrongful. After all, competent patients have the right to make unwise and risky medical decisions—decisions that can result in their death. To treat competent patients with mental illness or suicidal ideation any differently would amount to wrongful discrimination.

Finally, are his clinicians permitted to submit Malik to involuntary treatment, like administering a shot of haloperidol to calm him down? If Malik is competent, this will be permissible only if he poses a serious risk of harm to others, such as fellow patients or clinicians. Given the seriousness of this rights violation, Malik needs to be protected from unnecessary or excessive coercion. First, his clinicians ought to conduct a thorough, fair, and evidence-based risk assessment, one that Malik participates in (if he is able).[58] It is difficult to accurately predict the risk that any individual poses to others,[59] and so it is especially important that any risk identified is balanced against the risk of harm to Malik of unnecessary coercion (if the assessment is wrong) and the likelihood that he will not seek or comply with future care due to fear of coercion.[60] Finally, the team ought to draw up a risk-management plan that sets out how identified risks can be reduced or managed.[61] After this work is done, it may be evident that involuntary sedation is not the best way to reduce risk. Even if it is, the steps taken to reduce or manage risks should be the minimum needed to keep others safe. If Malik is not competent at the time, then his treatment will be governed either by judgments about what would be in his interests (and potentially those of other parties) or by his prior authorization (as discussed in section 5).

8. Conclusions

While codes of ethics for physicians have existed since antiquity, the requirement to obtain a patient's consent is of much more recent origin. In Western countries, it evolved from legal challenges and wider social changes, including civil rights movements. It is now widely accepted that in most circumstances a clinician may treat a competent adult patient only with that patient's valid consent. Agreement on that requirement still leaves many open questions. These include how to treat those with borderline or developing autonomy, such as children, how to make decisions on behalf of those who were competent but now lack decision-making capacity, and whether and when clinicians can employ methods that do not respect patient autonomy for the good of the patient or others.

Notes

1 The modern era of bioethics is widely agreed to have started in the 1960s. See Rothman, David J. *Strangers at the bedside: A history of how law and bioethics transformed medical decision making.* Routledge, 2017 and Jonsen, Albert R. *The birth of bioethics.* Oxford University Press, 2003.

2 Hippocrates. *Ancient medicine. Airs, waters, places. Epidemics 1 and 3. The oath. Precepts. Nutriment,* trans. W. H. S. Jones. Loeb Classical Library 147. Harvard University Press, 1923: 169.

3 In non-Western medical traditions the principle of beneficence also played a defining role. For example, ancient Chinese medical texts emphasize the beneficent virtues of humaneness, compassion, and a selfless dedication to the sick. See Tsai, Daniel F. "Ancient Chinese medical ethics and the four principles of biomedical ethics." *Journal of Medical Ethics* 25.4 (1999): 315–321. In classic Indian medical texts, the principle of beneficence was used to justify the practitioner's unilateral decision-making authority. See Wujastyk, Dagmar. *Well-mannered medicine: Medical ethics and etiquette in classical ayurveda.* Oxford University Press, 2012.

4 Percival, T. *Medical ethics: Or, a code of institutes and precepts, adapted to the professional conduct of physicians and surgeons*. J. Johnson, 1803.

5 Emanuel, Ezekiel J., and Linda L. Emanuel. "Four models of the physician–patient relationship." *JAMA* 267.16 (1992): 2221–2226.

6 Jay Katz recounts meeting a patient—"Iphigenia Jones"—during a panel discussion on the treatment of breast cancer. Jones's surgeon had given her the option of having a cancerous lump in her breast removed rather than having a mastectomy. She chose the breast preserving operation even though it was generally considered to be the second-best clinical option. When the wider medical community learned of this novel approach to medical decision-making, they were alarmed. Katz writes: "[t]he discussion from the floor was heated ... They were almost completely united on only one proposition: 'It is irrational to allow patients to make these decisions.' Some asked, 'If doctors have such trouble in deciding which treatment is best, how can patients decide? Are not patients' interests better served by trusting submission to their doctors' authority?'" Katz, Jay. *The silent world of doctor and patient*. JHU Press, 2002: 91.

7 Weindling, Paul J. "The Nazi medical experiments." In Ezekiel J. Emanuel, Christine Grady, Robert A. Crouch, Reidar K. Lie, Franklin G. Miller, and David Wendler (eds.), *The Oxford textbook of clinical research ethics*. Oxford University Press, 2008: 18–30.

8 Clancey, Gregory, and Rethy Chhem. "Hiroshima, Nagasaki, and Fukushima." *The Lancet* 386.9992 (2015): 405–406; Ohtsuru, Akira, et al. "Nuclear disasters and health: lessons learned, challenges, and proposals." *The Lancet* 386.9992 (2015): 489–497.

9 McBride, William Griffith. "Thalidomide and congenital abnormalities." *Lancet* 2.1358 (1961): 90,927–90,928; Lenz, Widukind. "Malformations caused by drugs in pregnancy." *American Journal of Diseases of Children*, 112.2 (1966): 99–106.

10 Kuhse, Helga, and Peter Singer. "What is bioethics? A historical introduction." In Helga Kuhse and Peter Singer (eds.). *A companion to bioethics*. Blackwell, 2009: 1–11.

11 Rhodes, Rosamond. "Bioethics: Looking forward and looking back." *The American Journal of Bioethics* 13.1 (2013): 13–16.

12 As early as 1767, in *Slater v. Baker and Stapleton*, patient consent was emphasized by the English courts and there were occasional successful lawsuits on the grounds of non-consent in various jurisdictions through the nineteenth and early twentieth centuries.

13 For example, by 1980 *informed* consent—specifically the disclosure of material risks—was legally established in South Africa (*Esterhuizen v. Administrator Transvaal* 1957 (2) SA 314 (A)), the United States (*Canterbury v. Spence*, 464 F.2d 772 (D.C. Cir. 1972); see also *Salgo v. Leland Stanford Jr. University Board of Trustees*, 317 P.2d 170 (Cal. Ct. App. 1957)) and Canada (*Hopp v. Lepp*, [1980] 2 S.C.R. 192 and *Reibl v. Hughes*, [1980] 2 S.C.R. 880).

14 Berg, Jessica W., et al. *Informed consent: legal theory and clinical practice*. Oxford University Press, 2001.

15 DeGrazia, David. "Value theory and the best interests standard." *Bioethics* 9.1 (1995): 50–61; Hawkins, Jennifer. "Theory without theories: Well-being, ethics, and medicine." *The Journal of Medicine and Philosophy* 46.6 (2021).

16 Faden, R. R, and T. L. Beauchamp. *A history and theory of informed consent*. Oxford University Press, 1986.

17 For discussion of cross-cultural variation, challenges, and adoption of Western informed consent practices in clinical care and research see, Levine, Robert J. "Informed consent: some challenges to the universal validity of the Western model." *Law, Medicine and Healthcare* 19.3–4 (1991): 207–213; Marshall, Patricia, and Barbara Koenig. "Accounting for culture in a globalized bioethics." *Journal of Law, Medicine & Ethics* 32.2 (2004): 252–266.

18 For discussion of these dual roles of the informed consent process see, Bromwich, Danielle, and Joseph R. Millum. "Informed consent to HIV cure research." *Journal of Medical Ethics* 43.2 (2017): 108–113.

19 Millum, J., and D. Bromwich. "Respect for persons." In A. S. Iltis and D. MacKay (eds.), *The Oxford handbook of research ethics*. Oxford University Press, 2024: 129–153.

20 For example, the World Medical Association's International Code of Medical Ethics states that "[t]he physician must respect the patient's decision to withhold or withdraw consent at any time and *for any reason*." World Medical Association. *International code of medical ethics*. World Medical

Association, 2022: principle 15 (emphasis added). This implies that the reason could be unwise but should still be respected.

21 Faden, Ruth R., and Tom L. Beauchamp. *A history and theory of informed consent*. Oxford University Press, 1986.

22 Mendelson, Danuta. "Historical evolution and modern implications of concepts of consent to, and refusal of, medical treatment in the law of trespass." *Journal of Legal Medicine* 17.1 (1996): 1–71.

23 For example, in healthcare systems in which patients pay at the point of service, scholars have questioned whether the cost of treatment options ought to be disclosed. See, for example, Hall, Alicia. "Financial side effects: why patients should be informed of costs." *Hastings Center Report* 44.3 (2014): 41–47.

24 Faden, Ruth R., et al. "Disclosure standards and informed consent." *Journal of health politics, policy and law* 6.2 (1981): 255–284; Katz, Jay. "Why doctors don't disclose uncertainty." *Hastings Center Report* (1984): 35–44, Dutton, Diana B. "Medical risks, disclosure, and liability: slouching toward informed consent." *Science, Technology, & Human Values* 12.3/4 (1987): 48–59.

25 *Bolam v. Friern Hospital Management Committee* [1957] 1 WLR 582.

26 *Sidaway v. Board of Governors of the Bethlem Royal Hospital* [1985] AC 871.

27 See, for example, Norrie, K. M. "Medical negligence: who sets the standard?" *Journal of Medical Ethics* 11.3 (1985): 135–137.

28 Farrell, Anne Maree, and Margaret Brazier. "Not so new directions in the law of consent? Examining *Montgomery v. Lanarkshire Health Board*." *Journal of Medical Ethics* 42.2 (2016): 85–88.

29 For South Africa, the United States, and Canada see *Esterhuizen v. Administrator Transvaal* 1957 (2) SA 314 (A)), *Canterbury v. Spence*, 464 F.2d 772 (D.C. Cir. 1972)), *Hopp v. Lepp*, [1980] 2 S.C.R. 192 and *Reibl v. Hughes*, [1980] 2 S.C.R. 880. Other examples include Australia (*Rogers v. Whitaker* (1992) 175 CLR 479) and India (*Samira Kohli v. Dr. Prabha Manchanda & Anr.* (2008) 2 SCC 1)

30 Faden, Ruth R., and Tom L. Beauchamp. *A history and theory of informed consent*. Oxford University Press, 1986, pp. 30–34. Each of these standards could be further subdivided into *interests* and *inducements* standards (see Chapter 4).

31 Adappa, R., et al. "Use of animal surfactant: should we seek consent?" *Archives of Disease in Childhood-Fetal and Neonatal Edition* 88.4 (2003): F351; Easterbrook, Catherine, and Guy Maddern. "Porcine and bovine surgical products: Jewish, Muslim, and Hindu perspectives." *Archives of Surgery* 143.4 (2008): 366–370.

32 United Nations. *Convention on the Rights of the Child*. 1989: Article 12.

33 Sigman, Garry S., and Carolyn O'Connor. "Exploration for physicians of the mature minor doctrine." *Journal of Pediatrics* 119.4 (1991): 520–525.

34 See, e.g., Consent to Treatment and Health Care Directives Act, S.P.E.I, 2024, c. 3 (1): Presumption of capacity.

35 Even so, the courts may still order treatment that is in a competent minor's best interests. For example, in *H. (P.) v. Eastern Regional Integrated Health Authority* the court in Newfoundland and Labrador considered the competence of a 16-year-old patient and found her incapable of making her own medical decisions. However, the judge maintained that he would have ordered treatment that was in her best interests even if she had been found capable.

36 See, for example, New Brunswick's Medical Consent of Minors Act, S.N.B. 1976 c. M-6.1 3(1).

37 They are allowed to consent to their own treatment earlier if they are "Gillick competent." That is, if they demonstrate sufficient understanding and maturity to make the decision. *Gillick v. West Norfolk and Wisbech Area Health Authority* [1985] 3 All ER 402.

38 Thornton, Rosy. "Multiple keyholders—wardship and consent to medical treatment." *The Cambridge Law Journal* 51.1 (1992): 34–37. See, also, Harris, John. "Consent and end of life decisions." *Journal of Medical Ethics* 29.1 (2003): 10–15.

39 For other ways to give a principled defense of this asymmetry, see Franklin-Hall, Andrew. "On becoming an adult: Autonomy and the moral relevance of life's stages." *The Philosophical Quarterly* 63.251 (2013): 223–247; Manson, Neil C. "Transitional paternalism: How shared normative powers give rise to the asymmetry of adolescent consent and refusal." *Bioethics* 29.2 (2015): 66–73; Skelton, Anthony, Lisa Forsberg, and Isra Black. "Overriding adolescent refusals of treatment." *Journal of Ethics and Social Philosophy* 20 (2021): 221–247; Tucker, Faye. "Developing autonomy and transitional paternalism." *Bioethics* 30.9 (2016): 759–766.

40 For an overview of the various decision-making standards for patients with no prior authorization, see DeGrazia, David, and Joseph Millum. *A theory of bioethics*. Cambridge University Press, 2021: 127–131.

41 Advance directives may also be called "living wills," "advance decisions," and various other names.

42 For example, while a patient in the Netherlands can legally bind themselves to specific psychiatric treatments that permit their clinicians to detain and treat them in the event of a future mental health crisis, advance psychiatric directives are not legally binding in the UK.

43 Dresser, Rebecca S., and John A. Robertson. "Quality of life and non-treatment decisions for incompetent patients: A critique of the orthodox approach." *Law, Medicine and Healthcare* 17.3 (1989): 234–244.

44 For a more extended discussion, including consideration of whether people with moderate or severe dementia might be different people than they were before, see DeGrazia, David, and Joseph Millum. *A theory of bioethics*. Cambridge University Press, 2021: 265–270.

45 Emanuel, Ezekiel J., and Linda L. Emanuel. "Proxy decision making for incompetent patients: An ethical and empirical analysis." *JAMA* 267.15 (1992): 2067–2071; Howard, Dana. "The medical surrogate as fiduciary agent." *Journal of Law, Medicine & Ethics* 45.3 (2017): 402–420.

46 Data show that the interactive features of the informed consent process—especially teaching back, testing, and giving feedback—are good to facilitate understanding of features that are important for good medical decision making. Glaser, Johanna, et al. "Interventions to improve patient comprehension in informed consent for medical and surgical procedures: an updated systematic review." *Medical Decision Making* 40.2 (2020): 119–143.

47 Ubel, Peter A. "Patient decision making." *Oncology: An Evidence-Based Approach* (2006): 177–183.

48 Fagerlin, Angela, Brian J. Zikmund-Fisher, and Peter A. Ubel. "Helping patients decide: ten steps to better risk communication." *Journal of the National Cancer Institute* 103.19 (2011): 1436–1443; Politi, Mary C., Paul K. J. Han, and Nananda F. Col. "Communicating the uncertainty of harms and benefits of medical interventions." *Medical Decision Making* 27.5 (2007): 681–695.

49 See, for example, the deliberative model of the doctor–patient relationship endorsed in Emanuel, Ezekiel J., and Linda L. Emanuel. "Four models of the physician–patient relationship." JAMA 267.16 (1992): 2221–2226.

50 A "nudge" is a small change made to the environment in which an agent makes a choice that alters that person's decision in a predictable way without taking away any of their options. See Sunstein, Cass R., and Richard H. Thaler. "Libertarian paternalism is not an oxymoron." *The University of Chicago Law Review* (2003): 1159–1202. Sometimes nudges are forms of rational persuasion in that they engage the person's rational processes, but often they are not. For an excellent discussion of manipulation, nudging, and framing effects, see Hanna, Jason. *In our best interest: A defense of paternalism*. Oxford University Press, 2018: ch. 8.

51 McNeil, Barbara J., et al. "On the elicitation of preferences for alternative therapies." *New England Journal of Medicine* 306.21 (1982): 1259–1262.

52 See, Testa, Megan, and Sara G. West. "Civil commitment in the United States." *Psychiatry* (Edgmont) 7.10 (2010): 30; McLaughlin, Paul, Domenico Giacco, and Stefan Priebe. "Use of coercive measures during involuntary psychiatric admission and treatment outcomes: data from a prospective study across 10 European countries." *PloS One* 11.12 (2016): e0168720; and Kisely, Steve R., Leslie A. Campbell, and Richard O'Reilly. "Compulsory community and involuntary outpatient treatment for people with severe mental disorders." *Cochrane Database of Systematic Reviews* 3 (2017).

53 Walker, Lenore E., et al. "Risk assessment and involuntary commitment." In *Introduction to forensic psychology: Clinical and social psychological perspectives*. Springer, 2020: 155–172.

54 Borecky, Adam, Calvin Thomsen, and Alex Dubov. "Reweighing the ethical tradeoffs in the involuntary hospitalization of suicidal patients." *American Journal of Bioethics* 19.10 (2019): 71–83.

55 See Millum, Joseph. "Consent under pressure: the puzzle of third party coercion." *Ethical Theory and Moral Practice* 17 (2014): 113–127. The view that consent under third party coercion is always invalid is a minority one. For alternative views, see Bajaj, Sameer, and Patrick Tomlin. "Consenting under coercion: the partial validity account." *The Philosophical Quarterly* 74.3 (2024): 709–731; Boonin, David. *Sexual ethics and problematic consent: When does yes mean no?* Oxford University Press, 2024: 63–84; Enoch, David. "Contrastive consent and third party coercion." *Philosophers' Imprint* 24 (2024); Kiener, Maximilian. "Consenting under third-party coercion." *Journal of Moral Philosophy* 19.4 (2021): 361–389.

56 In non-clinical scenarios, there may not be such a strong duty of beneficence, and so the correct action will depend on the other options that are open to the recipient of consent and the victim of coercion. See Millum, Joseph. "Consent under pressure: the puzzle of third party coercion." *Ethical Theory and Moral Practice* 17 (2014): 121–123.

57 Some clinicians deny this. In Europe, some argue that "mental capacity should not be the guiding principle when someone is at risk of suicide. Our first legal concern should be that of the European Convention on Human Rights (ECHR) and whether our operational duties under Article 2 are engaged. This means that we have a positive obligation to take 'operational steps to secure life' in the presence of sufficient risk." Beale, Chloe, et al. "Mental capacity in practice part 2: capacity and the suicidal patient." *BJPsych Advances* 30.1 (2024): 12.

58 It is common for patients to feel like risk assessments are done to them. And so, according to the Royal College of Psychiatrists, "for risk assessments to be accurate, patients must be engaged in their own risk assessment whenever possible … Too many patients view current risk-assessment processes as divorced from their clinical treatment." Royal College of Psychiatrists. *Rethinking risk to others in mental health services*. College report. Royal College of Psychiatrists, 2016: 22–23.

59 When the base rate of violence within a patient population is low, an individual risk assessment is typically of limited value. See Shergill, S, Szmukler, G. "How predictable is violence and suicide in psychiatric practice?" *Journal of Mental Health* (1998): 393–401.

60 Thornicroft, Graham. *Shunned: Discrimination against people with mental illness*. Oxford University Press, 2006.

61 Morgan, Steve. *Clinical risk management: A clinical tool and practitioner manual*. Sainsbury Center for Mental Health, 2000.

7 Consent to clinical research

1. Introduction

Every year, millions of people are enrolled into research. The studies in which they participate range from simple surveys of consumer preferences to the experimental insertion of electrodes into patients' brains and the intravenous administration of potentially toxic drugs. The involvement of human subjects in scientific research, especially medical experiments, has provoked considerable ethical concern among lay people and academics. This ethical concern has two primary sources. One is historical. In the words of bioethicist Carol Levine, research ethics was "born in scandal."[1] A long history of egregious experimentation on unsuspecting and vulnerable people has led to awareness of the potential dangers of leaving researchers to their own devices. The other source of concern has to do with the goals of research. While the primary goal of clinical care is to benefit the patient being treated, the primary goal of clinical research is to generate information that will ultimately benefit other people in the future. Benefiting research participants is, at best, a secondary goal. Clinical research consequently provokes particular ethical concern because of the potential for conflict between the interests of participants and the goal of acquiring knowledge.

In response to concerns about the actual and potential mistreatment of human research participants, most countries now have systems of legal and institutional protections in place.[2] These lay out the conditions under which research with human participants is permitted and typically require, for most types of research, prior review and approval by a research ethics committee.[3] International guidelines have also been promulgated by organizations such as the World Health Organization[4] and the World Medical Association.[5] A central plank of all these protections for participants is a requirement for *informed consent*. With limited exceptions, consent must be obtained from competent participants and from the legally authorized representatives of non-competent participants prior to commencing research.[6]

As a result of the scrutiny given to research and the incorporation of detailed consent requirements into policy and guidance, the consent process has been more formalized and better studied in the context of clinical research than anywhere else. In this chapter, we go into detail on how consent operates in practice in clinical research and examine some of the key ethical concerns that arise.

DOI: 10.4324/9781003287391-9

We begin with some brief history of how the consent requirement has developed in Western medical research. We then describe in some detail current practice for obtaining informed consent, the standard view on what is required, and describe how decision-making capacity is assessed for potential research participants whose competence is in question. We close with two cases. The first concerns what research participants understand about the studies in which they are enrolled. Data from numerous studies suggests that understanding is highly variable and very often inadequate according to the standards laid out by current guidance. Are these standards mistaken or is the dominant view of what is required for valid consent in error? The second case concerns the payment of healthy volunteers for high-risk research. Some argue that paying participants substantial sums is coercive or constitutes "undue influence," which may undermine the quality of their consent. We consider whether these charges have merit.

2. History

Early experiments

In clinical research, as in clinical care, the consent of participants has not always been regarded as a priority. In the nineteenth and early twentieth centuries, the majority of medical experimentation was carried out by physicians without much regard for what their subjects thought. It was quite normal for patients, in particular, to be experimented on without their knowledge. Subjects were often selected from among the most vulnerable individuals—prisoners, institutionalized children, and indigent patients. For example, in the US, hospitals were largely populated with very sick, poor patients. Some physicians considered that it was acceptable to experiment on these patients, given that they were receiving free care.[7] It was also standard practice to infect participants with dangerous diseases in the name of science. This was—for example—the accepted way in which someone could prove that they had identified the means of transmission of a disease.[8]

Despite all this, clinical research was not an ethics-free—or indeed a consent-free—zone. There were always dissenting voices. In 1897, the bacteriologist Giuseppe Sanarelli claimed to have identified the bacterium responsible for yellow fever. He had cultured *Bacillus icteroides* and injected it into five hospitalized patients, who then developed symptoms consistent with the disease. Three died.[9] These experiments were condemned by Sanarelli's contemporary, the renowned physician William Osler, who wrote: "To deliberately inject a poison of known high degree of virulency into a human being, unless you obtain that man's sanction, is not ridiculous, it is criminal."[10]

Albert Neisser, a professor of dermatology and venereology, carried out experiments involving inoculating prostitutes with cell free serum taken from patients with syphilis. The serum was unsuccessful and several of Neisser's subjects contracted syphilis.[11] Though defended by many of his contemporaries, Neisser was investigated by the Prussian public prosecutor and fined on the grounds that he should have obtained his subjects' consent. As a result of the public outcry following this case, in 1900, the government issued instructions to all medical facilities that would prohibit medical interventions "other than diagnosis, therapy, and immunization" if the person was a "minor or not competent for other reasons" or if the person "has not declared unambiguously that he or she consents to the intervention."[12]

It was a human infection study that involved the first known informed consent form.[13] Walter Reed, a US Army surgeon, and his colleagues on the Yellow Fever Commission became convinced that yellow fever was transmitted via mosquitos. In 1900, they carried out a series of experiments in Cuba to demonstrate this claim and to rule out alternative sources of transmission. These experiments included injecting participants with blood from infected patients and allowing "loaded mosquitos" to feed on them. Volunteers were offered $100 to participate and another $100 if they developed yellow fever. The money would go to the participant's next of kin if they died. Keen to avoid the criticism leveled at other scientists and to be able to demonstrate that his participants consented, Reed developed a written contract. Among other details it stated:

> The undersigned … here states by these presents, being in the enjoyment and exercise of his own very free will, that he consent to submit himself to experiments for the purpose of determining the methods of transmission of yellow fever… The undersigned understands perfectly well that in case of the development of yellow fever in him, that he endangers his life to a certain extent but it being entirely impossible for him to avoid the infection during his stay in this island, he prefers to take the chance of contracting it intentionally in the belief that he will receive from the said Commission the greatest care and the most skillful medical service.[14]

Even at the turn of the twentieth century, then, the notion that individual autonomy should be respected and so experiments should not be conducted without consent was widespread, even if not reflected in much of medical and research practice.

Codes of research ethics

Among the horrors perpetrated by the Nazi regime in the late 1930s and 40s, the experiments conducted by Nazi scientists and physicians are particularly gruesome.[15] A small fraction of the perpetrators were brought to trial at Nuremberg after the Second World War. In 1947, when rendering its judgment of the Nazi scientists, the International Military Tribunal also set out the "Nuremberg Code."[16] This statement of the ethical principles that should govern research began with an unequivocal statement of the fundamental importance of consent:

> The voluntary consent of the human subject is absolutely essential. This means that the person involved should have legal capacity to give consent; should be

> so situated as to be able to exercise free power of choice, without the intervention of any element of force, fraud, deceit, duress, overreaching, or other ulterior form of constraint or coercion; and should have sufficient knowledge and comprehension of the elements of the subject matter involved as to enable him to make an understanding and enlightened decision.[17]

Despite being the basis for legal verdicts at Nuremberg, the code did not have much immediate influence elsewhere in the world. In part, this is because the code was not widely promulgated. But, in part it is likely due to the widespread perception that the Nazi atrocities were a special case and that the code did not apply to well-meaning physician-scientists elsewhere in the world.[18]

The idea that medical research should not take place without the consent—let alone the *informed* consent—of participants would not be widespread in Western countries until at least the 1960s. In large part, this is due to the very different ways in which research with healthy volunteers—like those enrolled in the yellow fever study—was regarded versus research with patients.[19] Research with patients was usually considered to fall within the ethics of the physician-patient relationship. As noted in the previous chapter, this relationship was paternalistic and guided primarily by the clinician's judgment about what was best for the patient. Most physicians limited what they told patients for—they thought—the patient's own good. The presumption that it was up to the doctor to decide what to tell a patient and what medical interventions to attempt extended very naturally to research carried out by doctors on their patients.[20] However, as moral norms and legal precedents shifted within clinical care to increasingly emphasize the importance of patient autonomy, so they shifted within clinical research.

In 1964, the World Medical Association, the global body representing physicians worldwide, issued a set of "Recommendations guiding doctors in clinical research."[21] This document, known as the Declaration of Helsinki, has since been amended multiple times and is cited in regulations and relied upon by research ethics committees around the world. The original declaration instructed doctors to obtain the consent of research participants. However, it did still emphasize a "fundamental distinction" between therapeutic and non-therapeutic research—which, among other things, meant that doctors should obtain a patient's consent to research combined with care only when "consistent with patient psychology."[22]

Through the 1960s, a series of legal cases and public scandals concerning medical research, along with the changes in expectations surrounding clinical practice, led to substantial changes in the regulation of research in Canada, the UK, and the US.[23] In all three countries, questions of consent and of physician truth-telling were central issues. By 1966, all had established research ethics committees to carry out prior review of some clinical research, including the adequacy of plans to obtain informed consent. In 1972, news of the ongoing Tuskegee syphilis study broke in the US.[24] This experiment, carried out by the US Public Health Service, enrolled approximately 400 African American men with syphilis and 200 without in a 40-year natural history study. The men were not told about the experiment and did not give their consent. They were also not treated for syphilis. Indeed, when penicillin became widely available in the late 1940s, the researchers endeavored to prevent participants from getting access to it. The public outcry over this study led to the creation of the National Commission for the Protection of Human Subjects of Biomedical and Behavioral Research, whose recommendations would be the basis for the current US regulations governing research with human participants, including requirements for consent.

3. Current practice for obtaining consent to research

Most clinical research with human participants in almost all countries must now undergo prior review by a research ethics committee. Over the past few decades, this requirement has expanded to include other disciplines outside of medicine, including psychology, anthropology, and other social sciences.[25] Consequently, it is standard practice to expect that prospective participants' consent will be obtained before they are enrolled (or, for participants who lack decision-making capacity, the consent of a surrogate decision-maker).

There is considerable debate over exactly when exceptions should be made to this consent requirement. For example, some research questions can only be answered if participants are deceived about some aspect of the research.[26] Consider a study of altruistic behavior that involves observing how people behave when they discover unattended valuables. If participants knew that they were being watched, then they would almost certainly behave differently, thus ruining the experiment's results. As discussed in chapter 5, deception sometimes undermines the validity of consent. It will do so if prospective participants are deceived about what they are consenting to (i.e., the *understanding requirement* is not met) or if the deception leads them to consent when they otherwise would not (i.e., the *voluntariness requirement* is not met).[27]

There are also important outstanding questions about the scope of consent to research and when re-consent is required. For example, a biobank might collect data and biological specimens from a group of patients with the understanding that they will be used for research. However, the biobank will likely not know at the outset what research studies will be conducted. Often, biobanks offer their resources to outside researchers who can propose their own studies. Is it possible for participants to give consent to all and any uses of their specimens at the point of collection ("blanket consent")? Or is it impossible to give valid consent to research studies that are as yet unconceived, such that participants should be asked for consent each time their samples are used? The answer to this question is potentially very important, since requiring individual consent for each study will both slow down research and reduce the scientific value of sample collections (since there will always be *some* participants who refuse or do not respond to requests for consent). A variety of solutions have been proposed and practice across biobanks varies.[28] Our view on the understanding requirement has implications for this issue. As we argued in chapter 4, we think that broad consent is possible, but *what* is consented to depends on what was successfully communicated.

For research for which consent does have to be obtained, regulations and guidelines encourage comprehensive disclosure. For example, the 2024 version of the Declaration of Helsinki states:

> In medical research involving human participants capable of giving informed consent, each potential participant must be adequately informed in plain language of the aims, methods, anticipated benefits and potential risks and burdens, qualifications of the researcher, sources of funding, any potential conflicts of interest, provisions to protect privacy and confidentiality, incentives for participants, provisions for treating and/or compensating participants who are harmed as a consequence of participation, and any other relevant aspects of the research.
>
> The potential participant must be informed of the right to refuse to participate in the research or to withdraw consent to participate at any time without reprisal. Special attention should be given to the specific information and communication needs of individual potential participants as well as to the methods used to deliver the information.[29]

The required information is usually provided to participants in written form and they are asked to give a signature to signify consent.[30]

Due to the amount of information researchers are required to disclose to prospective participants, consent forms can be very long. A clinical research study that involves testing an experimental treatment against an active control might involve multiple interventions—not just to provide the experimental treatment but also in order to measure the effects of treatment and disease progression. Each intervention will need to be explained and will likely have its own set of risks (and possibly potential benefits). One study of oncology trials found that consent forms were a median of 5,129 words long (roughly the length of this chapter minus the footnotes).[31] Studies of consent forms for HIV and Covid-19 trials found them even longer.[32] Unsurprisingly, there are concerns that participants do not read these forms in their entirety and that the key information needed to make good decisions about enrolment may get lost.[33]

Guidance documents like the Declaration of Helsinki also claim that participants must *understand* all the information that is disclosed to them, a position that is also endorsed by many researchers and ethicists. Given the quantity of information provided, this is a challenge. Data suggest that many participants do not recall or never understood key details of the studies in which they are enrolled. In section 5, we consider what this data implies for the validity of consent to research.

4. Capacity assessments

In research, as in clinical care, it is presumed that adults are competent to give consent, unless there is some reason to doubt it. That is, the default is to assume decision-making capacity. Sometimes research studies will enroll a patient population whose condition is known to impair decision-making, such as patients with schizophrenia or dementia.[34] In other cases, a researcher may become concerned about capacity when interacting with a potential participant during the consent process. In these situations, where there is *uncertainty* about decision-making capacity, some sort of formal assessment is needed.

It is worth noting that a determination of competence or incompetence can be more significant in the context of decisions about research than clinical care. In clinical care, competent patients should be supported to make decisions that reflect their interests and values. Decisions on behalf of patients who are not competent should likewise reflect what the surrogate decision-makers think are the patients' interests and values. So, in most cases, the two ought to align since they typically aim at the same goal. Research has a different goal to care, and one which may not align with participants' interests, since it aims to generate knowledge to benefit other people, not the individuals being studied. Where research poses substantial net risks to participants, it may not be permissible to enroll them *unless* they have the capacity to make their own decisions.[35]

Capacity assessments generally break down capacity into component domains, as we discussed in Chapter 3. These domains reflect the relevant law concerning competence. So, in the UK, individuals whose capacity is in doubt are assessed on whether they can understand the relevant information, retain that information, use or weigh the information, and communicate a decision.[36] In North America, they more usually assess whether someone understands relevant information, appreciates how it applies to their situation, reasons, and expresses a choice.[37]

When someone's ability to consent to research is in question, the assessment will normally be tailored to the specific research study in which they are expected to enroll. They will be asked questions about, for example, their knowledge of the specific risks of *this* study, their reasons for considering enrolling in *this* study, and so forth. As a result, where there is some uncertainty about capacity, it cannot be evaluated without first educating the prospective participant about the study. For example, the study staff might first go through the consent form with the prospective participant, just as they would with someone whose capacity was not in doubt. Then, the individual would be interviewed by an assessor independent of the research team to evaluate their understanding, appreciation, and so on. If the individual did not pass some part of the assessment, they might be educated again on what they got wrong, and then retested. Thus, consent and capacity assessment can be part of an iterative process of education and testing, with the goal of helping someone with borderline decision-making capacity to reach the point where they can make their own decision.[38] A number of tools have been developed for assessing capacity to consent to research, which can be adapted to fit specific research studies.[39]

5. Case: the understanding of participants in clinical trials

Multiple studies have quizzed participants about their understanding of the clinical research in which they are enrolled. These studies have included research participants from many different countries and many types of research—including healthy volunteers in vaccine studies, the parents of premature newborns, and patients with cancer and other serious diseases. Though understanding is highly variable from one study to the next, it is often very poor. A substantial proportion of participants are unable to correctly answer simple questions about key facts, such as the purpose of the research, how it differs from clinical care, or major risks.[40]

To give one example, Rebecca Pentz and colleagues surveyed 95 patients with cancer who were enrolled into phase 1 clinical trials at a US medical center.[41] Phase 1 trials are designed to test dosing and toxicity. Efficacy is, at most, a secondary endpoint. Less than 5% of oncology drugs tested in phase 1 trials will ultimately be approved for use in patients.[42] These studies are therefore neither designed to benefit participants nor, realistically, likely to do so. Pentz and colleagues were interested in how well participants in these trials understood the difference between research and care. To assess this, they asked two questions:

(1) "Is the research study mostly intending to help research and gain knowledge or mostly intending to help you as a person?"
(2) "Does the research study or your physician decide the treatments?"

68% of their participants answered one or both of these questions incorrectly.

As discussed in Chapter 4, the standard view of the understanding requirement says that in order to give valid consent, participants must understand all the information that ought to be disclosed to them. Moreover, as we have seen, the canonical texts in research ethics—as well as most regulations—require a considerable amount of information to be disclosed to participants. Most of these texts also state that participants should understand the information that is disclosed to them. For example, after listing the many components of disclosure quoted above, the Declaration of Helsinki goes on: "*After ensuring that the potential participant has understood* the information, the physician or another qualified individual must then seek the potential participant's freely given informed consent."[43]

What, then, are we to make of the participants in research studies who appear not to know much of this important information? A natural reading of the standard view implies that the ignorant participants have not given valid consent to research. Thus, the injections, scans, and other invasive procedures that they undergo violate their rights and constitute egregious wrongs. However, perhaps surprisingly given the data, no one is calling for clinical research to be halted while we work out how to ensure that participants' rights are respected.

Other than calling for a moratorium on clinical research, there are two principled ways in which one might respond to the data showing low levels of participant understanding. One is to accept that consent is indeed frequently invalid, but argue that it is nevertheless permissible to proceed with clinical research. Franklin Miller and Alan Wertheimer argue that the regulatory framework for protecting human research participants is premised on this very idea.[44] Requiring prior review of studies by a research ethics committee, limiting the risks to which participants can agree, and similar protections, would be hard to justify if we thought that individuals' decisions about research enrolment are likely to be fully autonomous. They would constitute a form of hard paternalism (restricting the actions of autonomous adults for their own good). But we do not expect that every competent adult considering research participation will act autonomously. Most will not understand the science sufficiently to judge the risks and benefits, they may suffer from a therapeutic misconception, and so on.[45] Thus, Miller and Wertheimer argue, the protections for participants constitute a form of soft paternalism: "since we cannot count on the consent tokens of prospective subjects to constitute valid consent, we need independent risk-benefit assessment on soft paternalistic grounds."[46] More precisely, they think that these protections are a form of "group soft paternalism"—they are aimed at a group of individuals, some of whom will be decisionally impaired and some of whom will not.[47]

The other possible response, not incompatible with the first, is to revise one's view of the understanding requirement.[48] If it is not true that all the information that is disclosed to participants must also be understood, then some of these ignorant participants may in fact have given valid consent. This is the response that we prefer.

In Chapter 4, we argued that the disclosure and understanding requirements have different grounds. The disclosure requirement arises because omitting or misrepresenting information can deceive someone. Where that deception leads them to give consent it constitutes illegitimate control and thereby undermines the validity of the consent. Since for some research studies there are lots of facts that might be relevant to someone's decision about whether to enroll—including the risks, alternatives to being in research, the purpose of the study, and so on—the disclosure requirement can be quite extensive. By contrast, we argued that the understanding requirement is quite minimal. In order to give valid consent, someone need understand only: (1) that they are giving consent; (2) how to exercise their right in order to give or refuse consent; and (3) to what they are giving consent. We argued that the last of these conditions should be interpreted as understanding what rights are being waived through consent—e.g., that I am giving permission to have this nurse inject me with a drug.

If we are right about the informational requirements for valid consent, we can resolve the puzzle of why the data on participant understanding has not led to the outcry one might expect upon discovering that thousands of people are having their rights violated. Our view suggests that most of the time valid consent has in fact been given.[49]

Whether one agrees with Miller and Wertheimer, with us, or regards the data on participant understanding as an ethics scandal waiting to blow up, there are good reasons to try to improve understanding. Doing so will increase the likelihood that participants give valid consent and, importantly, improve the quality of their decision-making. Even if understanding, for example, the comparative risks and benefits of research enrollment versus usual care is not necessary for valid consent, it might still be needed in order for participants to make a good decision. And that is a worthy goal of the consent process, even if not as high stakes as a potential violation of bodily integrity.[50]

A number of interventions have been tested to try to improve the quality of informed consent to research. These include shorter consent forms, presenting information on forms in different ways, testing and re-educating potential participants, and providing information about studies through alternative media, such as video. For the most part, it turns out that alternative designs to consent forms—including reducing their length—do not improve comprehension.[51] It seems likely that the majority of research participants do not get their information about studies from reading the consent materials. There is now evidence that the use of alternative media, such as videos, increases what participants remember.[52] Interactive methods, such as testing participant understanding, targeted re-education, and retesting, improve understanding (as well as revealing exactly who might not know what they are agreeing to).[53] In general, consent processes that involve extended interaction with someone from the research team, improve understanding more than anything else.[54] This may be because people learn better from having key information conveyed in person, because it allows more active engagement, and because questions and responses can be tailored to the participant's specific needs. Such processes are, of course, more resource intensive than other ways to provide information. This may be the trade-off that is necessary, if we want research participants to give consent that is truly informed.

6. Case: paying healthy volunteers for high-risk research

In early 2021, in the midst of the global pandemic, researchers at Imperial College London began the world's first Covid-19 human challenge study.[55] Over the course of several months, 34 healthy, unvaccinated young adults with no history of SARS-CoV-2 infection were deliberately inoculated with the virus. Each was quarantined for two weeks in a hospital room and carefully monitored for markers of infection, immune responses, and adverse events.[56] The hope was that data from the study would prove valuable in the development of vaccines and treatments in future research. The research itself offered no benefits to participants, but each was paid £4565.

This was the first controlled human infection study using SARS-CoV-2, but such methods have been used to study many other infectious diseases, including cholera, malaria, influenza, and dengue fever.[57] By deliberately infecting healthy volunteers under carefully controlled conditions, researchers can gain insights into the progression of the disease and test vaccines and treatments much more efficiently than if they had to run a trial with people who were naturally infected.

Current controlled human infection studies are very different from the ones carried out by Sanarelli, Reed, and their contemporaries that we described above. Not only are they only carried out with competent consenting adults who are judged to be at the lowest risk for serious disease, scientists have many more tools for minimizing the risks. The studies often use weakened strains of the disease and only include diseases that we either know how to treat or are self-limiting.[58] Nevertheless, they raise understandable ethical concerns.[59] Participants are exposed to non-trivial risks. They also undergo considerable burdens by taking part in the research—two weeks in isolation is not to be sniffed at! It is therefore vitally important that their decision to enroll is voluntary.

One purported impediment to voluntariness that is often raised is the level of payment. £4565 is a lot of money. For comparison, median gross annual income for a full-time worker in the UK in 2021 was £31,285.[60] Moreover, the people who enroll in these sorts of studies are disproportionately likely to be poor and unemployed compared to the general population.[61]

Some commentators think that high levels of payment can be coercive. For example, the bioethicist Ruth Macklin argues: "The reason for holding that it is ethically inappropriate to pay patients to be research subjects is that it is likely to be coercive, violating the ethical requirement that participation in research should be fully voluntary."[62] This view is also widely held by research ethics committee members and researchers themselves.[63]

Is this concern warranted? In Chapter 5, we argued that the type of coercion that undermines consent essentially involves a threat. A threat is a proposal to make someone worse off if they do not comply with the coercer's demands. But payment for research participation is not a threat; it is an offer. If this analysis of coercion is correct, then the idea that payment undermines consent because it is coercive is just a non-starter.[64]

Chapter 5 also identified a form of coercion—eudaimonic coercion—that can occur via an offer. This form of coercion is bad for the victim because it makes them subject to someone else's will. If someone experiences eudaimonic coercion, they are harmed, whether or not they also experience deontic coercion, which is the sort of coercion that undermines voluntariness. Payment to potential research participants could constitute eudaimonic coercion, if they are in such desperate straits that the alternative to accepting the payment would be unacceptably bad for them (starvation, say). This situation will be rare—it is not true of most participants in phase 1 studies, even if they are poor. In addition, the correct response to such situations may not be refusing to pay (and thereby leaving the potential participants to their unacceptably bad alternative). Instead, it may be better to increase the level of benefits, so that the harm of being coerced is outweighed by the goods that the payment can provide.[65]

Instead of using the language of coercion, some articulate their concern about the influence of money on participants' decision-making in terms of "undue inducement." For example, the ethics guidelines from the Council for International Organizations of Medical Sciences state: "Monetary or in-kind compensation for research participants must not be so large as to persuade them to volunteer against their better judgment or deeply held beliefs ('undue inducement')."[66] The notion of undue inducement is much less clear and has been subject to much less analysis than that of coercion. One possibility is that undue inducement occurs when an offer is so attractive that it undermines an individual's decision-making capacity. It renders them incompetent with respect to this decision. That would explain both why they made a decision that was "against their better judgment" and why doing so might be evidence that payment rendered their consent invalid.

In evaluating this claim, we note first that there is no evidence that offers of payment undermine decision-making capacity. In experimental settings, understanding of risks is not reduced by higher offers of payment.[67] In fact, the opposite appears to be the case: higher payments are believed to be a signal that risks are higher, leading to greater scrutiny of the risks.[68] Further, participants who are primarily motivated by money appear to have better understanding of risks than those who are primarily motivated by, for example, altruism.[69]

The majority of health volunteers enrolling in phase 1 and challenge studies are motivated by payment, of course. Very few would volunteer for free. But the fact that payment is an inducement does not make it undue. It is perfectly reasonable to take the value of money into account when deciding whether to enroll in a study. By analogy, the vast majority of us would not go to work if we were not paid. That fact does not imply that our work is involuntary.[70]

A final worry that might be raised is that the participants in these studies are being *exploited*. Concerns about exploitation are a recurring theme in clinical research (and are borne out by some of the terrible historical examples of unethical research).[71] Exploitation can be broadly defined in terms of one party taking unfair advantage of another party.[72] It thus requires both that the exploited party is vulnerable in some way and that the exploiter uses that vulnerability to gain more from the exploited party than they should. Price gouging provides a classic example of exploitation. Suppose that, in the aftermath of a natural disaster, clean water is in short supply. Only one distributor controls the remaining source—a situation that will not change for the next few weeks, at least. Seeing that they have a monopoly on a basic necessity, the distributor jacks up their prices as high as the market will bear. People have no option but to pay the higher price, even though the costs to the distributor have not changed. This is exploitative and—we would judge—unethical.

It is possible that some participants are exploited by being paid to take on the risks and burdens of clinical research. However, note two points. First, it appears possible to give valid consent to exploitative terms. That the terms of a transaction are unfair does not entail that they undermine voluntariness.[73] So, someone might be treated wrongly because they are exploited but nevertheless give valid consent. Second, and more important in the present context, the simplest way to avoid exploiting research participants is to pay them *more*. If the benefits of enrolling in the research are high enough, then that will mean that the terms of the transaction are fair. Reducing payments to research participants will only make things worse. Lower payments are more likely to be unfair and so make exploitation more likely.

As far as we can see, paying research participants substantial sums of money does not coerce them or undermine their decision-making capacity. Still, even if their consent is valid that does not make these practices ethically neutral. As we have just noted, paying participants too little risks exploiting them. It also ensures that the population enrolling in high-burden studies—such as challenge studies and phase 1 studies—will not be representative of the wider population, even the healthy adult population. On the other hand, paying substantial amounts or offering participants other important benefits could lead to unnecessary harms if it motivates volunteers to conceal health problems that should exclude them from a study.[74] There are also potential problems if the incentives lead individuals to join multiple studies simultaneously. If someone is enrolled in more than one study at the same time, the scientific validity of all the studies may be undermined.[75] Questions about the ethics of payment for research participation are complex and merit nuanced discussion.

7. Conclusions

Most clinical research can proceed only with the valid consent of participants or their representatives. This is both a legal and an ethical requirement. Since most research with human participants is reviewed by a research ethics committee, the consent requirement for research has become heavily formalized and scrutinized. Nevertheless, getting valid consent to research remains challenging. There are unsettled questions regarding the scope of research consent, the informational requirements, and the effects of inducements, such as monetary payments to participants. As we have seen in this chapter, both empirical studies and conceptual analysis are needed in order to answer these questions.

Notes

1 Levine, Carol. "Has AIDS changed the ethics of human subjects research?" *Law, Medicine and Health Care* 16.3–4 (1988): 167.
2 US Department of Health and Human Services, Office for Human Research Protections. "International compilation of human research standards." 2024. Available at: www.hhs.gov/ohrp/international/compilation-human-research-standards/index.html.
3 Research ethics committees are also known as institutional review boards (IRBs) in the United States and research ethics boards (REBs) in Canada.
4 World Health Organization. "Standards and operational guidance for ethics review of health-related research with human participants." 2011. Available at: www.who.int/publications/i/item/9789241502948.
5 World Medical Association. "Declaration of Helsinki: Medical research involving human participants." 2025. Available at: www.wma.net/what-we-do/medical-ethics/declaration-of-helsinki.
6 Exceptions vary by jurisdiction, but might include, for example, low-risk research on anonymous data.
7 Blacksher, E., and J. D. Moreno, "A history of informed consent in clinical research." In E. J. Emanuel, C. C. Grady, R. A. Crouch, R. K. Lie, F. G. Miller, and D. D. Wendler (eds.), *The Oxford textbook of clinical research ethics*. Oxford University Press, 2008: 595.
8 E. Jamrozik and M. J. Selgelid. *Human challenge studies in endemic settings*. Springer, 2021: 11–13.

9 Lederer, S. E. "Walter Reed and the yellow fever experiments." In E. J. Emanuel, C. C. Grady, R. A. Crouch, R. K. Lie, F. G. Miller, and D. D. Wendler (eds.), *The Oxford textbook of clinical research ethics*. Oxford University Press, 2008: 10. Sanarelli was also mistaken about the cause of yellow fever.

10 Lederer, S. E. "Walter Reed and the yellow fever experiments." In E. J. Emanuel, C. C. Grady, R. A. Crouch, R. K. Lie, F. G. Miller, and D. D. Wendler (eds.), *The Oxford textbook of clinical research ethics*. Oxford University Press, 2008: 12.

11 Ligon, B. L. "Albert Ludwig Sigesmund Neisser: Discoverer of the cause of gonorrhea." *Seminars in Pediatric Infectious Diseases* 16.4 (2005): 336–341.

12 Ligon, B. L. "Albert Ludwig Sigesmund Neisser: Discoverer of the cause of gonorrhea." *Seminars in Pediatric Infectious Diseases* 16.4 (2005): 339.

13 Lederer, S. E. "Walter Reed and the yellow fever experiments." In E. J. Emanuel, C. C. Grady, R. A. Crouch, R. K. Lie, F. G. Miller, and D. D. Wendler (eds.), *The Oxford textbook of clinical research ethics*. Oxford University Press, 2008: 12.

14 Cutter, Laura. "Walter Reed, yellow fever, and informed consent." *Military Medicine* 181.1 (2016): 91.

15 Weindling, P. J. "The Nazi medical experiments." In E. J. Emanuel, C. C. Grady, R. A. Crouch, R. K. Lie, F. G. Miller, and D. D. Wendler (eds.), *The Oxford textbook of clinical research ethics*. Oxford University Press, 2008: 18–30.

16 The Nuremberg Code. In *Trials of war criminals before the Nuremberg Military Tribunals under Control Council Law no. 10. volume 2*. Washington, DC: U.S. Government Printing Office, 1949: 181–182.

17 The Nuremberg Code. In *Trials of war criminals before the Nuremberg Military Tribunals under Control Council Law no. 10. volume 2*. Washington, DC: U.S. Government Printing Office, 1949: Principle 1.

18 Again, however, views on the matter were far from uniform. Within the US Government, for example, the Atomic Energy Commission (AEC) developed rules in 1947 for research using radioactive isotopes that required "informed consent" from all participants. These rules were not widely disseminated. The policy of the National Institutes of Health Clinical Center, a federally-funded research hospital opened in 1953, required "voluntary agreement based on informed understanding" for all research participants. Blacksher, E., and J. D. Moreno, "A history of informed consent in clinical research." In E. J. Emanuel, C. C. Grady, R. A. Crouch, R. K. Lie, F. G. Miller, and D. D. Wendler (eds.), *The Oxford textbook of clinical research ethics*. Oxford University Press, 2008: 598.

19 The case of Henrietta Lacks illustrates the prevailing norms. Lacks was receiving care at Johns Hopkins Hospital for cervical cancer in 1951 when a sample of her cancer cells were retrieved for research purposes without her knowledge. The practice was common at the time, but we know about this research because, unlike every other cancer cell collected, Lacks' cells did not die; they multiplied. These "HeLa" cells became an essential biomedical tool—an immortal human cell line that has been and continues to be used in cancer research, infectious disease research, and the development of vaccinations. For an analysis of that case, and the ethical lessons for biospecimen policy today, see Beskow, Laura M. "Lessons from HeLa cells: The ethics and policy of biospecimens." *Annual Review of Genomics and Human Genetics* 17.1 (2016): 395–417.

20 Blacksher, E., and J. D. Moreno, "A history of informed consent in clinical research." In E. J. Emanuel, C. C. Grady, R. A. Crouch, R. K. Lie, F. G. Miller, and D. D. Wendler (eds.), *The Oxford textbook of clinical research ethics*. Oxford University Press, 2008: 599.

21 World Medical Association. "Declaration of Helsinki: Medical research involving human participants." 2025. Available at: www.wma.net/what-we-do/medical-ethics/declaration-of-helsinki.

22 The therapeutic/non-therapeutic distinction was removed only in the 2000 revision of the Declaration.

23 Blacksher, E., and J. D. Moreno, "A history of informed consent in clinical research." In E. J. Emanuel, C. C. Grady, R. A. Crouch, R. K. Lie, F. G. Miller, and D. D. Wendler (eds.), *The Oxford textbook of clinical research ethics*. Oxford University Press, 2008: 600; Hedgecoe, A. "A form of practical machinery: The origins of research ethics committees in the UK, 1967–1972." *Medical History*, 53.3 (2009): 331–350; Razumenko, Fedir. "The genesis and development of research ethics committees in Canada, 1960–1978." *European Journal for the History of Medicine and Health* 78.2 (2021): 330–352.

24 Jones, J. H. "The Tuskegee syphilis experiment." In E. J. Emanuel, C. C. Grady, R. A. Crouch, R. K. Lie, F. G. Miller, and D. D. Wendler (eds.), *The Oxford textbook of clinical research ethics*. Oxford University Press, 2008: 86–96.

25 For discussion, see Wassenaar, Douglas R. and Nicole Mamotte. "Ethical issues and ethics reviews in social science research" In Andrea Ferrero et al. (eds), *The Oxford handbook of international psychological ethics*. Oxford University Press, 2012: 268–282.

26 See, Wendler, David, and Franklin G. Miller. 2004. "Deception in the pursuit of science." *Archives of Internal Medicine* 164.6: 597–600.

27 For some discussion of the ethics of deception in research, see Athanassoulis, Nafsika, and James Wilson. "When is deception in research ethical?" *Clinical Ethics* 4.1 (2009): 44–49; Benham, Bryan. "The ubiquity of deception and the ethics of deceptive research." *Bioethics* 22.3 (2008): 147–156; Wendler, David, and Franklin G. Miller. "Deception in the pursuit of science." *Archives of Internal Medicine* 164.6 (2004): 597–600.

28 Grady, C., et al. "Broad consent for research with biological samples: workshop conclusions." *American Journal of Bioethics* 15.9 (2015): 34–42; Hansson, M. G., et al. "Should donors be allowed to give broad consent to future biobank research?" *The Lancet Oncology* 7.3 (2006): 266–269; Hirschberg, I., H. Kahrass, and D. Strech. "International requirements for consent in biobank research: qualitative review of research guidelines." *Journal of Medical Genetics* 51.12 (2014): 773–781.

29 World Medical Association. "Declaration of Helsinki: Medical research involving human participants." 2025. Available at: www.wma.net/what-we-do/medical-ethics/declaration-of-helsinki. Paragraph 26. Similarly extensive requirements for disclosure can be found in the widely cited guidance from the Council for International Organizations of Medical Sciences. "International ethical guidelines for health-related research involving humans." 2016. Available at: www.cioms.ch/ethicalguidelines-2016.

30 In some cases, the actual consent form may be separate from the pages of information given to participants. There are also a number of exceptions to requirements for *written* consent.

31 Duong, Quyen, et al. "Understanding verbosity: Funding source and the length of consent forms for cancer clinical trials." *Journal of Cancer Education* 36 (2021): 1248–1252.

32 Kass, Nancy E., et al. "Length and complexity of US and international HIV consent forms from federal HIV network trials." *Journal of General Internal Medicine* 26 (2011): 1324–1328; Emanuel, Ezekiel J., and Connor W. Boyle. "Assessment of length and readability of informed consent documents for COVID-19 vaccine trials." *JAMA Network Open* 4.4 (2021): e2110843.

33 Douglas, B. D., E. L. McGorray, and P. J. Ewell. "Some researchers wear yellow pants, but even fewer participants read consent forms: Exploring and improving consent form reading in human subjects research." *Psychological Methods* 26.1 (2021): 61–68.

34 There are also patient populations whose decision-making may be impaired by an acute condition that requires rapid intervention, such as people who have just experienced a stroke. There are additional complications in enrolling such patients into research, since rapid medical intervention is needed and so taking time to obtain consent or to assess decision-making capacity can itself pose a serious risk. Millum, Joseph, et al. "Emergency care research ethics in low-income and middle-income countries." *BMJ Global Health* 4.Suppl 6 (2019): e001260.

35 Regulations governing the enrolment of individuals who lack capacity vary. In most circumstances, however, research that poses more than "minimal risk" without compensating benefits for participants will not be permitted.

36 For England and Wales, see National Health Service. "Mental Capacity Act." 2024. Available at: www.nhs.uk/conditions/social-care-and-support-guide/making-decisions-for-someone-else/mental-capacity-act. For Scotland, see Scottish Government. "Adults with incapacity: Guide to assessing capacity." 2008. Available at: www.gov.scot/publications/adults-incapacity-scotland-act-2000-communication-assessing-capacity-guide-social-work-health-care-staff/pages/2. For Northern Ireland, see "Mental Capacity Act (Northern Ireland)." 2016. Available at: www.legislation.gov.uk/nia/2016/18/contents/enacted.

37 Legislation in this area in Canada and the US is by province/state. For the US, see Appelbaum, P. S. "Assessment of patients' competence to consent to treatment." *New England Journal of Medicine* 357.1836 (2007): 1834–1840. Canadian legislation focuses on whether the individual understands the information relevant to a decision and whether they appreciate the consequences of a decision or lack of decision. See, e.g., Health Care Consent Act, 1996, S.O. 1996, c. 2, Sched. A, s 4(1).

38 Of course, in some cases this will be unnecessary—it will very quickly become apparent that the person is unable to make their own decisions. This iterative process is ideal for participants who

have borderline capacity and can be supported to make their own decisions. See Chapter 3 for more discussion of scaffolded decision-making.

39 Dunn, Laura B., et al. "Assessing decisional capacity for clinical research or treatment: A review of instruments." *American Journal of Psychiatry* 163.8 (2006): 1323–1334; Matera-Vatnick, Mikaela, et al. "Evaluating the ability to consent to research: A twenty-year track record." *Ethics & Human Research* 44.2 (2022): 2–17.

40 Mandava, A., C. Pace, B. Campbell, E. Emanuel, and C. Grady. 2012. "The quality of informed consent: Mapping the landscape. A review of empirical data from developing and developed countries." *Journal of Medical Ethics* 38.6: 356–365.

41 Pentz, Rebecca D., et al. "Therapeutic misconception, misestimation, and optimism in participants enrolled in phase I trials." *Cancer* 118.18 (2012): 4571–4578.

42 Wong, Chi Heem, Kien Wei Siah, and Andrew W. Lo. "Estimation of clinical trial success rates and related parameters." *Biostatistics* 20.2 (2019): 273–286.

43 World Medical Association. "Declaration of Helsinki: Medical research involving human participants." 2025. Available at: www.wma.net/what-we-do/medical-ethics/declaration-of-helsinki. Paragraph 26 (emphasis added). See also The Nuremberg Code. In *Trials of war criminals before the Nuremberg Military Tribunals under Control Council Law no. 10. volume 2*. Washington, DC: U.S. Government Printing Office, 1949: Art. 1; Council for International Organizations of Medical Sciences. "International ethical guidelines for health-related research involving humans." 2016. Available at: www.cioms.ch/ethicalguidelines-2016. Guideline 9.

44 Miller, Franklin G., and Alan Wertheimer. "Facing up to paternalism in research ethics." *Hastings Center Report* 37.3 (2007): 24–34.

45 Miller, Franklin G., and Alan Wertheimer. "Facing up to paternalism in research ethics." *Hastings Center Report* 37.3 (2007): 29–30.

46 Miller, Franklin G., and Alan Wertheimer. "Facing up to paternalism in research ethics." *Hastings Center Report* 37.3 (2007): 33. Hard paternalism is typically understood as an act that interferes with a competent person's voluntary decision contrary to their wishes but for their own good. Soft paternalism, by contrast, is an act that interferes with a person's decision where they are thought to be acting non-voluntarily (whether for reasons of incompetence, lack of information, or illegitimate control). See Feinberg, Joel. *The moral limits of the criminal law, volume 3: Harm to self.* Oxford University Press, 1989: 12–16.

47 Miller, Franklin G., and Alan Wertheimer. "Facing up to paternalism in research ethics." *Hastings Center Report* 37.3 (2007): 28.

48 As argued in Millum, J., and D. Bromwich. "Informed consent: What must be disclosed and what must be understood?" *American Journal of Bioethics* 21.5 (2021): 46–58.

49 In a fascinating study on informed consent to biobank research, Laura Beskow and Kevin Weinfurt developed a consensus among experts on what facts needed to be understood for valid consent. Beskow, L. M., and K. P. Weinfurt. "Exploring understanding of 'understanding': The paradigm case of biobank consent comprehension." *American Journal of Bioethics* 19.5 (2019): 6–18. Presented with data showing that, even with education and retesting, a third of participants did not understand all these facts, a substantial fraction of the experts nevertheless agreed that it would be permissible to include them in the research. The experts were clearly pulled in two directions—feeling both that prospective participants should receive certain information and that they could nevertheless be enrolled in research without understanding all of it. Our view nicely reconciles these competing impulses.

50 See, Bromwich, Danielle, and Joseph R. Millum. "Informed consent to HIV cure research." *Journal of Medical Ethics* 43.2 (2017): 108–113.

51 Flory, James, and Ezekiel Emanuel. "Interventions to improve research participants' understanding in informed consent for research: A systematic review." *JAMA* 292.13 (2004): 1593–1601; Grady, C., et al. "A randomized trial comparing concise and standard consent forms in the START trial." *PLoS ONE* 12.4 (2017): e0172607; Perrault, Evan K., and David M. Keating. "Seeking ways to inform the uninformed: Improving the informed consent process in online social science research." *Journal of Empirical Research on Human Research Ethics* 13.1 (2018): 50–60.

52 Hall, E. W., et al. "Use of videos improves informed consent comprehension in web-based surveys among internet-using men who have sex with men: A randomized controlled trial." *Journal of*

Medical Internet Research 19.3 (2017): e64; Taylor, Holly A., et al. "Randomized comparison of two interventions to enhance understanding during the informed consent process for research." *Clinical Trials* 18.4 (2021): 466–476.

53 Flory, James, and Ezekiel Emanuel. "Interventions to improve research participants' understanding in informed consent for research: a systematic review." *JAMA* 292.13 (2004): 1593–1601; Geier, Caitlin, et al. "Informed consent for online research—is anybody reading?: assessing comprehension and individual differences in readings of digital consent forms." *Journal of Empirical Research on Human Research Ethics* 16.3 (2021): 154–164.

54 Flory, James, and Ezekiel Emanuel. "Interventions to improve research participants' understanding in informed consent for research: a systematic review." *JAMA* 292.13 (2004): 1593–1601.

55 Callaway, Ewen. "Scientists deliberately gave people COVID—here's what they learnt." *Nature* 602.7896 (2022): 191–192.

56 For a full report of the study and its findings, see Killingley, Ben, et al. "Safety, tolerability and viral kinetics during SARS-CoV-2 human challenge in young adults." *Nature Medicine* 28.5 (2022): 1031–1041.

57 Roestenberg, Meta, et al. "Experimental infection of human volunteers." *The Lancet Infectious Diseases* 18.10 (2018): e312–e322.

58 Roestenberg, Meta, et al. "Experimental infection of human volunteers." *The Lancet Infectious Diseases* 18.10 (2018): e312–e322.

59 World Health Organization. "WHO guidance on the ethical conduct of controlled human infection studies." 2022. Available at: www.who.int/publications/i/item/9789240037816.

60 Office for National Statistics. "Employee earnings in the UK: 2021." 2021. Available at: www.ons.gov.uk/employmentandlabourmarket/peopleinwork/earningsandworkinghours/bulletins/annualsurveyofhoursandearnings/2021.

61 Almeida, Luis, et al. "Why healthy subjects volunteer for phase I studies and how they perceive their participation?" *European Journal of Clinical Pharmacology* 63 (2007): 1085–1094; Kalbaugh, Corey A., et al. "Healthy volunteers in US phase I clinical trials: sociodemographic characteristics and participation over time." *PLoS One* 16.9 (2021): e0256994. Moreover, as part of research, these participants are likely to receive free healthcare. Where those enrolled have access to the care they need free at the point of service—as these UK participants did—this is not a concern. But it may be when enrolling people for whom medical costs represent a barrier to accessing the care they need. See, Cho, Hae Lin, Marion Danis, and Christine Grady. "The ethics of uninsured participants accessing healthcare in biomedical research: A literature review." *Clinical Trials* 15.5 (2018): 509–521.

62 Macklin, R. "The paradoxical case of payment as benefit to research subjects." *IRB: Ethics & Human Research* 11.6 (1989): 3.

63 Largent, E. A., C. Grady, F. G. Miller, and A. Wertheimer. "Money, coercion, and undue inducement: A survey of attitudes about payments to research participants." *IRB* 34.1 (2012): 1–8.

64 Wertheimer, Alan, and Franklin G. Miller. "There are (STILL) no coercive offers." *Journal of Medical Ethics* 40.9 (2014): 592–593.

65 For extended discussion, see Millum, Joseph, and Michael Garnett. "How payment for research participation can be coercive." *American Journal of Bioethics* 19.9 (2019): 21–31.

66 Council for International Organizations of Medical Sciences. "International ethical guidelines for health-related research involving humans." 2016. Available at: www.cioms.ch/ethicalguidelines-2016. Compare Ezekiel Emanuel's definition: "Undue inducement is when we offer people goods to assume clearly excessive and unreasonable risks." Emanuel, Ezekiel J. "Undue inducement: Nonsense on stilts?" *American Journal of Bioethics* 5.5 (2005): 11. Emanuel argues that if the risk/benefit ratio of a study is reasonable, then undue inducement is impossible.

67 Halpern, Scott D., et al. "Empirical assessment of whether moderate payments are undue or unjust inducements for participation in clinical trials." *Archives of Internal Medicine* 164.7 (2004): 801–803.

68 Cryder, Cynthia E., et al. "Informative inducement: Study payment as a signal of risk." *Social Science & Medicine* 70.3 (2010): 455–464.

69 Stunkel, Leanne, et al. "Comprehension and informed consent: assessing the effect of a short consent form." *IRB* 32.4 (2010): 1.

70 Eric Lee draws an analogy with being induced by potential therapeutic benefits and argues that it would be absurd to cap such benefits in order to protect the potential beneficiaries. Lee, Eric. "Our flawed approach to undue inducement in medical research." *Bioethics* 33.1 (2019): 13–18.

71 Hawkins, Jennifer S., and Ezekiel J. Emanuel, eds. *Exploitation and developing countries: The ethics of clinical research*. Princeton University Press, 2008.

72 Wertheimer, Alan. *Exploitation*. Princeton University Press, 1999.

73 We leave open the possibility that for individuals who are sufficiently desperate, exploitation might be both illegitimate and controlling and therefore invalidate consent. Our point here is simply that some instances of exploitation will not undermine voluntariness.

74 See, e.g., Mngadi, Kathryn T., et al. "Undue inducement: A case study in CAPRISA 008." *Journal of medical ethics* 43.12 (2017): 824–828.

75 Largent, Emily A., and Holly Fernandez Lynch. "Paying research participants: The outsized influence of 'undue influence.'" *IRB* 39.4 (2017): 1.

8 Consent online

1. The issue

People access many goods by using online technologies. They build personal and professional relationships on social media, watch their favorite shows and movies on streaming platforms, and even outsource their security, comfort, and energy monitoring to integrated smart home hubs. However, all this comes at a cost: when someone uses these apps, smart devices, and online platforms they provide technology companies and their third-party affiliates with access to personal data. Among other uses, this data may be used for targeted advertising, for training artificial intelligence, or for scientific research.

A lot of the information collected about people online is personal. It is protected by privacy rights. What, then, could make the collection, analysis, use, and trade of this data permissible? One common answer is: consent.

Sometimes online consent appears straightforward. For example, when Danielle shops with a retailer online, she will often be given the option of adding a card to her account. If she chooses to provide her payment details and click "Store my card," then it seems plausible to assume that she understands that she has given the company permission to retain this information. She will assume, correctly, that her card details will not be shared with anyone else. If she is concerned, there is usually a readily available privacy notice, in which the company discloses what personal information it collects, the purposes for which it is used, and the measures it puts in place to keep customer information secure. Though it is convenient to store her card details, it is not a huge burden to re-enter them either and there is no impediment to Danielle choosing to do so every time. In other words, there are no concerns about voluntariness.

Other cases are more problematic. In 2018, the Norwegian Consumer Council filed a complaint against Grindr, the popular LGBTQ+ dating app.[1] According to the complaint, Grindr had sold sensitive data about its users, including their HIV status and location, to third parties. Information about Grindr's data sharing practices was buried in their complex terms of service and privacy policies and there was no way to decline specific forms of sharing. Despite the fact that users had clicked to accept the terms of service, it was argued that they had not meaningfully consented. Grindr stopped sharing information about HIV status, but it was

DOI: 10.4324/9781003287391-10

later fined 65 million Norwegian krone (about US$6 million) by the Norwegian Data Protection Authority for selling information about users' locations and other data that could allow inferences to be drawn about their sexual orientation.[2]

The Grindr case illustrates a common challenge with online consent. Although the laws governing the right to use online data turn on users' consent, the validity of many online transactions seems questionable. Many people have a sense of the "surveillance capitalism" data economy—an inkling that technology companies make a profit by capturing and selling users' data to third parties for digital marketing, product development, and government surveillance. [3] Yet few users could outline the precise details of what happens to their information. Unlike adding card details to an online shop account—an action that sees the user actively and freely provide specific data in a context that clearly specifies the scope and purpose of the exchange—most data transactions are passive. We agree to have our data collected, retained, used, shared, and sold as a condition of using the technology. This leaves many of us unsure *whether* we have provided data, *what* kind of data we have provided, and with *whom* we have transacted. This is the *opacity* problem with online consent.

It is not the only problem. To be valid, consent needs to be given *voluntarily*, and yet we reside in digital societies built on surveillance technologies. While individual privacy notices emphasize our freedom not to use a company's technology if we disagree with the terms of use, it is practically impossible to access some essential goods and services while refusing to use the digital infrastructure surrounding them. In many countries, it is impossible to access public education while refusing to allow your child to use school computers fitted with surveillance software, get a college degree while refusing to use the institution of higher education's web-based virtual learning and management system, apply for a job while refusing to use prospective employers' recruitment and application software, or receive medical care while refusing an electronic medical record. Unlike choosing whether to use a specific online seller or declining to store card details, the consequence of not using some technology that collects one's data is tantamount, in many cases, to cutting off one's access to essential goods and services.

Finally, consent online poses challenges concerning the *competence* of the parties involved. These are twofold. One is that virtual interactions are by their very nature impersonal. When interacting with strangers online, it can be hard to be sure of who they are. This fact is exploited by bad actors in order to perpetrate scams and exploit vulnerable people. But it also leads to difficulties for well-meaning actors. When someone signs up for a service, how can the service provider know whether their new user is capable of giving their own consent? The other challenge concerns who should be allowed to give consent online. Children and adolescents are huge users of social media and many regard it as essential for their social lives. Yet data increasingly suggest that social media can be particularly harmful to young people.[4] How should those with questionable competence be protected online?

This chapter engages these three problems.[5] We begin with a discussion of privacy, since the right to control one's personal information is the main right implicated in online consent. We briefly summarize some key legal regimes governing data privacy. The complexity and ubiquity of online transactions have motivated some scholars to question whether traditional models of consent apply in the online context. We defend the applicability of our view of consent against more radical attempts to rethink consent in this domain. Then we consider the competence problem before discussing two hard cases that concern opacity and voluntariness. The first hard case analyzes the use of lengthy terms and conditions. We assess the ethical significance of signing up to a digital service after struggling to parse complicated and incomplete terms of service. The second concerns the voluntariness of online consent in the context of modern education. We outline the growing industry of educational technology and consider whether it is possible to opt out of its use or data collection while also accessing publicly funded education.

2. Privacy rights

Online consent mostly involves two sets of rights. One is our property rights, which are exercised when we engage in financial transactions online. The other is our *privacy rights*, where these concern our control over personal information.[6]

Philosophical accounts of informational privacy differ.[7] However, at their core, most hold that privacy involves restricting the access of others to information about oneself.[8] Much like the right to bodily autonomy, this establishes a default that other people are not permitted to collect or use our personal information. Our privacy rights also include a power that allows competent individuals to waive their rights and give others permission to collect and use pieces of personal information.

The information about an individual that is protected by their privacy rights—what we have labelled "personal information"—clearly has some limits.[9] Information that someone can readily ascertain about me simply by observing me in public presumably falls outside the information that I have a right to control. What I am wearing or the accent I speak with are clearly facts about me as an individual and in that sense *personal* to me. But they are not protected by privacy rights. On the other hand, what I wear or what I say in my home is private and I have the right that others not obtain that information without my explicit consent.[10]

One way to work out the scope of our privacy rights would be to look at the values they protect. The ability to control information about ourselves certainly has instrumental value. For example, it gives us the freedom to present ourselves to others in the ways that we choose, it facilitates intimate personal relationships whereby we allow some people but not others into our private sphere, and it protects us from being controlled by others who could use personal information to manipulate or threaten us. Privacy may also have intrinsic value—that is, it may be important in itself that we have the power to control access to information about ourselves.[11] We do not take a position on this latter question here.

Even if we agree on the values underlying privacy rights, there will remain questions about marginal cases, where it is unclear whether a piece of information about an individual falls within the scope of privacy. For example, do I have the right to refuse to have my picture taken if I am out in public? If I agree to be in someone's picture, do I retain the right to control whether they share it with others? The exact borders of the right will be important in some cases. However, in this chapter we will focus only on cases where it is uncontroversial that the information in question is personal and falls within the scope of privacy rights. The questions of consent are complex enough without us also having to resolve these difficult issues regarding the ultimate grounds of privacy rights.

One last important aspect of privacy rights concerns non-competent individuals. Decisions concerning the use of personal information sometimes have to be made on behalf of individuals who lack the ability to decide for themselves. For example, the caregiver of someone who is severely cognitively impaired must decide what information to reveal about them when they visit the doctor. Some of these decisions can have far-reaching consequences. Consider, for example, the personal information that a parent might reveal about their child to friends or to the public on Facebook. Some people share photographs and videos, origin stories, or even the child's medical history. When they are young, children may be indifferent to this. When they are older, they may care a great deal, but once revealed, it is very difficult to make information private again.[12] As a consequence, when considering whether to consent to the collection and use of data on another's behalf, proxy decision-makers have to take a long-term view of what is in the person's interests. This can prove challenging for families, where personal information about a child is also personal information about oneself. We do not think that a line is easy to draw here. Both the parent's and the child's interests are relevant and need to be weighed. At one extreme, we think that it will usually be unethical to share very private information widely online simply for the sake of entertaining others. At the other, it is surely permissible to share personal stories with one's close family, even if the child, when an adult, is likely to be embarrassed by them.[13]

3. Regulating online consent

Some sort of legal right to informational privacy is recognized in most jurisdictions.[14] Rights to privacy are also asserted in several international human rights documents, including the European Convention on Human Rights,[15] and the Universal Declaration of Human Rights.[16] Most countries have omnibus laws that govern the collection and use of personal data for all industries. These laws may then be supplemented by sector-specific regulation (for example, regarding medical information). Some countries, like the US, lack omnibus laws and rely solely on sectoral legislation—with specific laws regulating government surveillance, medical records, children under 13, and so on.[17]

Laws governing the collection and use of personal data online rely heavily on user consent. They usually adopt what is known as the "notice and consent" model: technology companies provide privacy notices and users read these and make decisions about whether to use the technology. In some jurisdictions, explicit requests for consent—to, say, use of non-essential cookies—must be made. Options are then provided for declining consent to specific collection or uses of data. For example, the GDPR requires "explicit consent" to the processing of sensitive personal data (such as regarding religious beliefs, health, or sexuality).[18] Where data protection laws are less strict, use of a website may be conditioned on agreement to provide one's data or it may be asserted that simply browsing past the homepage of the website constitutes consent to the terms and conditions listed in the privacy notice (so-called "browse-wrap" agreements).[19]

The GDPR includes requirements that personal data should be protected by design and by default.[20] Privacy by design involves building privacy protections into new information technologies and applications from the outset. In addition to minimizing the use of personal data, that means utilizing technology to keep data secure and to empower individuals to control their data.[21] Various standards and guidelines have been developed to help organizations to implement this.[22]

The GDPR also includes a right to be forgotten, that is, a right to demand that organizations delete personal data that they hold about you. The regulation states: "The data subject shall have the right to obtain from the controller the erasure of personal data concerning him or her without undue delay and the controller shall have the obligation to erase personal data without undue delay."[23] There are some exceptions, such as the data use being in the public interest or being used for establishing a legal defense. In general, however, this constitutes a way that consent to the *continuing* use of one's data can be revoked.

4. Alternatives to consent

In the introduction, we described three problems for online consent: the opacity, voluntariness, and competence problems. To some, the ubiquity of these problems suggests that valid consent to the collection and use of data online is a mirage—it is uninformed, involuntary, and often given by those who lack capacity. Yet online interactions involving the exchange of personal information are commonplace and treated by many of the parties involved as innocuous or, at worst, annoying.[24] In the face of the apparent verdict of mainstream consent theory that most online consent is invalid and the belief that the collection and use of personal data is nonetheless frequently morally permissible, some scholars have proposed alternative ethical frameworks that do not require consent.

For example, Bart Schermer, Bart Custers, and Simone Van der Hof argue at length against the *autonomous authorization* model of consent. On this model, competent individuals make the collection and use of their data permissible by exercising their wills through consent.[25] The view we have articulated and defended in the theory chapters of this book is a version of an autonomous authorization model. Schermer and colleagues argue that the model's use leads to an overload of consent transactions, an overload of information that people cannot hope to grasp, and an absence of meaningful choice. They propose as an alternative "a differentiated system of consent."[26] They write: "In this system, decisions only need unambiguous or explicit consent when it really matters, i.e., when decisions may involve serious risks or consequences for the person who consents."[27] In most cases, however, consent to the use of personal data would be implied—for example, by the fact that someone visits a website or signs up to a social media platform.

Of course, Schermer and colleagues are aware that not explicitly asking for consent could lead to the misuse of people's private information, as we saw in the Grindr case. They propose that we can avoid such misuse through an additional requirement: the collection and use of personal data without explicit consent will be permitted only insofar as it is *fair*. They write:

> For different scenarios (e.g. surfing the web, buying goods, using social media, et cetera) we must determine what is fair, when it comes to data processing. An example could be that when you share your personal data via a free social media platform, society deems it fair that the platform uses these data for targeted ads that generate revenue, as long as they exclude all sensitive data.[28]

This new system, Schermer and colleagues claim, would reduce the number of consent transactions and thereby reduce individual overload. It could also take into account the legitimate interests of the parties *requesting* data, as well as the interests of those providing it. After all, many of the services provided online are free to users. The business models of platforms like Facebook rely on targeted advertising and other means of monetizing personal data to be financially viable.

Lichelle Wolmarans and Alex Voorhoeve argue for a similar proposal.[29] Like Schermer and colleagues, they note the substantial challenges for meeting the standards for autonomous authorization in practice. They argue that improving the quality of consent—for example, by taking steps to ensure that users understand the pros and cons of exchanging information for services—would be "unduly burdensome and have inegalitarian impacts."[30] Requiring such understanding would prevent some potential users from making use of online platforms that they want to (ignorantly) use. Worse, it would disproportionately impact those with less education and less familiarity with online technology.

As an alternative, Wolmarans and Voorhoeve propose the "Value of Choice" account. On this account, what matters is not whether social networking sites get valid consent to data processing. Instead, they "gain permission to process users' personal data by providing users with sufficiently valuable opportunities to exchange access to personal data for services."[31] This means that the options that users are provided with online will be set up in such a way that the choices they make are likely to promote their goals. Whether they understand how their data will be used is neither here nor there.

It will be helpful to divide the claims made by these critics of current practice into two categories. First, the critics argue that obtaining meaningful consent for the collection and use of personal data online is often impossible. Fortunately, however, they also claim that it is often *unnecessary* in order to render transactions involving personal data ethically permissible. Second, they argue that consent is in any case *insufficient* to render such a transaction ethically permissible. Even valid consent would not protect users from exploitation, loss of privacy, and other woes. We consider these criticisms separately in the following sections.

5. Is valid consent necessary for ethical use of online personal data?

Why think that the collection and use of personal data online is permissible only if valid consent is given? To answer this question, consider a competent adult who is sharing some personal information online—for example, perhaps they are inputting their demographic information into a survey, or the website they are using is able to track their location, search terms, and purchase history. We assume that the individual has a privacy right with respect to this personal information. After all, if they do not start with a right against others accessing their information, then this whole discussion is moot.

Imagine now an online transaction in which the conditions for ethical permissibility on the fair transactions or value of choice accounts are met. The entity with access to this user's data would like to sell it to a carefully selected group of trustworthy business partners. Doing so is likely to promote the interests of our user and others. Not only are they receiving valued services for free from the service they have chosen to use—one which would not exist without the revenue from selling data—but these are socially beneficial businesses. They are developing sustainable, low-carbon, repairable, and in every way highly virtuous products. They use the personal data they receive to improve these products and identify potential users.

Suppose, however, that the user does not give valid consent to the onward sale of their personal information. Perhaps they are not asked, or they are asked but the website lies about whether the data will be sold on. It might even lie to users because if it told them the truth too many would refuse, so it manipulates their choice for the greater good.

What should we say about the permissibility of the collection and sale of users' personal information in a case like this? To us, it seems clear that it is still impermissible *even if* the transaction is otherwise fair or provides valuable choices. Each user has, we assumed, a privacy right with respect to the data. They have not given consent—if they had, then the views we are considering would not be giving *alternatives* to a consent requirement. That means that their right to privacy has not been waived. The entity with access to this data has not been released from the duty not to sell their information. Selling it to a third party would therefore violate this right.

Now, most people accept that there are conditions under which individual rights can be overridden for the greater good. For example, in the face of an infectious disease epidemic it might be permissible for the government to require that health care professionals share patient information to a centralized database, no matter whether individual patients object. Or it might enforce limitations on free movement, in order to reduce the transmission rate. But the cases we are considering are not so high stakes (and the proponents of non-consent models for online collection and use of personal data do not claim that this is a matter of overriding individual rights for some vitally important public good).

We conclude that where users have a privacy right with respect to a piece of personal information, it is normally wrongful to collect and use that information without their valid consent. In our discussion of the hard cases in the final sections of this chapter, we explain how online consent is also *possible*, even if current practice needs some tweaking.

6. Is valid consent sufficient for ethical use of online personal data?

While we disagree with the critics' claim that valid consent is not necessary for the collection and use of personal data to be ethical, we endorse their claim that it is not sufficient.

Throughout this book, we have emphasized that consent is not a panacea. Someone can give valid consent and thereby waive a right. But if that right is not the only moral consideration relevant to the interaction, knowing whether the consent was valid will not tell us whether the action that follows is right or wrong, good or bad. If Felipe gives valid consent to sex with Elena, she will still act wrongly by proceeding if she has promised to remain faithful to Hugo. Consent can be valid even though the act consented to is bad for the consent giver. It can be valid while the consent giver is treated unfairly, disrespected, or manipulated. And it can be ethically wrong to do what someone has consented to. The entities requesting personal data can and sometimes do act unethically even when they have obtained valid consent.[32]

The literature on online consent is littered with examples of ways in which people are mistreated. Some involve problems with the quality of consent; but others have different sources. For example, many websites provide a menu of options regarding their use of cookies and the sharing of data. Some set defaults to allow sharing and require users who do not want to share to untick a series of boxes. This is manipulative—since it makes the easiest choice for a user in a hurry the one that involves them giving up data—but we do not think it renders consent to sharing invalid. A dating app might require consent to targeted advertising in exchange for members using it for free. Someone might regard this as exploitative, especially if it is the go-to app for people from their community. Nevertheless, that would not render their consent invalid. A gambling company might target high-risk users who have recently deleted their app with marketing emails offering them free bets to rejoin. Repeated offers might induce a person with a gambling addiction to sign back up. Even if their consent is still sufficiently voluntary to be valid, using tracking data to identify vulnerable users—users who are seemingly trying to curb their gambling—and then bombarding them with incentives to download the app again is a particularly egregious form of exploitation.

These sorts of problems are common, in part, for systemic reasons. The business model of much of the internet is built on advertising revenue. This makes personal data monetizable and generates incentives to manipulate people into doing things that are inconsistent with their values. Consequently, reforms to current practice might need to be wide-ranging. Critics of the notice and consent model, like those we considered in section 4, have suggested some frameworks for how to think about such reforms. These frameworks remain valuable, even if we think that consent remains possible and necessary. Recommendations for reform range from the very broad, such as incorporating "privacy by design" into all online platforms, to the very specific, such as having time limits to consent or creating a privacy profile for each individual user.[33] Detailed consideration of possible reforms would, however, take us outside the scope of this book.

7. Competence and consent online

The consent exchanges that we discuss elsewhere in this book mostly happen in person. In person encounters usually provide a lot of clues about whether an individual giving consent has the capacity to do so. A discussion with a patient or potential research participant can reveal that they are having trouble understanding and trigger a capacity assessment. Whether a potential sexual partner is intoxicated or underage may be apparent at a glance. This is not to say that mistakes about competence are never made in person—they certainly are—but there is ample evidence readily available. Not so for most consent given online. That someone clicked "I agree" gives no information about whether they had decision-making capacity at the time.

This matters because many of the people who are online are not capable of giving their own consent. To give one example, in the UK, a quarter of 5–7-year-olds have their own mobile phone, and the proportion rises to 90% by age 11.[34] Half of all children under 13 use at least one social media platform.[35] Online services are also used by many adults with impaired decision-making capacity, whether congenital (e.g., people with Down syndrome), acquired (e.g., people with dementia), or self-induced (e.g., people who are intoxicated with alcohol or drugs). Many of these people benefit from their online activities. For example, people with dementia can find support and friendship through social networking sites, as well as maintaining their sense of self.[36] They are also at risk of exploitation by bad actors, loss of privacy, and having their data misused.

Most discussion of online consent by individuals who lack or may lack decision-making capacity has focused on children and adolescents. This is also the only group for which there are clear regulations and policies in place. For example, in the US, the Children's Online Privacy Protection Act (COPPA) requires commercial online service providers to obtain parental consent before they collect or use personal information about anyone under the age of 13.[37] The GDPR permits lower age limits between 13 and 16 for children to give their own consent to data processing. Different EU countries—and the UK—have set various ages within this range.

Ethically speaking, it makes sense to use age limits as rough proxies for competence when making policy. Just as with the legal age of consent to sex, medical care, or contracts, the law needs to draw a bright line between those who have the legal power and those who do not.[38] Whether current regulations draw this line in the correct place is up for debate.

Consider now how answers to the theoretical questions about the nature of competence can be relevant to these practical issues. On the view we defended in chapter 3, competence comprises two separate rights with separate grounds. There is the power to waive one's rights through consent and there is the claim against paternalistic interference with one's consent decisions. We argued that the power requires less extensive cognitive capacities than the claim against paternalism. This means, plausibly, that at some stages of development, a child will have the power to waive her rights, but others are permitted to interfere when she acts contrary to her interests. Likewise, for other individuals with borderline autonomy.

For young children, then, who lack both components of decision-making capacity, personal information should only be collected and used when their caregivers give consent on their behalf. Older children and adolescents likely have the capacities needed to have the power to give consent. Where making online choices for themselves is in their interests they can be permitted to make their own consent decisions. However, they lack the claim against paternalism. Those with responsibility for their care *and* those who are requesting the personal information are therefore permitted and sometimes obligated to interfere when sharing the information would be contrary to the young person's interests. Finally, once an adolescent has full decision-making capacity, including the capacities needed to be held responsible for their actions, they should have the same freedom as adults have online. Thus, policies that restrict social media use before a certain age could be ethically justified by our theory.

Multiple ethical and practical challenges remain. One is how to assess competency. Even for the rather crude marker of age, it can be difficult to ensure that a user is the age they say they are.[39] It is relatively straightforward for underage users to sign up for accounts with most of the major social media apps by, for example, simply entering a fake age.[40] Various solutions to this problem have been suggested, including using facial or speech recognition software that is designed to estimate age. For the most part, these would also be relatively easy to get around, quite apart from the additional issues concerning privacy that they would raise. This means that most of the responsibility for enforcement, in practice, falls on caregivers, such as parents, who can restrict what devices their children have and what apps they download.

We are aware of no comparable discussions of the question of whether and how to screen adults for impaired decision-making capacity when they sign up for services or purchase goods online. From the point of view of service providers, as long as someone has a mobile phone or a credit card, they are assumed to have capacity. Again, responsibility for assessing competence and putting limits on what a person does online rests with proxy decision-makers. This then poses the further challenge, for caregivers and other responsible third parties, of how to make these decisions. There are clearly benefits and risks to, say, being part of an online social network. Proxy decision-makers face the difficult task of balancing these benefits and risks, while also respecting—as far as possible—the privacy of the individuals for whom they are responsible.[41]

8. Case: terms and conditions

Rhonda is giving a talk on security systems at her local neighborhood watch. After her husband died, she signed up for Amazon Ring—a home security system composed of smart doorbells, cameras, lights, and alarms. She remembers finding Ring's terms of service hard to understand, but with the help of a lawyer friend, she learned what she wanted to know. While Amazon collect data amassed in connection with the use of these security services, they do not permit third parties to access individual devices, accounts, or the audio, video, and images its cameras record.

Some people at her talk are interested in Ring, but worried about unauthorized surveillance. Her neighbor Mike says, "Look, it's a nice bit of kit, I'll give you that, but why on earth would I install something that lets the police or the government spy on me?" In line with Amazon's disclosures, Rhonda explains that Amazon does not share users' data with law enforcement or anyone else. Instead, it facilitates the relationship between law enforcement and local communities via the Neighbors app—a free and integrated social networking app where Ring users can post footage from their devices, law enforcement can submit requests for video recordings, and the two parties can discuss matters of public safety in their local area.[42] She says, "You know, Mike, I used to share your concerns, and that's why I read the terms of service carefully. Amazon are actually very good on privacy."

In fact, matters were not so cut and dried. In a response to questions raised by Senator Ed Markey of Massachusetts in 2022, Amazon confirmed that US law enforcement could request videos through a process that did not require the consent of the device owner or a court order. The process just required that the police fill out a form and state that there was a life-threatening emergency. In response to Markey's questions, Amazon confirmed that it had complied with such requests 11 times from January to July 2022. This process was not detailed in Ring's terms of service.[43]

This case is an instance of the opacity problem. Most people do not know what personal data will be collected and how it will be used when they grant permissions online. Unlike Rhonda, very few people read privacy notices or statements of terms and conditions.[44] Indeed, to do so would require the average internet user to spend hundreds of hours reading.[45] Even then few would understand the implications of all the legal and technical jargon that is used. Rhonda struggled without the help of someone with legal training. Most people do not—and perhaps *could not*—know what they are getting into when they token "consent" online.

In Chapter 4, we developed an account of the informational requirements for valid consent that separates the disclosure and understanding requirements on the basis that they have different functions. We now consider what this account can tell us about consent to terms and conditions.

Though disclosure plays some role in achieving understanding, its primary function is to avoid invalidating consent through illegitimately controlling someone's consent decisions. A disclosure is rendered illegitimate, ethically speaking, by virtue of being deceptive. Deception can take various forms. It can involve outright lying, but it can also be achieved through misleading implications or through omitting information that the consent giver would reasonably expect to be told.

To avoid deception, information about what will be done with users' personal information needs to be made available in a manner which does not mislead them—actively or through omission—about any dealbreakers that the requestor of consent may reasonably expect them to have. Rhonda had a very common dealbreaker—that her Ring footage not be shared with third parties without her consent. It would be reasonable of her to expect to be told by Amazon that they had a process in place by which they gave the police access to her Ring data. Amazon did not *just* omit this information or bury it in technical language in the terms of service. They directed users to one set of disclosures that implied that they—*the user*—would have control over whether this data would be shared. At the same time, they directed law enforcement to another set of disclosures that explained that they—*Amazon Ring*—would share this data under certain circumstances without the knowledge or consent of the user.

The understanding requirement, in contrast to the disclosure requirement, is minimal. On our view, the person giving consent must understand only (1) that they are giving consent; (2) how to exercise their right to give or refuse consent; and (3) to what they are giving consent.

In some cases, users have no idea that what they are doing is taken to constitute consent. For example, we suspect that few users of the internet regard browsing past the landing page of a website as signifying consent to the collection and onward sale of their data.[46] If someone does not understand that what they are doing is giving consent, then it simply does not constitute consent, ethically speaking. There is no ethical basis for these practices. Understanding to what one is giving consent also means understanding what rights one is waiving—that is, what is the recipient of consent now permitted to do that they were not permitted to do before? When Rhonda signed up to Ring, she would need to know if Amazon would share her data with a third party. Since she did not, she might have waived her rights against Amazon collecting and storing her data but still not have given permission for them to share it.

9. Case: modern education

Tunde has become increasingly worried about protecting his children's privacy online. His oldest child is at primary school. When she enrolled he was asked to sign a consent form authorizing the school to create her Google Workspace for Education account. At the time, he did not give this a second thought, but he just learned that the Danish Data Protection Authority have banned Workspace after a parent complained that students' personal data was shared unlawfully.[47] Tunde looks back at the consent form he signed. After a little research, he notices that it is an adapted template that Google provides to schools. It links to a variety of Google's privacy notices, policies, and their terms of agreement with the educational institution, and it gives parents (and guardians) the option not to consent. Yet the form does not specify what the alternative to using Workspace would be. Given how integrated it is in every aspect of his daughter's schoolwork, he is not sure how he could opt out without negatively affecting her education. Tunde wonders whether he has an effective right to protect his children's privacy in education. Can he really opt out of technologies or digital partnerships that he suspects collect, use, and trade his children's personal data in ways he does not know about, while also ensuring that they receive the education to which they are entitled?

This case concerns the voluntariness of online consent in the context of modern education, as well as the ability of students, their guardians, and educational institutions to effectively protect students' autonomy rights.[48]

The UN Convention on the Rights of the Child (CRC) outlines three relevant rights of children. They have a right to education, a right to privacy, and a right to be protected from economic exploitation.[49] Since primary school children are usually no older than 11 years, many lack decision-making capacity. As a result, third parties—their parents, educators, regulators, and educational technology companies—have responsibilities to ensure their rights are protected. Yet the evidence suggests that a child's right to privacy and their right against economic exploitation are routinely violated while they learn in specially designed digital workspaces for education.[50]

In 2022, a group of researchers at the Digital Futures Commission conducted a series of studies with children aged 9–12 in publicly funded UK schools that used the standard (free) version of Google Workspace for Education.[51] They found that, despite being within this protected Workspace, when a child accessed educational links provided to them by their teachers, "the child's user journey and Google Classroom interfaces showed no notifications or warnings that the child was stepping out of Google Classroom's high privacy-by-default environment."[52] Instead of having their access restricted to that environment, they were free to navigate to websites with extensive cookie surveillance. One 9-year-old's "visit to Vimeo and YouTube following a teacher's announcement resulted in cookie surveillance by 92 third-party sites."[53]

The children's privacy does not seem to be well-protected here and—given the commercial value of children's data to third parties—we might regard this as economic exploitation. Yet, the parents and educational institutions did agree to use Google Workspace for Education. What are we to make of their consent?

In Google's promotional materials, the 9-year-old's parents and educators were told the following:

> There are no ads in Google Workspace for Education core services, and core service data is not used for advertising purposes. Also in additional services, primary and secondary (K-12) school students' personal information is not used for ads targeting."[54]

Google also assured "transparency and compliance with regulations like GDPR as well as privacy and security best practices" on the same page.

On the basis of these statements, it would be natural for a parent or educator to think that a child is protected if they are operating *within* Google Workspace for Education. It would also be natural to assume that, in compliance with GDPR and rights-respecting best practices, children would be denied access to sites engaged in surveillance capitalism while they are learning with the Workspace. Neither assumption, it turns out, is true. These promotional materials falsely imply that Google Workspace respects and ensures children's privacy rights and protects them from online economic exploitation. Given that educational institutions would not—or should not—use these tools as designed if they knew about the default loopholes that allow children to venture into low-privacy online environments, this marketing material is not only illegitimate, it is controlling.

One might object that this is why parents, educators, and data controllers ought to peruse Google's privacy policies. But this just reveals the depth of the problem. While Google's promotional materials are clear and accessible but misleading, their privacy statements are convoluted, dense, and incomplete. The Digital Futures Commission researchers—a team of experts composed of policymakers, regulators, and academics—say:

> We estimate that it would take a lawyer with expertise in privacy law a week to read and comprehend the different intersecting policies and potentially months to analyse the extent of the implications for children's rights in a given school, especially as data is transferred to a number of sub-processors and stored in the USA.[55]

When these experts worked to decipher Google's privacy policy, they were still unclear *exactly* what data is collected and used:

> Since our expert lawyers could not ascertain what data Google Classroom actually collects and how it handles these data, including when the data are shared with others (e.g., the government or future universities, employers or, indeed, data brokers or other businesses), it is no wonder that schools struggle to grasp the nature, purposes or consequences of education data processing.[56]

We think Tunde is right to be concerned about his children's privacy in their digital education. It is highly unlikely, given the Digital Futures Commission's findings, that he has given valid consent to the school creating and maintaining a *data collecting* Google Workspace for Education account. It is also unclear what, if anything, he has authorized Google to do with his daughter's data.

Is he also right in thinking that he has no option but to agree to Google's demands in order to ensure his children can access education to which they have a right? It is increasingly difficult to educate children in publicly funded school systems while opting out of educational technology. Modern primary and secondary school is thoroughly digital in some regions. Estimates vary, but in the UK in 2021, one in three 16–17-year-olds used Google Workspace for Education.[57] Suppose, then, that Tunde's catchment area was served exclusively by schools with this digital partnership in place. Opting out would either require home schooling, private schooling, or a special non-digital accommodation with the school.

Take the first two alternatives: private schooling and home schooling. Given the financial cost of private schooling, and the financial and time costs of home schooling, it is plausible to suppose that neither are a reasonable option for Tunde. Since his children have a right to education, and since the costs of declining public education partnered with Google would be too high, if these are the only two options then it seems very likely that Tunde has been coerced into agreeing to Google's demands in order to access compulsory education for his children.

However, whether he is faced with a "take it or leave it" coercive proposal depends on specific conditions that we have not fleshed out. It depends on whether he could secure his daughter a place at this school while opting out of Google Workspace *without* that resulting in her receiving a sub-standard education—that is, an education that falls short of what she has a right to receive.

10. Conclusions

These hard cases might leave the reader skeptical about the possibility of valid consent online. We are not so skeptical. Even in these cases, Senator Ed Markey's work has resulted in Amazon Ring making changes to its disclosure practices that make valid consent more likely,[58] and the Danish and Dutch Data Protection Authority's interventions have resulted in Google making technical changes to Workspace that protect children's privacy more effectively.[59] We believe that thorough regulation can result in changes that make valid consent possible. This is vital because, as we have argued, given that much personal data online is private, valid consent is necessary—though not sufficient—for permissible data transactions online.

Notes

1 Norwegian Consumer Council. "Filing complaint against Grindr's sharing users' HIV-status and sexual preferences." April 3, 2018. Available at: www.forbrukerradet.no/side/filing-complaint-against-grindrs-sharing-users-hiv-status-and-sexual-preferences.

2 Norwegian Consumer Council. "Grindr is made to pay after a complaint from the Norwegian Consumer Council." July 1, 2024. Available at: www.forbrukerradet.no/side/the-district-courts-judgment-in-the-grindr-case.

3 Zuboff, S. *The age of surveillance capitalism: The fight for a human future at the new frontier of power.* Profile Books, 2019.
4 See, for example, Riehm, Kira E., et al. "Associations between time spent using social media and internalizing and externalizing problems among US youth." *JAMA Psychiatry* 76.12 (2019): 1266–1273, Hunt, Melissa G., et al. "No more FOMO: Limiting social media decreases loneliness and depression." *Journal of Social and Clinical Psychology* 37.10 (2018): 751–768; and Dyer, C. "Social media content contributed to teenager's death 'in more than a minimal way,' says coroner." *BMJ* (Clinical research ed.), 379 (2022): o2374.
5 These same three problems are identified by various authors, particularly legal scholars. See, e.g., Richards, Neil and Woodrow Hartzog. "The pathologies of digital consent." *Washington University Law Review* 26 (2019).
6 Note that in the United States, the right to privacy has come to have several meanings. In addition to the informational privacy that we discuss here, it also refers to *decisional privacy*—the right to make decisions about one's private life without interference by others. This is the right to privacy that was referenced in legal rulings by the US Supreme Court in *Griswold v. Connecticut* (381 U.S. 479) and *Roe v. Wade* (410 U.S. 113) and established various sexual freedoms, as well as the right to an abortion (up until *Dobbs v. Jackson Women's Health Organization* (597 U.S. 215) in 2022).
7 Roessler, Beate and Judith DeCew. "Privacy." *The Stanford Encyclopedia of Philosophy* (Winter 2023 edition), ed. Edward N. Zalta and Uri Nodelman.
8 See, e.g., Allen, Anita L. "Privacy-as-data control: Conceptual, practical, and moral limits of the paradigm." *Conn. L. Rev.* 32 (1999): 861–875.
9 See, e.g., Parent, W. A. "Privacy, morality, and the law." *Philosophy & Public Affairs* 12.4 (1983): 269–270. Parent defines "personal information" as "*facts* about a person which most individuals in a given society at a given time do not want widely known about themselves."
10 Someone might argue that by going out in public or by speaking within earshot of another person, one consents to being observed and so all this information is actually private. We doubt that this is the right way to think about privacy. After all, I cannot avoid leaving the house and speaking in public without incurring substantial costs. Nor do I have the option of going out but explicitly rescinding consent: people in the streets would be very confused if I were to tell them I did not consent to be looked at or listened to.
11 Gavison, Ruth. "Privacy and the limits of law." *The Yale Law Journal* 89.3 (1980): 421–471.
12 The EU's General Data Protection Regulation (GDPR), discussed in the next section, includes a "right to be forgotten." (Regulation (EU) 2016/679 (General Data Protection Regulation): Article 17). This gives individuals the legal power to have organizations delete personal data about them under certain conditions. It does not, and could not, give them the power to make those who know the information forget it; it just makes it harder for other parties to find it out.
13 For one view on how parents should take the interests of family members, including themselves, into account when making decisions on behalf of their children, see Millum, Joseph. *The Moral foundations of parenthood.* Oxford University Press, 2017: 128–153.
14 UN Trade and Development. "Data protection and privacy legislation worldwide." 2021. Available at: https://unctad.org/page/data-protection-and-privacy-legislation-worldwide.
15 European Convention on Human Rights: Article 8. Available at: www.echr.coe.int/european-convention-on-human-rights.
16 Universal Declaration of Human Rights: Article 12. Available at: www.un.org/en/about-us/universal-declaration-of-human-rights.
17 Solove, Daniel J., and Paul M. Schwartz. *Privacy law fundamentals*, 6th edition. International Association of Privacy Professionals, 2022.
18 Regulation (EU) 2016/679: Article 9.
19 Hartzog, Woodrow. "The new price to play: Are passive online media users bound by terms of use?" *Communication Law and Policy* 15.4 (2010): 405–433.
20 Regulation (EU) 2016/679: Article 25.
21 Cavoukian, A. *Privacy by design.* Information and Privacy Commissioner of Ontario, Canada, 2009.
22 For background and some of the relevant philosophical issues, see van den Hoven, Jeroen, Martijn Blaauw, Wolter Pieters, and Martijn Warnier. "Privacy and information technology." *The Stanford Encyclopedia of Philosophy* (Winter 2024 edition), ed. Edward N. Zalta and Uri Nodelman: section 3.1.

23 Regulation (EU) 2016/679: Article 17.

24 Norberg, Patricia A., Daniel R. Horne, and David A. Horne. "The privacy paradox: Personal information disclosure intentions versus behaviors." *Journal of Consumer Affairs* 41.1 (2007): 100–126.

25 See, e.g., Miller, Franklin G., and Wertheimer, Alan, "Preface to a theory of consent transactions: Beyond valid consent." In Franklin G. Miller and Alan Wertheimer (eds.), *The ethics of consent: Theory and practice*. Oxford University Press, 2009: 81.

26 Schermer, Bart W., Bart Custers, and Simone Van der Hof. "The crisis of consent: How stronger legal protection may lead to weaker consent in data protection." *Ethics and Information Technology* 16.2 (2014): 180.

27 Schermer, Bart W., Bart Custers, and Simone Van der Hof. "The crisis of consent: How stronger legal protection may lead to weaker consent in data protection." *Ethics and Information Technology* 16.2 (2014): 180.

28 Schermer, Bart W., Bart Custers, and Simone Van der Hof. "The crisis of consent: How stronger legal protection may lead to weaker consent in data protection." *Ethics and Information Technology* 16.2 (2014): 180. They describe their proposal as based on Miller and Wertheimer's "fair transaction" model of consent transactions. See Miller, Franklin G., and Wertheimer, Alan, "Preface to a theory of consent transactions: Beyond valid consent." In Franklin G. Miller and Alan Wertheimer (eds.), *The ethics of consent: Theory and practice*. Oxford University Press, 2009.

29 Wolmarans, Lichelle, and Alex Voorhoeve. "What makes personal data processing by social networking services permissible?" *Canadian Journal of Philosophy* 52.1 (2022): 93–108.

30 Wolmarans, Lichelle, and Alex Voorhoeve. "What makes personal data processing by social networking services permissible?" *Canadian Journal of Philosophy* 52.1 (2022): 98.

31 Wolmarans, Lichelle, and Alex Voorhoeve. "What makes personal data processing by social networking services permissible?" *Canadian Journal of Philosophy* 52.1 (2022): 106.

32 For another argument that valid consent to the collection and use of data online is possible and necessary, and yet that it is not the only ethical consideration that matters, see Mills, Kevin. "Consent and the right to privacy." *Journal of Applied Philosophy* 39.4 (2022): 721–735.

33 Custers, Bart. "Click here to consent forever: Expiry dates for informed consent." *Big Data & Society* 3.1 (2016): 2053951715624935; Custers, Bart, Francien Dechesne, Wolter Pieters, Bart Schermer, and Simone van der Hof. "Consent and privacy." In Andreas Müller and Peter Schaber (eds.), *The Routledge handbook of the ethics of consent*. Routledge, 2018: 247–258.

34 Ofcom. *Children and parents: Media use and attitudes report*. Ofcom, 2024: 10. Available at: www.ofcom.org.uk/siteassets/resources/documents/research-and-data/media-literacy-research/children/children-media-use-and-attitudes-2024/childrens-media-literacy-report-2024.pdf.

35 Ofcom. *Children and parents: Media use and attitudes report*. Ofcom, 2024: 13. Available at: www.ofcom.org.uk/siteassets/resources/documents/research-and-data/media-literacy-research/children/children-media-use-and-attitudes-2024/childrens-media-literacy-report-2024.pdf.

36 Johnson, Jazette, et al. "'It's a lonely disease': Cultivating online spaces for social support among people living with dementia and dementia caregivers." *Proceedings of the ACM on Human–Computer Interaction* 6.CSCW2 (2022): 1–27; Talbot, Catherine V., Daisy Roe, and Melissa Brunner. "Navigating who I was and who I am online: How people with dementia use social media platforms to support identity." *Dementia* (2024): 14713012241292659.

37 Van der Hof, Simone. "I agree, or do I: a rights-based analysis of the law on children's consent in the digital world." *Wis. Int'l LJ* 34 (2016): 422–423.

38 Individual cases might be evaluated more carefully by the courts, of course, as when a minor is deemed able to give their own consent to receive or refuse medical care; but it would be impossible to evaluate the decision-making capacity of an entire population.

39 Schneble, Christophe Olivier, et al. "Social media terms and conditions and informed consent from children: Ethical analysis." *JMIR Pediatrics and Parenting* 4.2 (2021): e22281.

40 Pasquale, Liliana, et al. "Digital age of consent and age verification: can they protect children?" *IEEE software* 39.3 (2020): 50–57.

41 For some discussion, see Batchelor, Rachel, et al. "Challenges of ethical and legal responsibilities when technologies' uses and users change: social networking sites, decision-making capacity and dementia." *Ethics and Information Technology* 14 (2012): 99–108.

42 As of the start of 2024, Ring no longer allows law enforcement to request video recordings using Neighbors. See "Ring to stop allowing police to request videos from security cameras." *The New York Times*, January 28, 2024. Available at: www.nytimes.com/2024/01/28/business/amazon-ring-doorbell-camera-police.html.

43 Details of this case, including Senator Ed Markey's correspondence with Amazon and their response, can be found in Hollister, Sean. "Today I learned Amazon has a form so police can get my data without permission or a warrant." July 15, 2022. Available at: www.theverge.com/2022/7/14/23219419/amazon-ring-law-enforcement-no-warrant-no-consent. In their response, Amazon note that their publicly available law enforcement guidelines disclose that "Ring reserves the right to respond immediately to urgent law enforcement requests for information in cases involving imminent danger of death or serious physical injury to any person." See www.markey.senate.gov/imo/media/doc/amazon_response_to_senator_markey-july_13_2022.pdf. However, this disclosure was not in the terms of service and Ring employees—not a court—decide what constitutes an emergency of the sort that justifies sharing.

44 Solove, D. "Privacy self-management and the consent dilemma." *Harvard Law Review* 126 (2013): 1183–1185.

45 McDonald, Aleecia M., and Lorrie Faith Cranor. "The cost of reading privacy policies." *Isjlp* 4 (2008): 543.

46 In fact, terms of use can be wide-ranging: "The agreements typically involve obligations regarding how the parties will settle disputes, licensing (and sub-licensing) of a user's copyrighted work, restrictions on use of the Web site and of the site's content, limitations on a Web site's liability, and notifications regarding how the user's personal information can be used." Hartzog, Woodrow. "The new price to play: Are passive online media users bound by terms of use?" *Communication Law and Policy* 15.4 (2010): 405–433.

47 In 2022, the Danish authority banned the use of Google Chromebooks and Google Workspace for Education in the Helsingør Municipality due to unlawful processing of students' personal data. For more on this case, and many others, see Livingstone, Sonia, et al. "The Googlization of the classroom: Is the UK effective in protecting children's data and rights?" *Computers and Education Open* 7 (2024): 2–3.

48 In 2017, three years after launching, it was estimated that more than 30 million children in US primary and secondary schools learned within Google Classroom. See Singer, N. "How Google took over the classroom." *New York Times*, May 13, 2017. As of 2024, it is estimated to be used by over 150 million students. Shimalla, Alexandra. "How is Google Workspace for Education digitally transforming K-12 environments?" *Ed Tech*, June 18, 2024.

49 These are Articles 28, 16, and 32 of the Convention on the Rights of the Child (1989). For discussion of children's rights in digital education, see Zeide, Elana. "Education technology and student privacy." In Evan Selinger, Jules Polonetsky, and Omer Tene (eds.), *The Cambridge handbook of consumer privacy*. Cambridge University Press, 2018: 70–84; Van Der Hof, Simone, et al. "The child's right to protection against economic exploitation in the digital world." *The International Journal of Children's Rights* 28.4 (2020): 833–859.

50 Privacy and data protection cases have been brought against Google's use of children's data in the US, France, Germany, the Netherlands, and Iceland. For a summary and discussion of these cases, see Livingstone, Sonia, et al. "The Googlization of the classroom: Is the UK effective in protecting children's data and rights?" *Computers and Education Open* 7 (2024): 1–8.

51 Hooper, L., S. Livingstone, and K. Pothong. *Problems with data governance in UK schools: the cases of Google Classroom and ClassDojo*. Digital Futures Commission/5Rights Foundation, 2022.

52 Hooper, L., S. Livingstone, and K. Pothong. *Problems with data governance in UK schools: the cases of Google Classroom and ClassDojo*. Digital Futures Commission/5Rights Foundation, 2022: 29.

53 In response to challenges from the Dutch Data Protection Agency, Google made changes that resulted in far less data surveillance. The authors of this study revisited the primary school again in 2024 and found that "children had access to significantly fewer Google additional services compared to our findings in 2022; for example, neither child had access to YouTube, Google Maps or Google Hangouts, all of which had been available to the 9-year-old previously." See Livingstone, Sonia, et al. "The Googlization of the classroom: Is the UK effective in protecting children's data and rights?" *Computers and Education Open* 7 (2024): 5.

54 Quoted in Hooper, L., S. Livingstone, and K. Pothong. *Problems with data governance in UK schools: the cases of Google Classroom and ClassDojo.* Digital Futures Commission/5Rights Foundation, 2022: 28.
55 Hooper, L., S. Livingstone, and K. Pothong. *Problems with data governance in UK schools: the cases of Google Classroom and ClassDojo.* Digital Futures Commission/5Rights Foundation, 2022: 38–39.
56 Livingstone, Sonia, et al. "The Googlization of the classroom: Is the UK effective in protecting children's data and rights?" *Computers and Education Open* 7 (2024): 4.
57 Hooper, L., S. Livingstone, and K. Pothong. *Problems with data governance in UK schools: the cases of Google Classroom and ClassDojo.* Digital Futures Commission/5Rights Foundation, 2022.
58 See www.markey.senate.gov/news/press-releases/senator-markey-renews-investigation-into-amazon-rings-surveillance-practices-and-cooperation-with-police.
59 See Livingstone, Sonia, et al. "The Googlization of the classroom: Is the UK effective in protecting children's data and rights?" *Computers and Education Open* 7 (2024): 5.

9 Consent to sex

1. Introduction

What makes it permissible for one person to have sex with another? The popular slogan "Yes means yes"[1] seems to point us in the right direction: the consent-giver's agreement. But this can be no more than a partial answer. After all, sexual desire, arousal, and attraction starts before puberty,[2] and these feelings are also experienced by people with substantial intellectual and cognitive impairments. Few people think that the agreement of a person with severe dementia, let alone a child's, could justify another person having sex with them. Similar worries arise about intoxicated consent. Drink and drugs can impact decision-making capacity, and given that some substances lower inhibitions, enhance sexual desire, and increase impulsivity there are also worries about the voluntariness of inebriated consent.[3] Even in the best-case scenario—one in which amorous partners are competent, sober, and willing—the question remains: what exactly have they agreed to when they have agreed to sex? Sex includes a wide range of activities, and without a clear answer to that question it is unclear which acts consenting parties have waived their rights against.

In this chapter, we explore consent to sex. Starting with the law, we outline the way in which modern thinking about sexual autonomy coupled with civil rights, feminist, and LGBTQ+ activism has transformed Western attitudes towards permissible sexual relations. Turning next to ethics, we consider the radical view that valid consent is not necessary for permissible sexual relations. Against this view, we argue that consent is necessary, just not sufficient: some important questions about the ethics of sex are not primarily about consent. We then turn to the necessary conditions for valid consent. We explore current debates that concern the *understanding* and *voluntariness* conditions, before exploring the *disclosure* and *competence* conditions in two hard cases. Our first hard case concerns sex and deception. Whereas in other contexts, deception renders consent invalid, it is commonly thought that lying about one's profession, age, or marital status to get someone into bed is at worst bad behavior. We consider whether deceiving someone into sex invalidates their consent and what implications this has for the disclosure of private information. The second case addresses inebriated consent. Can someone who is conscious, but drunk or high, still give valid consent to sex?

DOI: 10.4324/9781003287391-11

2. Socio-legal history of consent to sex

The central goal of civil rights movements that rose to prominence in the mid-twentieth century was equality before the law.[4] The legal recognition of autonomy rights—including sexual autonomy rights—emerged as a primary struggle of feminist and LGBTQ+ movements.[5] Activists and scholars fought to make intimate practices that violated sexual autonomy illegal. Marital rape, forced marriage, and, more recently, revenge porn are now against the law in many jurisdictions.[6] The same movements fought to overturn moralistic laws prohibiting sexual practices that consenting adults willingly engaged in or partnerships they wanted to enter or exit. Sodomy laws and adultery laws have been widely repealed, and some jurisdictions have also decriminalized sex work.[7] Inter-racial marriage, same-sex marriage, and divorce are now legally recognized in many countries, and there is growing scholarly debate about alternative forms of marriage, including among more than two people.[8]

At the heart of this political and legal liberalism is the view that *valid* consent is what distinguishes permissible from impermissible sex. It is for this reason that liberals reject legal moralism. As Robin West puts it:

> Consensual sex, perhaps quintessentially for contemporary liberal legalists, wherever it happens, and whatever its form, and whatever the motivation—whether it be in cars, in bordellos, or on screen sets; whether it be between persons of the same sex, opposite sex, or no discernible sex; whether it be anal, oral, vaginal, missionary, marital, nonmarital, vanilla, nonvanilla, sadomasochistic, or something other; whether it be for pleasure, for reproduction, for money, for status, for friendship, or for the approval of one's peers—should be deregulated.[9]

While liberals maintain that *consensual* sex is no business of the state, they argue that non-consensual sex ought to be. The law ought to recognize that violations of sexual autonomy are seriously wrong.

Consent was also central to earlier civil and criminal laws governing intimate relations. For example, irregular marriages—common in parts of Europe up until the nineteenth century—were established informally by mutual consent. But without any public or formal solemnization, deception and betrayal were commonplace. When a union was contested, the courts looked for evidence of *valid* consent.[10] If they were satisfied that one party had communicated consent or a promise to marry, they recognized these irregular marriages as legal unions even if one party had no private intention of marrying. Indeed, consistent with the performative view of consent that we defended in chapter 2, in *Dalrymple v. Dalrymple* in 1811 the courts rejected the idea that private intention could determine the meaning of the speech act of consent. The judge ruled that it could not be:

> represented as the law of any civilized country that in such a transaction a man shall use serious words, expressive of serious intentions, and shall yet be afterwards at liberty to aver a private intention … to avoid a contract which was differently understood by the other party.[11]

More recent debates about the law turn on whether valid consent is all that should matter to whether sex should be criminalized.[12] While it is widely agreed that sexual autonomy requires legal protection, precisely whether and how acts that undermine that autonomy should be treated by the law is vexed. For example, even if we agree that sexual deception can invalidate consent to sex this does not settle whether and which kinds of sexual deception should be criminalized. Legal practice showcases a range of different views. In some jurisdictions, like in England and Wales, only deception about the nature of the sexual act itself can invalidate consent, not deception about other material facts.[13] Other jurisdictions have taken a more expansive view.[14] We explore the ethics of deceptive sex in section 8.

3. Is consent ethically necessary?

In recent years, some have argued that the liberal emphasis on consent as distinguishing permissible from impermissible sex is mistaken.

One line of criticism comes from those who think that consent is unnecessary or inappropriate for good sex.[15] Good sex, it is argued, is a joint activity—something that two people do together. But in giving consent, one party permits another party to do something to them (paradigmatically in a sexist culture, a woman permits a man to do something to her).[16] This is not ideal. Tanya Palmer writes:

> In reality, sexual encounters often develop organically and mutually, without the parties taking on fixed active or passive roles. Thus, while consent is clearly absent from the worst sexual encounters it will also be absent in the most positive sexual encounters jointly instigated by mutually active partners, because both partners are in a state beyond consent, a state of active involvement and participation rather than reaction or submission.[17]

Similarly, John Gardner argues: "Ideally, I suggest, the question of consent does not arise between sexual partners, for the question of consent belongs to sex individualistically, even solipsistically, conceived, to sex conceived as something that one person does to another."[18]

Are these writers correct that it is sometimes permissible to have sex without valid consent? We think not. Our view is that someone gives valid consent when they successfully waive a right through a speech act that signifies consent.[19] However, as we have emphasized, there are many ways to communicate giving, refusing, or retracting consent. The speech act token of consent does not have to be verbal. In the right context, consent can be communicated through a nod, a touch, or simply by leaning in for a kiss. What counts as a token of consent is likely to vary from context to context and from partner to partner. Crucially, though, there must be *some* act by which the individual waived their right.

The sexual acts that we are concerned with in this chapter are all acts that would be rights violations if carried out without permission. Each of us has the right not to be kissed, the right not to be touched in a sexual way, and so on. When sexual encounters go well, those rights are waived in very specific ways (i.e., with respect to a particular act, a particular person, and at a particular moment). The waiver is carried out by the autonomous individual whose rights they are. It seems, then, analytic that the explanation for how the rights are waived is that consent was given.

It is open to someone to argue that there are other speech acts that involve waiving a right but which are not consent. For example, Quill Kukla argues that consent involves one party making a request and another agreeing to it or refusing it.[20] They think that good sex is more often initiated by "invitations and gift offers."[21] Here we may simply have a disagreement in linguistic intuitions. We think that there are multiple ways in which consent can be given, including speech acts that do more than one thing at once. For example, an invitation can be *both* a request and a token of consent, as when someone says, "Do come in!" or "Kiss me!"[22]

Alternatively, the consent sceptic might argue that the acts in question are not individual acts—they are joint acts. It therefore does not make sense to say that the acts were made permissible by individuals waiving their individual rights. As Gardner writes: "In the case of good penetrative sex ... the activity as a whole is not something that is done by one partner to the other, nor, strictly speaking, by each to the other, but rather by both together ... the question is not 'what is he up to?' or 'what is she up to?' but 'what are we up to?'"

We think this is mistaken. Following Karamvir Chadha, we think that the joint actions involved in good sex are constituted by individual actions, each of which requires consent. Chadha draws an analogy to two people tangoing:

> Each of these actions—Amelia's placing her hands on Bert's shoulders, and Bert's placing his hands on Amelia's waist—partly constitutes their joint action of tangoing together, and each of these actions is something that one does to the other. ... So, although neither person does the joint action to the other, the joint action is partly constituted by individual actions in which each of them does something to the other.[23]

Likewise, when two people kiss, each pushes their lips against the other's. Though the kissing is a joint action, there are individual component actions that constitute it. Those individual actions are the ones that require consent: each individual has a right that the other not kiss them and each of them waives that right so that they can jointly make out.

We conclude that valid consent is indeed necessary for permissible sex. However, that does not entail that valid consent is sufficient for sex to be ethically permissible.

4. Is consent ethically sufficient?

Is valid consent all there is to permissible sex? We think not. As noted above, the question of consent has come to dominate discussions of how the law should treat sexual acts. It is equally dominant in discussions of the ethics of sex. To some extent, this emphasis is welcome. It has led to the acknowledgement of marital rape and other forms of intimate partner violence. It has also provided a powerful case against legal sexual moralism. However, the emphasis on consent can give the misleading impression that sexual ethics is only about consent and that if someone gives valid consent then sex is ethically permissible.[24] This conclusion would overreach.

Take a humdrum example: an adulterer in a monogamous relationship. He and his lover might succeed in waiving relevant rights, releasing each other from their directed duties not to trespass on each other's bodies. Yet, our adulterer does something morally wrong when he has sex with his lover: he breaks a promise to his spouse. The correct explanation of what makes this sexual encounter wrong has nothing to do with consent.

Student–professor relations provide another example. University students are normally over the age of consent and likely to be competent. In some cases, a faculty member might proposition a student that they are teaching or supervising. The implicit threat that saying no would risk a bad grade or professional consequences could constitute coercion and so render the student's agreement invalid. But this would not explain what—if anything—is wrong with a teacher dating a student over whom they wield no power or with a teacher dating a student who propositioned them. Consent theory does not provide the resources to analyze such cases. Any wrongs are more likely to be a matter of exploitation (the teacher taking advantage of their student) or failures in professional duties (such as duties of care towards all students at one's institution).[25]

The other problem with focusing only on consent is that it leads not just to a sexual ethics that *reduces* all sexual wrongs to consent violations, but one that *inflates* consent to explain all good sexual relations.[26] Take the idea of "enthusiastic consent." It is widely agreed that good sex involves more than a mere successful rights waiver. However, if valid consent were sufficient for good sexual relations, then it would need amending to account for this. Hence, we end up with the view that to be valid, consent must be *enthusiastically* given. This collapses the distinction between permissible and ideal sexual relations.

This is a problem. Sexual autonomy—just like autonomy more generally—allows us to live our lives in accordance with our preferences, values, and interests. Ideally, that will involve giving enthusiastic consent to sexual encounters that are fulfilling, pleasurable, and serve one's interests more generally. However, we often waive our rights against acts that we are indifferent to, hostile towards, or to serve other interests. For example, it is possible to give valid consent to a root canal, a deeply unpleasant experience but one that is preferable to the agony of later tooth pain. Likewise, a sex worker might waive their rights against sex for money, a bad friend might waive their rights against sex with their friend's ex to hurt them, and someone in a stale relationship might waive their rights against unimaginative mid-week sex because they could not think of anything better to do on a Tuesday evening. Meaningful autonomy protects the right to make these decisions. Just as a competent adult has the right to make risky financial decisions, or make overly optimistic treatment decisions, so they have the right to make less than ideal sexual decisions too.

5. What is needed for valid consent to sex

The theory chapters of this book analyzed five necessary and jointly sufficient conditions for valid consent: competence; disclosure; understanding; voluntariness; and a token of consent. Sex raises perplexing questions for each of these conditions. What is expected in other areas of life, like medical care, may appear unrealistic and naive when we move into the sexual arena. Inebriation, seduction, and outright deception are commonly accepted features of sexual encounters. Yet, we would be horrified by a doctor who lied and manipulated drunk patients into agreeing to unnecessary medical procedures.

As we have already seen, there are many ways to token consent, refusal, or retraction to sexual acts, both verbal and non-verbal. However, unlike other contexts in which consent is a one-off occurrence (e.g., consent to surgery), sex often involves multiple acts and a series of opportunities to ask for, give, refuse, and retract consent—all while engaging in sexual activity. Surgeons rarely have to revisit consent unless something has dramatically changed; not so for sexual partners.

In the sections that follow we consider how the other conditions should be interpreted in the context of consent to sex. This leads us to doubt some common views regarding sexual consent.

6. Sex and understanding

Even if someone agrees to sexual relations, it is sometimes unclear *precisely* what they have agreed to. Sexual activity includes a wide range of acts—kissing, caressing, penetrating; also, spanking, slapping, biting. Data suggest that "rougher" acts are increasing in prevalence in some populations. For example, among U.S. undergraduates, reports suggest that choking appears to be a relatively common, if gendered, act in casual sex.[27] Does a college student agree to sexual asphyxiation when they agree to sex with a peer? We think not. The challenge is to explain why. In doing so, we can get clear on what needs to be understood to give valid consent to sex.

As we saw in chapter 4, there are maximalist and minimalist views of the understanding requirement. However, in contrast to medicine, few scholars hold maximalist views about consent to sex. It is largely taken for granted that parties can give valid consent to sex even if they are ignorant of the purpose of the activity for their partner or the risks and benefits associated with the sexual acts.[28] Provided that the disclosure requirement has been fulfilled, we agree.

In Chapter 4 we argued that successfully waiving your rights through consent requires that you understand only three things: first, that you are giving consent; second, how to give consent; and third, to what you are giving consent. The primary issue, in the domain of sexual relations, turns on how to understand the first and third conditions.

Understanding that one has given consent and to *what* one has given consent is a matter of what is successfully communicated.[29] Take the first condition: understanding *that* you are giving consent to sex. Once you understand that that is what you are doing with this speech act, you can succeed in proffering consent non-verbally, via conversational implicature, and even tacitly. Consider, for the purposes of illustration, the communicative shorthand that can develop between long-standing sexual partners. Perhaps, after a period of making out, it is mutually understood that the question "Do you have the condoms?" means consent to penetrative sex with protection and producing a condom in response signifies consent by the other party. The consenting parties do not say "yes" in response to an explicit and precisely worded invitation to protected penetrative sex. However, they share an understanding *that* they have consented to sex, and this familiar conversational exchange in this context is *how* they do it. Of course, if one of them were to ask this question of the other in the pharmacy, it would not communicate consent to sex right now in Aisle 7. In this context, it is mutually understood to be a question about whether they still need to add some condoms to their shopping basket. Moreover, if they were a new couple, that question would not reliably communicate consent to sex either. Some sort of follow up question—like "Do you want to have sex?"—would be required to check whether what one party thinks has been communicated has, in fact, been communicated.

Between our long-standing sexual partners, it is plausible to think that they also understand *what* they have waived their rights against, even though nothing is explicitly stated. For example, given their sexual history, it is probably mutually understood what *kind* of protected penetrative sex has been authorized. Suppose, for instance, that they are a heterosexual couple who have only ever had vaginal sex. The question "Do you have the condoms?" was definitely not consent to penetrative anal sex. Engaging in that sexual act would misinterpret what had been communicated and constitute a clear rights violation. Moreover, during sex, the communicative shorthand that has developed between this couple might mean that their agreement to different types of sex (e.g., moving from vaginal to oral sex) or different positions might proceed through facial expressions, moans, or touch—mutually understood non-verbal communication.

While these sorts of communicative shorthand develop over time, it takes work to ensure that they do not develop in ways that lead to reliable *miscommunication*. A lot of shared work may be required before they could ground mutual understanding of when and to what consent has been given. There are clear barriers to doing this work: people are often embarrassed to talk explicitly about sex, and they also worry about being shamed, not living up to expectations, or even hurting their partner by being frank about their sexual preferences. Some may even believe that such conversations are unnecessary: it is commonly assumed that good sex simply involves being in the moment, making a connection, reading another's body and mind.

However, it is not that simple. Successful communication involves recognizing, and sometimes working to overcome, problematic sociolinguistic conventions that may exist between oneself and one's partner. Our sexual relations take place against a backdrop of regressive, patriarchal, and deeply misogynistic social scripts, conventions, and communicative practices.[30] Given how pervasive these are, otherwise good actors can fall foul of them—like the man who believes (without malice) that a woman's lack of resistance to a sexual advance is itself consent to that act. In fact, not only does silence, inaction, or a lack of resistance not reliably communicate tacit consent, some people who have experienced sexual trauma can also experience tonic immobility, a temporary freezing in response to sexual touch.[31]

This reveals a common problem: an unjustified assumption of shared shorthand. Communicative shorthand is *earned.* First-time or new sexual partners have no reason to think that they can successfully communicate non-verbally, reliably read each other's minds or body, or rely on shortcuts. This explains why clear and explicit communication is required—just as it would be if our long-standing partners were trying something new or unusual for their relationship. This applies before sex, but also checking in during sex, to ensure that what is being communicated is being interpreted correctly (for example, through questions like: "You mean, like this?"; "Does *that* feel good?"; "Tell me if that's too much?").

We are now able to answer our earlier question: does the college student consent to sexual asphyxiation when they consent to sex? If the couple had talked through their sexual preferences, boundaries, and their preferred ways of communicating during sex, and the relevant party had told their partner that they enjoyed being choked during sex, certain non-verbal moves might reliably indicate consent to this act. For instance, one party might gently place their hands on their partner's neck and raise a questioning eyebrow, before getting a receptive grin in response. A risky act of this sort—one in which the partner's preferences, tolerance, or safety might change quickly—requires frequent checking-in and stopping if there is no clear indication of agreement. On the other hand, if there is no history and no prior conversation, but one partner just starts to choke the other during otherwise consensual sex, then this act would just constitute assault. The normative difference between these two instances of sexual asphyxiation is explained by what is successfully communicated.

7. Sex and voluntariness

Some acts clearly undermine voluntariness. The use of force or the threat of force is coercive and agreement given under any serious threat will be invalid. Rape, sexual assault, and sexual harassment remain huge problems in every society.[32] Their consensuality is not in question and so we do not discuss them at length here.[33] We considered the wrongness of non-consensual acts in Chapter 2, where we suggested why some violations are worse than others.

Other cases are more philosophically puzzling. People tend to be much more forgiving of certain forms of influence in the sexual realm than they are in other realms, such as clinical care or research.

Consider some non-violent threats. Suppose Simon and Karolina have been dating for a few months, but Karolina is reluctant to get more intimate. Simon threatens to break up with her if she will not agree to sex. She might regard losing the relationship as worse than giving in to his overtures. If so, has he coerced her such that her consent to sex is invalid? Or suppose they are already in a sexual relationship, but Karolina does not want to have sex tonight because she is sensitive just after her period. Simon might make it clear that he is going to sulk all week if he does not get his way. If she then agrees, was that coercion?

In order to invalidate consent a threat must be both controlling and illegitimate. It might well be that the threat of losing a relationship is bad enough to be controlling.[34] However, Simon has the right to leave the relationship if he chooses. He is therefore not threatening to make Karolina worse off than she ought to be. In other words, though this feels like a threat, philosophically speaking it is not (as discussed in Chapter 5).[35] Karolina's consent would therefore be valid. Similar points apply to sulking. Simon is presumably within his rights to sulk.[36] In addition, the consequences do not seem bad enough that they would even count as controlling.[37]

So, Simon acts within his rights and Karolina's consent would be valid. That does not stop us from judging Simon's actions negatively. He is clearly being a bad boyfriend and treating Karolina badly. He ought not to control her decisions about sex in this way.

Turn now to manipulation. Manipulating another person into sex is often admired, even desired. It is called *seduction*.[38] The "victim" of seduction may welcome their manipulation. It is nice to be flattered, put in the mood, and swept off one's feet. Someone may feel valued when their date shows up in sexy clothes, wearing sensuous scents, and proposes romantic locations for their activities together. But all of these actions are designed to influence the seductee's desires in ways that bypass their reasoning. They therefore appear to be manipulative and, according to the analysis of chapter 5, pro tanto wrongful.

In fact, we think that whether manipulating someone to consent to sex is wrongful will depend on the attitude of the person who is manipulated. Manipulation is wrongful insofar as it disrespects autonomy. This suggests that we can distinguish between manipulation that is welcome and manipulation that is not. Where it is welcome, the person being manipulated has endorsed the way that their decision-making is being influenced. It can therefore still be ultimately respectful of their autonomy because they are still able to govern their own life (even if, on this occasion, they govern it by letting themselves act on their immediate desires).

On the other hand, not all seductive strategies are welcome. Someone might put their prospective partner in a situation where it would be socially awkward to turn them down. No threat need be involved, but motivating someone in this way would be unwelcome and so disrespectful of their autonomy. Similar points apply to some of the techniques of the "pick-up artists" that became notorious in the 2000s, such as "negging" (using back-handed compliments to undermine someone's self-esteem and make them seek approval).[39]

In brief, then, for the reasons discussed in Chapter 5, manipulating someone into sex will not normally invalidate consent (where they are not also deceived or coerced). It may be permissible or wrongful nevertheless, depending on whether the manipulation is welcome.

8. Case: deceptive sex

We have all feigned interest in boring conversations, paid insincere compliments, and embellished a tall tale to get more laughs. Many people meet their sexual partners online and, if the data are to be believed, few people are scrupulously honest in their profiles. Men tend to lie about their height, women their weight, and everyone seems to lie about their interests—there are a lot of hikers out there![40]

These lies are often cut moral slack even if they lead to sex.[41] Even if lies can invalidate consent, and it is seriously morally wrong to have sex without valid consent, it seems like moral overkill to claim that consent to sex could be invalidated by pretending, say, to like a particular genre of music. Consider such a case.

Kyle fancies Tajay. After some social media sleuthing, Kyle learns that Tajay is a massive fan of UK garage music. Kyle is indifferent to the genre, but he edits his dating profile to fit Tajay's. After they match, he wears a specially purchased t-shirt embossed with an esoteric garage DJ's logo and pretends that he too had a misspent youth as a London club rat and pirate radio obsessive. Tajay feels the connection, and later that evening they have sex.

Had Tajay known Kyle was indifferent to UK garage, perhaps he would have lost interest in sex, perhaps it would have made no difference whatsoever, or perhaps it would have been just one factor among many that could have swayed him either way.

It is fair to assume that Kyle does not have a legitimate interest in keeping his taste in music private. Sometimes, however, one party does have a privacy right over information that would be relevant to another's consent decision. Consider the following example from Emily Tilton and Jonathan Ichikawa:

> *Passing:* Greg is romantically interested in Laura, a trans woman. Laura generally "passes"—that is, she is typically not read as trans. Greg is unaware that she was designated male at birth. They go on a date and have sex. Throughout the encounter, Greg remains ignorant that Laura is trans. Had Greg known that she was trans, he would not have agreed to have sex with her.[42]

The fact that Laura is read as female is not deceptive.[43] However, if Laura has reason to believe Greg would not have sex with a trans woman, then her failure to disclose might look like the kind of deception that we argued can invalidate consent in Chapters 4 and 5. In cases like this, the information that is relevant to someone's decision about whether to agree to sex is private. The only way they could have known more is if their potential sexual partner had *disclosed* it to them. However, unlike other cases we have considered thus far in the book, Laura appears to have a legitimate interest in keeping this information private. This seems to be a case in which her autonomy is in tension with Greg's.

These two are both hard cases. While it might be tempting to think of Kyle's deception as just part and parcel of the permissible art of seduction, a lenient attitude towards even minor sexual deception is puzzling. When we turn our attention to other domains in which consent operates, we see that it is taken very seriously.[44] Absent an explanation that accounts for the difference between the conditions for valid consent to sex when compared to a contract or a medical procedure, we should either take a more lenient stance towards deception in those other domains or we should take the minor sexual deception in the UK garage case more seriously. And yet doing so might have unpalatable implications for *Passing.* If Laura believes that her potential sexual partner would not have sex with a person assigned male at birth, does she need to refrain from sex altogether or disclose that she is trans (and, in doing so, assume the associated risks that come with that disclosure)? These options seem unjust and unfair: she—much more than Greg—faces barriers to accessing the good of sexual relations and, even though these barriers are transphobic, she risks wronging Greg if she ignores them.

Such problems have led some to doubt that these hard cases should be analyzed in terms of either dealbreakers or validity.[45] We are not so pessimistic. We think that philosophical progress can be made by appropriately distinguishing between the informational requirements for valid consent.

Start with the understanding requirement. What is consented to is a matter of what is successfully communicated, but what is communicated is *more* than what is literally said. If Issa says to Kabir, "Hey, would you mind massaging my shoulders?," and he says "Sure," then what is implicated, but not said explicitly, is that she would like that massage *now*, not in an hour, not next Tuesday, not in a year's time. This goes without saying *because* this information is conversationally implicated by the relevance of her request as it is worded. However, the same cannot be said of specific, idiosyncratic dealbreakers. The request for a massage does not conversationally implicate that she would retract her consent if she knew he had had coffee with an old flame (even if that is true). If there is a problem with consent in these cases, it is not a problem with understanding.

As we argued in Chapter 4, the manipulation of information invalidates consent by way of disclosure. If I know some fact that is relevant to your consent decision, and if I have reason to think it would be dispositive, then I am in a position to exercise control over whether you give or refuse consent. Kyle suspects that music is important to Tajay—that is *precisely* why he goes out of his way to create a false impression that he, too, is a big fan of UK garage. By deceiving Tajay, he does something wrongful, and he knows that the deception misrepresents a fact that is likely relevant to whether Tajay would have sex with him. Our view does not imply that Kyle is under a general obligation to disclose his musical tastes. He exercises no illegitimate control over Tajay if he simply does not broach the subject during their date. He is only under an obligation because he has created a false impression that ought to be corrected.[46] This explains the UK garage case: Kyle's deception is wrong, and it potentially invalidates Tajay's consent by exercising illegitimate control over his decision.

Passing is a more complicated case. To avoid exercising illegitimate control over Greg's consent decision, Laura ought to disclose that she was designated male at birth if and only if she has reason to think that that information is relevant to his decision, and she judges that he would reasonably expect to be told it. Dating norms are variable, but we think it would be odd for Greg to *expect* to be told this information. He should no more expect to learn this on a first date than to be told who Laura voted for in the last election, or her degree classification, or how she feels about her mother. Hence, in most cases, her non-disclosure is unlikely to be *deceptive*. That means that her non-disclosure would not invalidate Greg's consent to sex.[47]

But suppose that Greg asked Laura directly whether she is a trans woman. *Now* Laura does have reason to think that this information is relevant; she also has reason to think that Greg expects an honest answer. And yet disclosing her trans identity requires her to put his autonomy before her own. It might also require her to put herself at serious risk of harm.

In Chapter 4, we argued that deception can be permissible if it is the only reasonable way to protect a privacy right. In this case, Laura cannot keep her trans identity to herself without lying or engaging in some sort of deceptive evasion. That deception is therefore not illegitimate. That implies, on our view, that her deception does not invalidate Greg's consent to sex. And yet, we think that if she were to pursue sex with Greg, she would do something bad. She has reason to suspect that he would not have sex with her if he knew the truth. If she ignores that and has sex with him anyway, she acts selfishly. This is another example in which consent underdetermines the ethical analysis of sexual relations. This would be an instance of bad consensual sex.

9. Case: intoxicated sex

Xiao Wen has been out celebrating with her colleagues. In the early hours, she gets a taxi home from the bar. When the driver asks for her address, she slurs a little in response, and she notices that her tongue feels thick in her mouth. To her surprise, she feels unsteady on her feet as she exits the taxi, and she drops her keys twice in her rush to enter the apartment. She has been thinking of her girlfriend, Kaya, all night. She gets into bed, Kaya gives her a kiss goodnight, and Xiao Wen responds with passion. She feels good—libidinous, but uncharacteristically disinhibited. On smelling the alcohol on her breath, Kaya tells her to stop. Realizing that Kaya is refusing to have sex with her because she has been drinking, Xiao Wen reacts angrily. "Are you serious?! Yes, I've had a few drinks, but I'm not drunk! Do you have any idea how insulting you're being?" she shouts, as she stumbles off to spend the night on the sofa.

Intoxicated sex is common. Many people drink to relax, to facilitate intimacy, or to lower inhibitions. Others take specific substances to enhance the pleasure and prolong the experience of sexual activity. However, drugs and alcohol impair our decision-making capacity, and when inebriated we are vulnerable to poor decision-making, harmful exploitation, and even non-consensual sex. Alcohol use by one or all parties is a well-documented factor in sexual assaults, and the risk of non-consensual sexual activity increases in contexts in which binge drinking is common (e.g., college campus party culture) or sexual encounters in which sobriety is less common (e.g., casual hook-ups).[48]

These risks, together with the prevalence of sexual assault on college campuses, have seen some institutions of higher education prohibit intoxicated sex.[49] The prohibitions are typically grounded in contested claims about consent. For example, members of Beliot College are informed that "[i]ndividuals who are below their normal cognitive function, inebriated, mentally or physically impaired or incapacitated, have a mental illness or deficiency, are unconscious for any reason, or are physically unable to communicate are assumed to be incapable of giving consent."[50] Such policies give us a clear verdict on cases like ours: Kaya, the recipient of consent, ought to assume that Xiao Wen is incapable of giving valid consent to sex because she is intoxicated and so below her normal level of cognitive functioning.

However, the discussion of competence in Chapter 3 gives us reason to doubt this verdict. Clearly someone who is drunk or high to the point of passing out cannot consent, but it is fair to presume—contra Beliot's policy—that there is a consumption level at which a consenting party can be intoxicated, but still capable of exercising their rights. This follows from the fact that sober, competent adults naturally vary in their decision-making abilities. It must therefore be possible for someone to worsen their decision-making on a particular occasion but still be above the threshold of competence.

Is that the case for Xiao Wen? We, like other consent scholars, think that her level of intoxication presents a hard case.[51] The details focus our attention on what makes it so. The main issue is not one of understanding. After all, since Xiao Wen and Kaya are in a relationship, we can assume that they are not engaged in a one-off casual sexual encounter. If the consenting parties know each other well and have developed a successful communicative shorthand, then successful communication of consent, refusal, or even retraction is likely to be possible even when somewhat inebriated.

It is not voluntariness either. Even though we may make poor decisions when inebriated, we may also make decisions that align with our interests, preferences, and values. Alcohol has made Xiao Wen feel disinhibited. This might be deeply valuable to her, especially if she judges her sexual self-consciousness to be an obstacle to achieving physical intimacy with Kaya. Moreover, as the case illustrates, the intoxicated party might *really* want to have sex and, if there is no illegitimate control from the recipient, there is no problem from the point of view of voluntariness.

The central issue is competence. We can distinguish four questions. First, is someone as intoxicated as Xiao Wen *capable* of waiving her rights against sexual trespass? Second, are other parties permitted to interfere by preventing an intoxicated person from having sexual relations? Imagine that Xiao Wen was out drinking with her colleagues and they saw her about to leave the bar with an ex-boyfriend. Would her sober colleagues be permitted to shoo him away, put Xiao Wen in a taxi home, or otherwise interfere to prevent her from hooking up with her old flame? Third, is Kaya, the recipient of intoxicated consent, permitted to have sexual relations with Xiao Wen? Finally, is Kaya guilty of wrongful paternalism when she refuses to accept the token of consent if her primary reason for doing so is Xiao Wen's wellbeing?

Consider the first two questions. On most views of competence, the answer to the first question determines the answer to the second: if the intoxicated person is capable of consenting to sex, then third parties have no right to interfere with their consent decision. The primary disagreement on most views of competence, then, is *what* capacities Xiao Wen would need to retain in order to waive her rights against sexual trespass.

More demanding views of competence are unlikely to find Xiao Wen capable of consenting to sex. After all, on these views, the consenter must be able to appreciate their situation and the consequences of different choices. These abilities are precisely what alcohol impairs. *Alcohol myopia* refers to the tendency of an intoxicated person to be overly attendant to their occurrent mental state (e.g., hunger) or factors in their immediate environment (e.g., this glistening, juicy, fragrant beef burger on the grill) and less responsive to more abstract commitments (e.g., I am a vegetarian) and consequences of those commitments (e.g., I will regret having eaten meat when I sober up).[52] In the original case, the strength of Xiao Wen's reaction to Kaya gives us *some* reason to doubt that she can appreciate why someone who cares for her may not want to have sex with her when she is impaired. And, in the variant on the case, her other signs of impairment suggest that, if she was feeling lustful, nostalgic for the times when her ex was sweet, or swayed by his charming chat, she might struggle to reason through the consequences of letting her guard down versus keeping her resolve not to sleep with him again. All this suggests that she is incapable of consenting to sex on a demanding view. Since she is incapable of altering her claim against interference, her colleagues would also be permitted to prevent her from going home with her ex.

More liberal views would likely find Xiao Wen capable of consenting to sex. After all, in the original case she appears to be pursuing something she values—namely, disinhibited physical intimacy with her girlfriend. And, if she is capable of valuing in this state, then she is still capable of acting autonomously. She is, then, also capable of consenting to sex with her ex. As a result, it would be wrongfully paternalistic for her sober colleagues to prevent her from leaving the bar with him.

The reader will be unsurprised to learn that we think this case is ripe for analysis in terms of the two separate rights that comprise competence: the power to give consent and the claim against paternalistic interference. It is very likely that Xiao Wen has retained the capacities necessary to be able to alter her claims against sexual trespass. This gives us an answer to the first question: yes, someone as intoxicated as Xiao Wen is still capable of waiving her rights against sexual trespass. However, this does not determine the answer to the question of whether other parties are permitted to interfere to prevent an intoxicated person from having sexual relations. Since it is plausible that Xiao Wen no longer has the capacities necessary for a claim against paternalistic interference, her colleagues are in a position to consider whether there are any paternalistic reasons to intervene. Of course, to justify interference, these reasons would need to be weighty enough to outweigh the benefits to Xiao Wen of being able to make her own decisions, and the benefits of being allowed to pursue disinhibited sex. Depending on the situation—are they confident that she will regret it? Is this likely to damage her current relationship?—her colleagues might be justified in preventing her from leaving the bar to have sex with her ex. Even so, paternalistic interference should be their last course of action. They first ought to try to remind Xiao Wen of *her* reasons why leaving with him would be a bad idea. But since she no longer has a claim against paternalism, they would be permitted to intervene if the risks to her were weighty.

Turn now to the ethics of Kaya's actions. If Xiao Wen is capable of consenting but not capable of being responsible for her decisions, then Kaya also has to decide whether sex would be bad for Xiao Wen. If so, she might have paternalistic reasons for saying no. No matter Xiao Wen's state, however, we can give a negative answer to our final question—whether by refusing to have sex Kaya would be guilty of wrongful paternalism. Unlike the other questions, this one is answered by considering what consent is—the topic of Chapter 2. If valid, Xiao Wen's consent waives her right and releases Kaya from the duty that right imposed not to have sex with her. That is all Xiao Wen's rights waiver does. It does not also make a claim on Kaya that they have sex with Xiao Wen. A rights waiver is not also a demand. This means that when Kaya refuses the invitation of sex, she does not violate a claim, and so she is not guilty of rights-violating paternalism. All this is compatible with Xiao Wen feeling the *insult* of paternalism[53]—but she is mistaken if she thinks that Kaya's refusal to accept her token of consent, or indeed Kaya's refusal to reciprocate consent, wrongs her.

It is worth closing with a final virtue of this detailed analysis. Thus far, the discussion has focused on Xiao Wen's competence to *consent*, but not her competence to *refuse* sexual relations or *revoke* her consent to those relations. On our view, consent and refusal are on a par: someone who has the power to consent also has the power to refuse to consent. This means that Xiao Wen retains the power to refuse or revoke her consent to sexual relations even when she is this intoxicated. Moreover, since there is *never* a paternalistic reason to override a person's refusal of sex or retraction of consent to sex, her intoxicated refusal or retraction is normatively decisive.

10. Conclusions

Valid consent is necessary, but not sufficient, for permissible sexual relations. Yet every necessary condition for valid consent—competence, disclosure, understanding, voluntariness, and tokening consent—raise distinct challenges in this domain. Even when these issues are settled—for example, that illegitimate deception can invalidate consent to sex—the question of whether and how the law should reflect the ethics of non-consensual sexual relations remains vexed.

Notes

1 The slogan is intended to be read as *only* yes means yes. Friedman, Jaclyn, and Jessica Valenti (eds.). *Yes means yes! Visions of female sexual power and a world without rape*. Seal Press, 2019.

2 McClintock, Martha K., and Gilbert Herdt. "Rethinking puberty: The development of sexual attraction." *Current Directions in Psychological Science* 5.6 (1996): 178–183.

3 Wertheimer, Alan. "Intoxicated consent to sexual relations." *Law and Philosophy* (2001): 373–401.

4 Tsesis, Alexander. *We shall overcome: A history of civil rights and the law*. Yale University Press, 2008.

5 D'emilio, John, and Estelle B. Freedman. *Intimate matters: A history of sexuality in America*. University of Chicago Press, 1997; Stein, Marc. *The Stonewall riots: A documentary history*. New York University Press, 2019. For an argument that the sexual revolution started much earlier, see Dabhoiwala, Faramerz. *The origins of sex: A history of the first sexual revolution*. Oxford University Press, 2012.

6 Randall, Melanie, Jennifer Koshan, and Patricia Nyaundi (eds.). *The right to say no: Marital rape and law reform in Canada, Ghana, Kenya and Malawi*. Bloomsbury Publishing, 2017; Dauvergne, Catherine, and Jenni Millbank. "Forced marriage as a harm in domestic and international law." *The Modern Law Review* 73.1 (2010): 57–88; Mania, Karolina. "The legal implications and remedies concerning revenge porn and fake porn: A common law perspective." *Sexuality & Culture* 24.6 (2020): 2079–2097.

7 For discussion of prostitution and the law, see Anderson, Scott A. "Prostitution and sexual autonomy: Making sense of the prohibition of prostitution." *Ethics* 112.4 (2002): 748–780; Flanigan, Jessica. "The case for decriminalizing sex work." *The Routledge handbook of philosophy of sex and sexuality*. Routledge, 2022: 527–537.

8 Calhoun, Cheshire. "Who's afraid of polygamous marriage—Lessons for same-sex marriage advocacy from the history of polygamy." *San Diego Law Review* 42 (2005): 1023, Brake, Elizabeth. "Minimal marriage: What political liberalism implies for marriage law." *Ethics* 120.2 (2010): 302–337, Den Otter, Ronald C. *In defense of plural marriage*. Cambridge University Press, 2015.

9 West, Robin. "Sex, law, and consent." In Franklin Miller and Alan Wertheimer (eds.), *The ethics of consent: Theory and practice*. Oxford University Press, 2010: 222.

10 Kennedy, Chloë. *Inducing intimacy: Deception, consent and the law*. Cambridge University Press, 2024: 27–118.

11 Quoted in Kennedy, Chloë. *Inducing intimacy: Deception, consent and the law*. Cambridge University Press, 2024: 97.

12 Green, Stuart P. *Criminalizing sex: A unified liberal theory*. Oxford University Press, 2020; Chadha, Karamvir. "Criminalizing sex: Is consent all that matters?" *Criminal Law and Philosophy* (2024): 1–13; Tolley, Rachel C. "Harmfulness and wrongfulness in sex-by-deception." *Criminal Law and Philosophy* (2024): 1–15.

13 See *R v. Lawrance* [2020] EWCA Crim 97.

14 Pundik, Amit, Shani Schnitzer, and Binyamin Blum. "Sex, lies, and reasonableness: The case for subjectifying the criminalisation of deceptive sex." *Criminal Justice Ethics* 41.2 (2022): 167–189.

15 See, e.g., Gardner, John. "The opposite of rape." *Oxford Journal of Legal Studies* 38.1 (2018): 48–70; MacKinnon, Catharine A. "Rape redefined." *Harvard Law & Policy Review* 10 (2016): 431; Palmer, Tanya. "Distinguishing sex from sexual violation: Consent, negotiation and freedom to negotiate." In Alan Reed et al. (eds.), *Consent: Domestic and comparative perspectives*. Routledge, 2017.

16 Compare Ichikawa who claims that the language of consent presupposes that someone consents at another's behest ("Consent … is typically a response to a request, an instruction, a command, or the like. When you are considering doing something at another's behest, the question of consent is an appropriate one. When you are considering doing something for your own reasons, the question doesn't even arise." Ichikawa, Jonathan Jenkins. "Presupposition and consent." *Feminist Philosophy Quarterly* 6.4 (2020): 6–7. Ichikawa also endorses the idea that there can be permissible sex without consent.

17 Palmer, Tanya. "Distinguishing sex from sexual violation: Consent, negotiation and freedom to negotiate." In Alan Reed et al. (eds.), *Consent: Domestic and comparative perspectives*. Routledge, 2017: 13.

18 Gardner, John. "The opposite of rape." *Oxford Journal of Legal Studies* 38.1 (2018): 60.

19 This rules out purely attitudinal views of consent. These are views that hold that it is possible to give or retract consent by thought alone. We argued against these views in Chapter 2.

20 Kukla, Rebecca. "That's what she said: The language of sexual negotiation." *Ethics* 129.1 (2018): 75–76.

21 Kukla, Rebecca. "That's what she said: The language of sexual negotiation." *Ethics* 129.1 (2018): 81.

22 For those who doubt this, note that even a response to a request—that is, the sort of speech act that Kukla and Ichikawa regard as constituting consent—can perform multiple functions. "May I kiss you?" Axl asks. "Please do!" Alex replies, thereby both consenting to and inviting the kiss. Indeed, Kukla concedes: "Sexual activity is only ethical if everyone involved has communicated successfully that they want to engage in it and is doing so autonomously and willingly. If this broad point is all we mean by saying that all sex must be consensual, then consent is a necessary condition for the ethical acceptability of any sexual activity." Kukla, Rebecca. "That's what she said: The language of sexual negotiation." *Ethics* 129.1 (2018): 92.

23 Chadha, Karamvir. "Sexual consent and having sex together." *Oxford Journal of Legal Studies* 40.3 (2020): 628.

24 Classic feminist critiques of consent-centered sexual ethics include: Paterman, Carole. *The sexual contract*. Stanford University Press, 1988, MacKinnon, Catharine A. *Toward a feminist theory of the state*. Harvard University Press, 1989; Alcoff, Linda Martín. *Rape and resistance*. John Wiley & Sons, 2018.

25 For discussion, see McArthur, Neil. "Relationships between university professors and students: Should they be banned?" *Ethics and Education* 12.2 (2017): 129–140; Srinivasan, Amia. "Sex as a pedagogical failure." *Yale Law Journal* 129 (2019): 1100.

26 Anderson, Ellie. 2022. "A phenomenological approach to sexual consent." *Feminist Philosophy Quarterly* 8.2.

27 Herbenick, Debby, et al. "Diverse sexual behaviors in undergraduate students: Findings from a campus probability survey." *The Journal of Sexual Medicine* 18.6 (2021): 1024–1041.

28 Of course, this likely depends on dealbreakers. On some views, there may be a lot that needs to be understood. See, for example, Dougherty, Tom. "Sex, lies, and consent." *Ethics* 123.4 (2013): 717–744. However, even on views like these, if there are no dealbreakers, it would be possible to give valid consent ignorant of risks or purpose.

29 For more on how we use language and pragmatic norms in sex, see Kukla, Rebecca. "That's what she said: The language of sexual negotiation." *Ethics* 129.1 (2018): 70–97.

30 Sometimes these are used by bad actors to minimize the sexual harassment, abuse, or assault of women. For example, take the hateful and disingenuous phrase—"She was asking for it." It is used to excuse non-consensual sexual acts on the grounds that consent was non-verbally communicated by a woman's dress, behavior, or mere existence. See, for analysis, Tilton, Emily C. R. "Rape myths, catastrophe, and credibility." *Episteme* 21.2 (2024): 408–424.

31 Marx, Brian P., et al. "Tonic immobility as an evolved predator defense: Implications for sexual assault survivors." *Clinical psychology: Science and Practice* 15.1 (2008): 74.

32 Dworkin, Emily R., Barbara Krahé, and Heidi Zinzow. "The global prevalence of sexual assault: A systematic review of international research since 2010." *Psychology of Violence* 11.5 (2021): 497.

33 A number of philosophers have engaged philosophical questions about rape, including on how it should be defined, what makes it distinctively wrong, and the social structures and societal norms that enable it. See, e.g., Alcoff, Linda Martín. *Rape and resistance*. John Wiley & Sons, 2018; Hänel, Hilkje Charlotte. *What is rape? Social theory and conceptual analysis*. transcript, 2018.

34 From the outside, one might think that it would not in fact be that bad for Karolina if Simon broke up with her. After all, he is the sort of boyfriend who uses the threat of abandonment to pressure a partner into unwanted sex—she'd be better off without him! In that case, he is really making an offer, not a threat. We invite such readers to tweak the case in order to make it so that she will definitely be worse off. Perhaps they are living together in his house and he will kick her out if they break up.

35 For analysis of how such proposals can still be coercive, even though they do not involve threats to violate any rights, see Garnett, Michael. "Coercion: The wrong and the bad." *Ethics* 128.3 (2018): 545–573.
36 Cf. discussion in Boonin, David. *Sexual ethics and problematic consent: When does yes mean no?* Oxford University Press, 2024: 52–59.
37 Cf. Wertheimer, Alan. *Consent to sexual relations*. Cambridge University Press (2003): 170; Scheidegger, Nora. "Of nagging and guilt-tripping. Lack of consent in one's own activities?" *Consent and Sexual Offenses*. Nomos, 2022. For an argument that sulking can constitute consent-undermining coercion, see Patwardhan, Sumeet. "Sulking into sex: Blame, coercion, and consent." *Journal of Ethics & Social Philosophy* 28 (2024): 357.
38 Conly, Sarah. "Seduction, rape, and coercion." *Ethics* 115.1 (2004): 96–121.
39 Woolf, Nicky. "'Negging': the anatomy of a dating trend." *New Statesman* May 25, 2012.
40 Toma, Catalina L., Jeffrey T. Hancock, and Nicole B. Ellison. "Separating fact from fiction: An examination of deceptive self-presentation in online dating profiles." *Personality and Social Psychology Bulletin* 34.8 (2008): 1023–1036; Ellison, Nicole, Rebecca Heino, and Jennifer Gibbs. "Managing impressions online: Self-presentation processes in the online dating environment." *Journal of Computer-Mediated Communication* 11.2 (2006): 415–441.
41 For discussion in the context of how differently the law on sexual consent does and should treat deception and coercion, see Wertheimer, Alan. *Consent to sexual relations*. Cambridge University Press (2003): 193–214.
42 Tilton, Emily C. R., and Jonathan Jenkins Ichikawa. "Not what I agreed to: content and consent." *Ethics* 132.1 (2021): 133.
43 Tilton and Ichikawa's example focuses on trans identity, but the reader could substitute this for racial identity, social class, disability, or any other group that Greg would not consent to sex with but to which Laura belongs.
44 A seemingly trivial but fraudulent misrepresentation can render a legal contract null and void. A benevolently motivated but minor deception on the part of a doctor to persuade you to agree to a much-needed surgery could render your subsequent consent invalid.
45 Tilton, Emily C. R., and Jonathan Jenkins Ichikawa. "Not what I agreed to: content and consent." *Ethics* 132.1 (2021): 127–154.
46 Compare with Alexandra Lloyd's discussion of a couple meeting at a vegan convention, but one party is not vegan. Lloyd, Alexandra. "Elusive consent." *Public Affairs Quarterly* 35.4 (2021): 297–314.
47 For alternative analyses of cases like these, see Lazenby, Hugh, and Iason Gabriel. "Permissible secrets." *The Philosophical Quarterly* 68.271 (2018): 265–285; Fischel, Joseph J. *Screw consent: A better politics of sexual justice*. University of California Press, 2019: 94–116.
48 Abbey, A. "Alcohol-related sexual assault: A common problem among college students." *Journal of Studies on Alcohol Drugs* 14 (2002): 118–128; Mellins, Claude A., et al. "Sexual assault incidents among college undergraduates: Prevalence and factors associated with risk." *PLoS One* 12.11 (2017): e0186471; Flack, W. F., Jr, et al. "Risk factors and consequences of unwanted sex among university students: hooking up, alcohol, and stress response." *Journal of Interpersonal Violence* 22 (2007): 139–157.
49 For a representative sample of these policies and discussion, see Director, Samuel. "Sober thoughts on drunken consent." *Social Theory and Practice* 48.2 (2022): 235–261.
50 Beliot College. "Policy against sexual harassment and associated grievance procedures." Effective since August 14, 2020. Available at: www.beloit.edu/live/blurbs/733-policy-against-sexual-harassment-and-associated-grievanc.
51 See, for example, Wertheimer, Alan. "Intoxicated consent to sexual relations." *Law and Philosophy* (2001): 373–401; Dixon, Nicholas. "Alcohol and rape." *Public Affairs Quarterly* (2001): 341–354; and Director, Samuel. "Sober thoughts on drunken consent." *Social Theory and Practice* 48.2 (2022): 235–261.
52 Steele, Claude M., and Robert A. Josephs. "Alcohol myopia: Its prized and dangerous effects." *American Psychologist* 45.8 (1990): 921.
53 See, Shiffrin, Seana Valentine. "Paternalism, unconscionability doctrine, and accommodation." *Philosophy & Public Affairs* 29.3 (2000): 205–250.

10 Consent to government

> We hold these truths to be self-evident, that all men are created equal, that they are endowed by their Creator with certain unalienable Rights, that among these are Life, Liberty and the pursuit of Happiness.—That to secure these rights, Governments are instituted among Men, deriving their just powers from the consent of the governed.
>
> —United States Declaration of Independence

> I, [name], swear by Almighty God that, on becoming a British citizen, I will be faithful and bear true allegiance to His Majesty King Charles III, His Heirs and Successors according to law … I will give my loyalty to the United Kingdom and respect its rights and freedoms. I will uphold its democratic values. I will observe its laws faithfully and fulfil my duties and obligations as a British citizen.
>
> —Oath of Allegiance and Pledge of Loyalty, required for naturalization as a British citizen

1. Introduction

What gives the government the right to make the laws? What gives its agents—like the police—the right to enforce them?

If you live in a functioning democracy, you might answer that the government's authority comes from the fact that it won an election. Elections express the will of the people (or at least those who can vote). Because each person has one vote, they give each person an equal say in who will govern them. Those who vote thereby agree to be bound by the results of the election. And so, if elections are sufficiently free and fair, they therefore involve the people giving authority to govern to the winners. Through elections, we *consent* to be governed and we waive certain rights so as to permit the state to enforce its laws.

Set aside, for now, any qualms you might have about the conduct of actual elections. Even in the best case, this answer may not be fully satisfying. After all, elections take place within a territory that is already fixed and with a state that already exists. No matter the results of the national parliamentary polls, this book's

DOI: 10.4324/9781003287391-12

authors will still live in the United Kingdom and be subject to its laws. What justifies that?

This question became pressing in the West during the Enlightenment, as intellectuals tried to reconcile nascent liberal ideas about individual rights and freedom with the reality of—mostly—autocratic rule. In the first of his *Two Treatises on Government*, John Locke dismantles Sir Robert Filmer's attempt to justify government by appeal to the divine right of kings. In the second, Locke confronts the challenge of what could make a state legitimate. His answer is that we must give consent to be governed:

> Men being, as has been said, by nature all free, equal, and independent, no one can be put out of this estate and subjected to the political power of another without his own consent, which is done by agreeing with other men, to join and unite into a community for their comfortable, safe, and peaceable living, one amongst another, in a secure enjoyment of their properties, and a greater security against any that are not of it.[1]

In this chapter, we consider whether consent theory has anything to tell us about the authority of governments to regulate the lives of the people within a state. We briefly summarize some of the history of the consent theory of political authority and identify its key challenges. These challenges invoke familiar concepts from the analyses given earlier in this book—of understanding, communication, and voluntariness. Some modern political philosophers have attempted to revive the consent theory of political authority. We argue that they fail to show that most individuals have actually given consent to the state in which they live. If consent is to ground state authority substantial reforms would be necessary in order to obtain it and render it morally transformative.

This chapter's first difficult case takes the best case for government authority on the basis of consent—a referendum—and asks whether the results of a referendum have special authority because they directly express the will of the governed. We consider the UK's referendum on European Union membership in the light of concerns raised about misinformation, which might in other contexts be thought to invalidate consent. The second difficult case concerns a rather different issue: whether it is possible to give consent when threatened with legal sanctions for refusal. We focus on laws requiring drivers to agree to blood alcohol tests. Does the fact that agents of the state issue the threat mean that consent to such a test is still valid?

A brief note on terminology.[2] We will talk of states and their governments as being *legitimate* or *illegitimate*. At a minimum, if a state and its government are legitimate this means that the government has the *authority* to make and enforce laws for its citizens and residents. Authority here functions as a normative concept, not just a descriptive one—that is, a government has authority in this sense if it is morally permissible for it to make and enforce laws. Note, further, that to have such authority does not mean that the government can permissibly makc absolutely any law it likes. What the government is morally permitted to do will still be limited by considerations of justice.[3]

The question of legitimacy and authority is at least conceptually distinct from the question of what obligations citizens have. Some writers think that the authority to make and enforce laws goes hand in hand with the obligation of citizens to obey those laws.[4] Others think they can come apart, so that it would be possible to have a legitimate government without even a *prima facie* moral obligation to obey it.[5] We do not take a stand on this issue. Philosophers writing on this topic also use the term *consent* in differing and often wider senses than in other areas of life that we have covered in this book.[6] Consent to be governed centrally involves giving the state permission to make and enforce just laws. But for some writers it also involves taking on an obligation to obey the laws and so looks like it is exercising an additional normative power—one more akin to promising.[7] A. John Simmons writes:

> Let us say, more precisely, that consent is the deliberate (and communicatively successful) performance of acts or omissions whose conventional or contextual point is to communicate to others the agent's intention to undertake new obligations and/or convey to others new rights (with respect to the agent).[8]

For those who think that citizens have obligations arising through consent, we might then think of consent to be governed along the lines of a contract—where someone may both suspend or give up rights and commit to certain acts. This would be consent in *both* the promissory and the permissive senses that we distinguished in Chapter 2.

2. Historical context

In Western political thought, the idea that the law applies to competent, adult citizens in virtue of their consent traces back to Plato. In *Crito*, Socrates explains his reasons for refusing to escape Athens and thereby escape his death sentence.[9] Socrates has been brought up receiving the benefits of the city's laws, he has seen how the laws function, and he has had the opportunity to leave the city and settle elsewhere. By remaining under these circumstances, Socrates claims, he has agreed to abide by the laws of the city.

Over two thousand years later, John Locke considered what could justify the existence of the state, if not a divine right of the monarch to rule. Like other *social contract* theorists, he used the device of a "state of nature" to represent the world prior to government. Persons living in a state of nature, all of whom are naturally free and equal, can only have their freedom curtailed by a government if they agree to it. And there are, of course, good reasons why people would agree to form a state.

But given his commitment to the natural freedom and equality of all, Locke also faced the problem of how to justify government authority to those who never had a choice about leaving the state of nature. In Locke's time, as in our own, very few people appeared to have actually given express consent to a government. Did that mean that the government was actually illegitimate? No, Locke argued. Instead, people have given tacit consent to be governed:

> every man that hath any possession or enjoyment of any part of the dominions of any government doth hereby give his tacit consent, and is as far forth obliged to obedience to the laws of that government, during such enjoyment, as any one under it, whether this his possession be of land to him and his heirs for ever, or a lodging only for a week; or whether it be barely travelling freely on the highway; and, in effect, it reaches as far as the very being of any one within the territories of that government.[10]

Thus, being in a territory or, perhaps, enjoying the benefits that territory's state provides, counts as giving consent to the territory's government. Our choice to remain in our country of birth constitutes consent to the rule of UK government. On this view, governments are indeed legitimate in virtue of the consent—albeit tacit—of those they govern.

Two main objections have been raised to Locke's consent theory, which challenge consent theorists to this day. Both were pithily stated by David Hume in his *Of the Original Contract*. The first, the *no token* objection, concerns whether someone living within a territory or accepting the benefits of the state can accurately be described as giving consent. As discussed in Chapter 4, even the most minimal understanding condition includes the understanding that one's act signifies giving consent. Yet, people do not seem to take themselves as consenting via residence. Hume writes:

> It is strange, that an act of the mind, which every individual is supposed to have formed, and after he came to the use of reason too, otherwise it could have no authority; that this act, I say, should be so much unknown to all of them, that, over the face of the whole earth, there scarcely remain any trace or memory of it.[11]

If people do not think that their act signifies consent, then is it plausible to claim that it is?

The second objection—the *voluntariness* objection—is that even if consent were given through, say, the act of continued residence in a territory, that consent would not be freely given:

> Can we seriously say, that a poor peasant or artisan has a free choice to leave his country, when he knows no foreign language or manners, and lives, from day to day, by the small wages which he acquires? We may as well assert, that man by remaining in a vessel, freely consents to the dominion of the master; though he was carried on board while asleep, and must leap into the ocean, and perish, the moment he leaves her.[12]

In order for the decision to remain in a country to count as valid consent, it must be voluntary. But for many people, the consequences of leaving the country in which they live would be terrible. They would be leaving behind their friends, family, and community. They would be leaving their livelihood. Moreover, since the habitable landmass of the earth is now covered by states, someone choosing to dissent from their government's rule would have to find another acceptable state to take them in. Otherwise, they would be stuck floating around in international waters.[13] As we can clearly see in the plight of modern refugees who flee persecution, this in itself is no straightforward task and the choice of receiving state is limited for all but the luckiest of those who leave.

3. Responding to the objections

In the face of the *no token* and *voluntariness* objections, philosophers have taken one of four routes.

First, many regard the objections as fatal for consent theory. They believe that neither the authority of governments to make and enforce laws nor the obligations of citizens and residents to obey them rest on the consent of the governed. Some philosophers argue for alternative grounds for state authority and citizens' obligations, such as "fair play."[14] Others, convinced that the consent of the governed would be necessary for a legitimate state, become "philosophical anarchists"—"according to which real citizens generally lack political obligations and real states or governments generally lack the authority or legitimacy that correlates with those obligations."[15]

Second, some argue that the actual consent of the governed is not what is required. Instead, what matters is what persons *hypothetically would* consent to under certain conditions or *should* consent to under actual conditions. For example, John Rawls's contractualism models principles of justice on what individuals in very idealized circumstances would consent to.[16] Meanwhile, David Estlund argues that sometimes someone morally ought to consent and their non-consent therefore is "null."[17] They are then in the same normative situation as if they actually gave consent. This, he argues, is the situation that individuals are in with respect to some appropriately democratic political institutions.[18]

The third and fourth routes try to rescue actual consent as the basis for political legitimacy. Route three involves arguing that the *no token* and *voluntariness* objections fail: in fact, most people in sufficiently just democracies do give morally valid consent to the rule of the state they are in. Route four accepts that few people give morally valid consent to be ruled but argues that there could be practical reforms so that they could consent. Given the importance of obtaining the consent of the governed, proponents of route four think that these reforms ought to be implemented. We discuss routes three and four together over the course of the next two sections—first considering possible responses to the *no token* objection and then responses to the *voluntariness* objection.

4. Responding to the *no token* objection

Defenders of the view that we consent to be governed must show that residents of a state typically give actual consent and that this consent is sufficiently voluntary to be valid. The first challenge is dealing with the *no token* objection. Many countries already require immigrants who naturalize to swear oaths of allegiance as part of the process of becoming a citizen—as illustrated by the UK's oath of allegiance quoted at the beginning of this chapter. In them, they generally promise, among other things, to obey the laws of their new country.[19] We might reasonably take the swearing of such an oath as also constituting consent to the authority of the state. After all, it would make little sense to promise to obey the law if one did not also grant the government permission to make and enforce laws (within, as noted, the parameters of justice). We have, then, a clear model for express speech acts of consent to be governed. Unfortunately, most natural-born citizens in modern democracies have not taken similar oaths.[20] Neither of the authors of this book, for example, has expressly agreed to obey the laws or accept the government of the United Kingdom.

If not an express speech act of consent, what then might constitute the token of consent to be governed for natural-born citizens? Locke's answer, as we have seen, was that residence in a country constituted tacit consent. Alternative answers might say that accepting the benefits that the state provides or taking part in political processes like voting constitute tokens of consent. But, as far as we know, none of these acts are generally understood to indicate consent. This implies that the acts cannot *mean* "I consent."

One response to this objection is to argue that whether or not people *actually* think they are consenting through continued residence, they *should* know that that is what they are doing and that is enough.[21] This response relies on three key premises. First, that in order to consent to *x* by *y*-ing, one need not know that *y*-ing constitutes consent, it must only be the case that one ought to know. Second, that residing in a country constitutes consent to be governed. And third, that most adults in modern democracies ought to know that so residing constitutes consent. But even if the first and second premises were true,[22] the third is belied by the existence of the debate about consent and political legitimacy. If even philosophers who have spent years thinking about the question are largely skeptical that residence entails consent, then how can we say that most adults ought to have inferred that it does?

Instead, one might lean more on the idea of tacit consent. In certain circumstances, not dissenting constitutes tacit consent. For example, when the chair of a meeting proposes a course of action and asks if there are any objections, silence—non-dissent—is consent. Might the lack of dissent among citizens play the same role with respect to the state?[23] This could only be plausible in states where the risks and costs of expressing dissent are sufficiently low, of course. But we might expect that any state that is sufficiently just to be legitimate should be one where dissent can be safely expressed. It is also plausible that widespread and ongoing popular dissent is an indicator that the people do not consent. The challenge, yet again, is to show that not expressing dissent *means* consenting to the state that one is in. Expressions of dissent in well-functioning democracies rarely take the form of dissenting to be ruled—protests usually target specific policies that the rulers plan to enact.[24] The French *gilets jaunes* protests, for example, aimed to change economic policies and enact constitutional reforms, but protesting did not appear to signify rejecting the French state overall.[25]

A final possibility is that participating in the political processes of one's state constitutes giving consent to the results of that process. No additional speech act is required. Just as by joining a game one thereby consents to be bound by the rules of the game (assuming one joins voluntarily, understands the rules, and so forth), so by voting in elections one thereby consents to be bound by the results. Peter Steinberger writes:

> The fact is that going to the polls and casting a vote in an election is analogous to sitting down at the poker table. It is a kind of engagement that signals a prima facie belief in the legitimacy of the electoral process and a willingness to accept its outcomes.[26]

As a justification for the legitimacy of the state, this analogy falls short. One typically has a choice about whether to join a game of poker and thereby signal that one has accepted the rules and outcome of the game. Most people do not have such a choice with respect to whether to be part of a modern state—they are already in it. Voting in an election is not like joining the game, it is like making a move in a game one is already a part of. This is not to say that voting is irrelevant however. We return to the question of whether voting might constitute consent to *something* later in the chapter.

While it seems implausible that most citizens in modern democracies have tokened consent to being governed, reform in this regard seems like it would be straightforward. We have already noted that many countries require oaths of allegiance for naturalizing immigrants. Requiring such oaths could simply be extended to all competent citizens at the age of majority. Someone who thinks that consent is a necessary condition for the legitimacy of the state could advocate for this reform to be made.

5. Responding to the *voluntariness* objection

Even if reforms were instituted so that all competent adult citizens were asked for their consent to be governed, the voluntariness objection would remain. Would the token of consent be valid, given the consequences of dissent for many people? Clearly, being cast into international waters would be bad. But exile would be bad even for those who could actually find another country willing to take them in. They would have to leave behind family, friends, and community, become an alien in a new culture, lose their job and find new employment, and possibly learn a new language. Plus, as non-citizens in their new home, they would very likely have even fewer political rights than in the country they left. A threat with consequences as severe as these would normally be taken to render consent involuntary.

In response, one might argue that the state's "take it or leave" proposal is in fact an offer, not a threat. It is true that the consequences of saying "no" are terrible. But, as we have seen in previous chapters (e.g., Chapter 5), that is not sufficient to render a request for consent coercive. After all, the innocent surgeon, asking for consent to life-saving surgery, makes an offer and consent proffered to her is valid. The surgeon's proposal is an offer because she is not responsible for the bad consequences attendant on refusal. Likewise, one might argue, it is not the fault of the state that the consequences of leaving are so bad. It did not make the oceans inhospitable, the other territories unwelcoming, or stop one's friends and family from leaving too. The proposal to receive all the benefits of democratic government in exchange for being subject to the law is therefore an offer.

Tempting though this line of argument might seem, we do not find it convincing. First, consider the plight of those who cannot find another state to take them in or do not want to be ruled by any government. Though it is not the fault of any particular state that the habitable land of the world is now divided up into states, so that there is nowhere else to live, it *is* plausible that the global order is maintained jointly by the various countries of the world. Collectively, they are responsible for it being impossible to live anywhere without being governed.

Second, and more damning, for many liberals it will seem like begging the question to describe the state's proposal as an offer. This is because it seems to assume that the state has legitimate title to rule the territory that its putative citizens inhabit. If, instead, these citizens have prior claims to be in the territory, then saying, "If you don't like being governed, then leave!" will indeed be a threat. It will be a proposal to violate people's rights, if they do not comply. As Nicolás Maloberti puts it:

> Thus, if individuals indeed have pre-existing rights to their persons, properties, and to protect those rights by just means, the case of a state would not be like the case of a customer going to a restaurant. It will be like the case of a restaurant demanding a payment for a meal that the customer prepares at his own home.[27]

Grant, then, that someone who consented to be governed only because of the terrible consequences of emigration would have been coerced. There is one further argumentative strategy for the defender of the view that consent to government is voluntary. Stephen Puryear argues that if one does what one wants to do, then one's action will be voluntary.[28] Someone who remains in a room because he wants to be there, remains there voluntarily, even if the exits are blocked so that he cannot leave. His remaining is only involuntary if he remains because the exits are blocked. With respect to coercion, we might argue that a threat only renders an action involuntary if the action is the result of the threat. I cannot be coerced into doing something that I was going to do anyway. Moreover, Puryear thinks that most citizens of liberal democracies are in exactly this situation:

> Most Americans, I suspect, would decline to emigrate to another country or even to some libertarian paradise in another part of the world, even if the respective governments made this a ready possibility, because most of them genuinely want to be here, whether out of nationalistic loyalty, a deep connection to place or people or culture, or even just inertia.[29]

Intuitions might vary regarding whether we can be coerced into doing what we already prefer to do. Even if we accept that we cannot, problems remain. One is that even if the majority would stay, some people would surely prefer to leave their native country if the conditions elsewhere were not so bad. Something must be said to these dissenters. The other is that the question may still seem to be begged in favor of the state's right to govern. What is at issue is not just whether someone would choose to remain in a particular territory, culture, and community, but whether they would, given the option, prefer to be governed by this state. Even more people might reject the state, if they could still stay in the same place.

We do not find these responses to the voluntariness objection compelling. What about proposals for reform? Just as it would be possible to reform current practice so that all competent adults were asked for consent to be governed, perhaps it would be possible to institute reforms so as to make dissent voluntary.

A small literature addresses what reforms would be necessary and what their prospects are.[30] These include, in addition to the option of emigration, giving groups within a territory the right to secede, and making provisions for dissenters who wish to remain within the territory. Such dissenters—non-citizens with the right to remain—could be denied the benefits of government, provided that their prior rights were still respected. Naturally this would pose some practical challenges. One is that it would be very hard to deny dissenters some of the benefits of government, including public goods and the positive externalities of living in modern economies with all their material benefits. Meanwhile, dissenters would have some advantages over citizens, such as freedom from taxation. If the government could not make citizenship sufficiently attractive, there might be too many dissenters to make the state viable.

6. Consent within the state

If the consent of the governed is necessary for government to be legitimate, then it is unlikely that we have any legitimate states. It is possible that reforms could be instituted in order to obtain the morally valid consent of citizens and residents of existing states. Those reforms would be challenging to institute in a way that deals with the voluntariness concerns and there are no signs that they are actually being considered. One possibility, then, is that all existing states are in fact illegitimate.[31] Another is that consent is not in fact necessary for legitimacy. There is some other ground for the authority to make and enforce laws (and for the obligations of citizens and residents to obey them). Exploring this option would take us away from discussing consent and into political philosophy more broadly. Instead, we now leave the question of whether consent can legitimize the state as a whole and move to more specific cases involving consent within existing states.

The first case concerns referendums. Even if one doubts that consent can legitimize the state, one might still think that voting authorizes an existing state to carry out certain policies. We consider the UK's Brexit referendum in the light of this possibility: did the vote in favor of leaving the EU constitute consent to the government's subsequent actions?

The second case concerns what policies the state is permitted to enact. Many countries have laws against driving while under the influence of alcohol. Enforcing these rules involves asking people who are not known to have committed any crime to submit to a blood-alcohol test. There are penalties for refusal. On its face, this seems coercive. May a legitimate state impose sanctions on individuals if they refuse to consent to a bodily intervention? Or are such actions problematic—because they violate individual rights—in the same way as they would be if the threats were not made by agents of the state?

7. Case: a referendum

On June 23, 2016, a referendum was held in the UK concerning the UK's membership of the European Union (the so-called "Brexit referendum"). Voters were asked a simple question: "Should the United Kingdom remain a member of the European Union or leave the European Union?" Turnout was high: 33.6 million people voted, which was 72% of the electorate. In a shock result, the Leave option won by 52% to 48%. Though the referendum was not binding, the government considered itself bound to respect the result. The UK ultimately left the EU on December 31, 2020.

Assume for the sake of argument that existing democratic states are legitimate. This means that they have the right to make and enforce laws, provided that those laws are sufficiently just. We leave open how far justice constrains which laws are permissible to enact (and which laws are so unjust that individuals may refuse to obey them). In these states, adults with the right to vote are regularly asked to make choices. Sometimes those choices are about who will represent them and potentially govern. Sometimes, though, they are about specific policies, as in a referendum, where voters are asked to choose among a small number of policy options.

We choose referendums for discussion because they seem like the most likely candidates for individual citizens giving consent to a law. It is common for a referendum to give voters just two options, one of which is the status quo. This was the case for the Brexit referendum. Effectively, then, each voter is being asked—Do you agree to this proposed policy?—and if sufficiently many dissent, the policy is not enacted. Moreover, it seems clear what the voters are being asked to agree to and how it is that they token their agreement. If any individual democratic act is giving consent, voting in a referendum is surely it.

Assuming, then, that the state itself is legitimate, does a referendum result favoring a new policy give the state any additional authority to enact that policy?

Challenges to the idea that consent might do some work here immediately arise. Suppose that someone takes part in a referendum and votes "No." They appear to have dissented. But let us suppose the majority vote "Yes." Why, the dissenting individual might ask, does the majority now get to impose on me against my will? The whole point of asking for individual consent is supposed to be that individuals get to decide what happens to them. Here, someone was asked, but their answer was ignored.

In response, someone might say that the dissent was not ignored. It was counted. So was everyone else's vote. And the will of the majority was respected. Were dissenters to have been in the majority, their opinion would have been imposed on everyone else.

This response is not satisfactory as regards individual consent. If a vote is a request for consent, consent has clearly been refused by answering "No." Two possibilities present themselves. One is that the majority represents "the will of the people" and it is the people who have consented or dissented through a vote. Such a view would require a pretty robust idea of the electorate as a single agent.[32]

The other possibility is that *taking part* in a referendum entails accepting its results. Just as if one plays a game one implicitly agrees to abide by its rules, so by taking part in an election one implicitly agrees to accept its results. The act of consent here is not consent to, say, leave the EU, but consent to accept the referendum results.[33] A key problem with this alternative is that for an act to count as a token of consent, there must also be an option to dissent. If taking part in the election is agreeing to its results, then not taking part must be refusing to accept its results. And yet, it does not appear that non-participation is held to *mean* refusal. Much of the time, it is taken as indifference or apathy.[34]

Strictly speaking, then, referendums do not involve consent. Nevertheless, our prior discussion of the conditions under which consent is valid may still prove valuable. Even if voters are not consenting, there may be good reasons for thinking that it matters what the majority chooses. A referendum might plausibly enhance the authority of the government to enact the preferred policy, just as an election might enhance the authority of those who take power as a result.

We see three types of reason for caring about what citizens want, as expressed through their votes, even if they do not literally consent that way. First, there are epistemic reasons.[35] For example, what someone wants is a good guide to what is good for them. It is an even better guide when they choose voluntarily and on the basis of full information. Second, there are intrinsic reasons. Democratic representation may be important in itself in order to justify the imposition of the preferences of the majority (within the constraints of what is just). Third, the very fact that people are being asked to make a choice provides reasons to respect that choice. It is true that we, the people, have not consented to the game that we are now part of. Yet, the game purports to be one that involves us exercising our autonomy. It would be disrespectful to ignore or undermine that exercise.

Importantly, we do not need to choose among these reasons. For each, the relevant value will be undermined insofar as the autonomous choice of voters is undermined. Badly informed voters are likely to make worse decisions. The value of democracy lies in people choosing themselves and according to their values. The game of voting claims to be one in which people make autonomous decisions. Thus, insofar as the exercise of autonomy by voters is undermined, it seems fair to say that the legitimacy of an election or referendum result is reduced.

Return now to the Brexit referendum. Both the campaign and the aftermath of the vote were marked by acrimony. Both sides accused each other of lying to voters and multiple organizations were fined for campaign finance violations. Claims were also raised and investigated regarding misuse of personal data—including by Facebook—and possible foreign interference.[36] It turned out that the implications of the referendum result were also unclear, since the terms under which the UK would leave the EU depended on negotiations and parliamentary approval that took place in the years following the vote. The final agreement—a so-called "hard Brexit"—entailed a greater separation between the UK and EU than was originally anticipated. For example, pro-Brexit leaders before the referendum gave very different and opposing answers to the question of whether leaving the EU would mean leaving the single market.[37]

Thinking about the Brexit referendum campaign in terms of the conditions for the validity of consent, we can see two main sources of problems—concerning disclosure and concerning understanding. We consider them in turn.

From the point of view of exercises of autonomy—including those involved in consent—the central concern about disclosure is when it leads to illegitimate control of one person's decision by another party. A central case is when misleading or false information is deliberately and successfully used to cause someone to act differently than they would otherwise have done.

Take a possible case of such deceit. In the run-up to the referendum, politicians campaigning to leave the EU increasingly emphasized concerns about immigration. In May 2016, Vote Leave—the official campaign to leave the EU—claimed that Turkey was about to join the EU.[38] They said:

> Since the birthrate in Turkey is so high, we can expect to see an additional million people added to the UK population from Turkey alone within eight years. This will not only increase the strain on Britain's public services, but it will also create a number of threats to UK security. Crime is far higher in Turkey than the UK. Gun ownership is also more widespread. Because of the EU's free movement laws, the government will not be able to exclude Turkish criminals from entering the UK.[39]

Besides being racist and stoking anti-immigrant sentiment, the statement is highly misleading. In particular, it was not true that Turkey was about to join the EU, so the speculative claims that a million Turks would move to the UK were wholly unfounded. Given that the statement was put out by a campaign that included government ministers and given the prompt media fact-checking, it seems clear that Vote Leave knew their claims were false. Thus, this constitutes deception.

One might think that context matters a lot here: politics is very different from medicine. People generally accept politicians making claims to voters that they would never tolerate a doctor making to her patients. Yet, we still think that outright lying by politicians is wrongful. Talk of a "post-truth" era notwithstanding, it also seems that most people agree—politicians are negatively judged for being dishonest. Insofar as deceit by politicians is wrongful, they cannot escape the charge of illegitimate control by claiming it is not unethical. Instead, the question is whether a lack of trust in politicians means that their lies are liable to be unsuccessful—that is non-controlling. This is an empirical question. However, it is at least plausible that lies told about immigration affected how some individuals voted on Brexit.[40] In this respect, their autonomy and the authority conferred on the government by the referendum result would be undermined. It is, of course, a further empirical question whether enough people were influenced to change the referendum result.

Turn now to understanding. On its face, what was being asked in the referendum was pretty clear: "Should the United Kingdom remain a member of the European Union or leave the European Union?" In the aftermath of the vote to leave, it became rapidly apparent that the meaning of leave was quite unclear. This is because there would have to be some enduring relationship between the UK and the rest of Europe. It might be on the model of Norway (part of the European Economic Area and so accepting free movement of goods and people, while not coming under the EU's common trade policy, foreign policy, and the like), or Switzerland (member of the European Free Trade Area but not the European Economic Area), or some other negotiated variant that preserved a substantial amount of the existing legal relationship. Or, as it turned out, it might be a more dramatic severing of ties with the EU, so that both free movement of goods and people would cease. We take it that the post-referendum uncertainty about what would and should be negotiated with the EU is evidence that the meaning of the vote was vague.

It therefore seems unlikely that the UK government had a clear mandate from the referendum, given uncertainty about what the result meant. It is like a doctor saying, "Do you want the treatment?" when the patient has multiple treatment options. Insofar as the referendum is supposed to add anything to what the government is already authorized to do, it seems to lack force: for any content given to "Leave" we just cannot know that a majority of voters meant that content.

8. Case: drink driving

So far, we have talked about whether people can give consent to be governed or for their government to enact specific policies. Legitimate states have the authority to make laws and, crucially, to enforce them. Our final case concerns this enforcement. We examine the status of laws requiring drivers who have not been convicted of any crime to submit to chemical tests for blood alcohol levels. The tests would normally require consent but are administered under threats of penalties. Is there something special about the state that means such consent can still be valid?

The evidence that alcohol consumption impairs the ability to drive and therefore increases the risk of traffic accidents is incontrovertible.[41] This is the basis for the criminalization of driving under the influence of alcohol, even when the driver has not yet caused any harm. In many countries, driving with a blood alcohol content over a specified amount is itself an offence. For example, the legal limit is 0.08% blood alcohol content in England, Wales, and Northern Ireland, and 0.05% in Scotland. Whether a driver is over the limit is ascertained through the administration of a chemical test. This is usually a breath test, though under some circumstances blood or urine might be tested. Since blood-alcohol levels diminish over time, it is important that a sample is obtained relatively quickly.

Administering a breath test to a conscious individual requires their consent (as does the collection of blood or urine). In the US and UK a driver can refuse to give a breath sample, but there are severe sanctions for refusal except in exceptional circumstances.[42] In the UK refusing to provide a specimen is a criminal offence, punishable by a driving ban of a year or more, a fine, and potentially imprisonment.[43] In the US, laws vary by state, but all include a lengthy suspension of the refuser's driving license.[44] Interestingly, US states treat driving a motor vehicle as "implied consent" to chemical testing for alcohol or drugs:

> Any person who operates a vehicle upon the highways of this State shall be deemed to have given consent to a test or tests of such operator's blood or breath, for the purpose of determining the operator's alcohol concentration, and to a test or tests of such operator's blood, urine, or other bodily substances for purpose of detecting the presence of drugs. The test or tests shall be administered at the direction of a law enforcement officer who has arrested that person for, or has probable cause to believe, that the person has operated a vehicle under the influence of alcohol and/or drugs or other controlled substance ...[45]

Ethically speaking, it is implausible that the alleged implied consent is valid in most cases.[46] This is because most drivers are probably unaware of the implied consent rule.[47] In any case, the implied consent would only be relevant in cases where a driver is incapacitated.[48] Otherwise, they normally have the option to refuse and so the question of consent is live again at the point of the request for a specimen. We therefore focus on that request.

What are we to make of the validity of a driver's agreement to undergo testing? What is being requested is relatively clear—that is, the understanding requirement is probably satisfied. In some cases, there may be problems with disclosure. Being stopped by the police can be a scary experience and what drivers are told regarding their rights and the consequences of refusal may not be clear.[49]

Even in a case where disclosure is impeccable, we might think that the driver is coerced into consenting. The consequences of refusal are severe. For many people, even the minimal penalty of a year's suspension of their driving license would have a massive impact on their lives. The consequences are therefore bad enough to undermine consent. They are also, we expect, sufficient to determine many drivers' decisions. The driver's decision is therefore controlled. But is it illegitimately controlled?

The answer to this question depends on whether the consequences constitute a *threat* in the sense discussed in Chapter 5. There, we argued that a threat is best analyzed against a normative baseline. Would carrying out the threat make the individual worse off than they ought to be? In this case, the baseline depends on the moral authority of the state. Does the state have the right to impose the proposed penalties on a driver who refuses to give consent? If so, then the consent will not be illegitimately controlled and so could be valid. If not, then, despite the option to refuse, the driver's rights are being violated by making them submit to the test.

This question goes to the heart of discussions about coercion and the state. For many philosophers, it is axiomatic that the state coerces citizens.[50] In an effective state, laws are backed up by sanctions, which are ultimately backed up by the use of physical force. For other philosophers, the fact that a legitimate state has the right to impose sanctions entails that doing so is not coercive (or, at least, not coercive in a consent-undermining sense).[51] As Vinit Haksar puts it: "the state is not making a coercive proposal when it proposes fairly and justly that it will not put X in jail if he is law abiding."[52]

Suppose, for the sake of argument, that Haksar is correct. This idea can be very helpful for analyzing policies like the drink-driving laws under discussion.

First, the nature of an actor affects what sort of sanctions they can legitimately apply. As a private individual, I could not take away your driving license or impose a fine on you for driving without a license. I simply lack the requisite power to do so. Only for a government body is this an option. Second, some sanctions are easier to justify than others. The fact that driving licenses are granted by the state in the first place makes it plausible that the state can permissibly suspend or revoke them (provided it does so in a way that is non-discriminatory, and so on). Moreover, it seems reasonable that people should need licenses to drive, given how dangerous driving is. A prison sentence, on the other hand, would seem like it required a higher bar for justification. The state does not grant individuals freedom from imprisonment—a permission it is then at liberty to revoke. Rather the normative baseline is freedom.

Taken together these points suggest that proposing to suspend someone's license if they refuse a breath test might not constitute a threat, whereas a prison sentence might. Agreement in the former case, but not the latter, would therefore constitute valid consent. We leave it to the reader to consider whether they agree with our analysis here.

9. Conclusions

The idea that governments are legitimate if and only if they have the consent of the governed has a long history. It remains very contentious among political philosophers. Those who defend it face serious challenges. They must either accept that all actual governments are illegitimate or show that consent has in fact been given. As this chapter has shown, the latter thesis is difficult to defend. Our cases show that the topic of consent to government is richer than just the question of overall political legitimacy. We can still ask of specific policies or elected representatives whether they have greater legitimacy if they were selected through a fair election. Consent theory appears relevant to such questions. And it is also clearly relevant to questions regarding what the state or its representatives are permitted to do. When asked for consent by the police or some other state functionary, refusal may have consequences. It is important to analyze when those consequences invalidate consent and when they do not in order to assess the limits of permissible state actions.

Notes

1 Locke, John. *Two treatises on government.* Awnsham Churchill, 1690: s. 95.
2 For a helpful overview of the different ways in which philosophers have understood legitimacy, authority, and related concepts, see: Peter, Fabienne. "Political legitimacy." *The Stanford Encyclopedia of Philosophy* (Summer 2017 edition), Edward N. Zalta (ed.). Available at: https://plato.stanford.edu/archives/sum2017/entries/legitimacy. Our definition in this chapter is stipulative, but is not intended to beg any important questions of relevance to the arguments that follow.
3 van der Vossen, Bas. "Consent to unjust institutions." *Legal Theory* 27.3 (2021): 236–251.
4 E.g., Simmons, J. *Justification and legitimacy: Essays on rights and obligations.* Cambridge University Press, 2001: 130.
5 Edmundson, William A. *Three anarchical fallacies.* Cambridge University Press, 1998.
6 Cf. Chapter 2, section 2.
7 E.g., Raz, Joseph. "Authority and consent." *Virginia Law Review* (1981): 103–131.
8 Simmons, A. John. "Political obligation and consent." In Franklin Miller and Alan Wertheimer (eds.), *The ethics of consent: Theory and practice.* Oxford University Press, 2010: 306.
9 Plato, *Crito*, 51 c–e.
10 Locke, John. *Two treatises on government.* Awnsham Churchill, 1690: s. 119.
11 Hume, David. "Of the original contract." In David Hume, *Political essays*, ed. K. Haakonssen. Cambridge Texts in the History of Political Thought. Cambridge University Press, 1994: 189.
12 Hume, David. "Of the original contract." In David Hume, *Political essays*, ed. K. Haakonssen. Cambridge Texts in the History of Political Thought. Cambridge University Press, 1994: 193.
13 Locke, incidentally, was perfectly aware of this problem when he wrote *Two Treatises*, but was more optimistic about the options for dissent: "For there are no examples so frequent in history, both sacred and profane, as those of men withdrawing themselves and their obedience from the jurisdiction they were born under, and the family or community they were bred up in, and setting up new governments in other places." Locke, John. *Two treatises on government.* Awnsham Churchill, 1690: s. 115.
14 Klosko, George. "The principle of fairness and political obligation." *Ethics* 97.2 (1987): 353–362.
15 Simmons, A. John. "Political obligation and consent." In Franklin Miller and Alan Wertheimer (eds.), *The ethics of consent: Theory and practice.* Oxford University Press, 2010: 325.
16 E.g., "Together with the veil of ignorance, these conditions define the principles of justice as those which rational persons concerned to advance their interests would consent to as equals when none are known to be advantaged or disadvantaged by social and natural contingencies." Rawls, John. *A Theory of Justice.* Revised Edition. The Belknap Press of Harvard University Press, 1999: 17.
17 Estlund, David. "Political authority and the tyranny of non-consent." *Philosophical Issues* 15 (2005): 351–367.
18 For critiques of Estlund, see Edmundson, William A. "Consent and its cousins." *Ethics* 121.2 (2011): 335–353; Sreenivasan, Gopal. "'Oh, but you should have': Estlund on normative consent." *Iyyun: The Jerusalem Philosophical Quarterly* (2009): 62–72.

19 For an argument that immigrants making such oaths are in fact performing morally transformative speech acts, see Lovett, Adam, and Daniel Sharp. "What immigrants owe." *Ergo* 8 (2022). Lovett and Sharp think that the normative inequality between immigrants who have taken on obligations to the state and natural-born citizens who have not is unfair. They deny that this unfairness should be addressed by having natural-born citizens take oaths of allegiance on the grounds that the costs of dissent would be too high.

20 In the United States, the "Pledge of Allegiance" is recited by schoolchildren, by members of the armed forces, and before some government meetings, such as the opening of Congressional sessions. It is not recited by most adult, natural-born Americans.

21 See, e.g., Puryear, Stephen. "Consent by residence: A defense." *European Journal of Political Theory* 20.3 (2021): 529–546.

22 The first is clearly inconsistent with most views of the understanding requirement for valid consent, including our own (Chapter 4).

23 Cibik, Matej. "Tacit consent and political legitimacy." *European Journal of Political Theory* (2022): 14748851221143612. Relatedly, Mark Murphy argues that by accepting the decisions of the government as authoritative, e.g., with respect to drink driving limits, citizens thereby consent in the "acceptance sense." Murphy, Mark C. "Surrender of judgment and the consent theory of political authority." *Law and Philosophy* 16 (2005): 115–143. No explicit speech act of consent is needed. It remains to be shown that all or most citizens of modern democracies do accept the government's determinations in the way Murphy requires for his view.

24 The exception is in territories that have active secessionist movements. Protests that demand an independent state seem like much better candidates for dissent to living under the current state and its government.

25 Chrisafis, Angelique. "Who are the gilets jaunes and what do they want?" *The Guardian*, December 7, 2018. Available at: www.theguardian.com/world/2018/dec/03/who-are-the-gilets-jaunes-and-what-do-they-want.

26 Steinberger, Peter J. "Political obligations and derivative duties." *Journal of Politics* 64.2 (2002): 460. See also Plamenatz, J. P. *Consent, freedom and political obligation*, 2nd edition. Oxford University Press, 1968: 1–25.

27 Maloberti, Nicolás. "The fallacy of consent." *The Journal of Value Inquiry* 44.4 (2010): 475.

28 Puryear, Stephen. "Consent by residence: A defense." *European Journal of Political Theory* 20.3 (2021): 540–542.

29 Puryear, Stephen. "Consent by residence: A defense." *European Journal of Political Theory* 20.3 (2021): 540.

30 See, e.g., Beran, Harry. *The consent theory of political obligation*. Croom Helm, 1987; Klosko, George. "Reformist consent and political obligation." *Political Studies* 39.4 (1991): 676–690; Otsuka, Michael. *Libertarianism without inequality*. Clarendon Press, 2003; Walzer, Michael, "Political Alienation and Military Service." In *Obligations: essays on disobedience, war, and citizenship*. Harvard University Press, 1970: 99–119.

31 Simmons, A. John. "Political obligation and consent." In Franklin Miller and Alan Wertheimer (eds.), *The ethics of consent: Theory and practice*. Oxford University Press, 2010.

32 For discussion, see Volmert, Andrew. "The puzzle of democratic authorization." *Political Studies* 60.2 (2012): 287–305.

33 For further discussion of what this can and cannot mean, see Goodin, Robert. *Consent matters*. Oxford University Press, 2024: 206–220.

34 Sometimes attempts are made to organize a boycott of an election or a referendum in order to delegitimize its results. It is at least possible that where this is the reason for many people abstaining from voting and it is widely understood that this is why they abstain, that constitutes a form of dissent from the system that is normatively significant. It would not imply the converse—that voting implies consent—unless it were also widely understood that voters on this occasion are endorsing the electoral process as well as their preferred candidate or policy.

35 Estlund, David. *Democratic authority: A philosophical framework*. Princeton University Press, 2008.

36 For a list see "Allegations of unlawful campaigning in the 2016 EU referendum." Available at: https://en.wikipedia.org/wiki/Allegations_of_unlawful_campaigning_in_the_2016_EU_referendum (accessed 8 September 2023).

37 Full Fact. "What was promised about the customs union before the referendum?" October 26, 2018. Available at: https://fullfact.org/europe/what-was-promised-about-customs-union-referendum.
38 A Vote Leave poster showed a British passport as an open door and the words: "Turkey (population 76 million) is joining the EU. Vote Leave, take back control."
39 Boffey, Daniel, and Toby Helm. "Vote Leave embroiled in race row over Turkey security threat claims." *The Guardian*, May 22, 2016.
40 The testimony of some individuals involved in the Leave campaign suggests that they thought messages about the NHS and immigration were particularly effective. Fletcher, Martin. "Dominic Cummings has admitted the Leave campaign won by lying—we should never forgive him." *The New Statesman*, July 23, 2021).
41 Taylor, Benjamin, and Jürgen Rehm. "The relationship between alcohol consumption and fatal motor vehicle injury: high risk at low alcohol levels." *Alcoholism: Clinical and Experimental Research* 36.10 (2012): 1827–1834.
42 For example, someone with advanced lung disease might reasonably decline a breath test. They would then be obliged to submit to a blood test instead.
43 Lawtons Solicitors. "Failing to provide a specimen of breath: Sentencing guidelines." November 3, 2020. Available at: www.lawtonslaw.co.uk/resources/failing-to-provide-a-specimen-of-breath-sentencing-guidelines.
44 Voas, Robert B., et al. "Implied-consent laws: A review of the literature and examination of current problems and related statutes." *Journal of Safety Research* 40.2 (2009): 77–83. In a couple of states there is no option for refusal: drivers suspected of driving under the influence of alcohol who refuse a breath sample may be forced to give a blood sample. However, requiring a blood sample requires a warrant.
45 National Committee on Uniform Traffic Laws and Ordinances, Uniform Vehicle Code (2000): S.11–904.
46 For discussion of cases in which someone is treated as having given consent for *legal* purposes, even though they have not actually given consent, see Westen, Peter. *The logic of consent: The diversity and deceptiveness of consent as a defense to criminal conduct*. Routledge, 2017: 309–349.
47 The tone of this law blog is typical: "Fun Fact most motorists don't know when they get their license for the first time: Every license holder, upon registration, has given his or her consent to take a chemical test for blood alcohol concentration (BAC) upon arrest by the police for suspicion of driving under the influence." Hammond, Donald. "Warning! You've consented to California drawing your blood!" June 24, 2019. Available at: www.donhammondlaw.com/blog/implied-consent-law.
48 In 2019, the US Supreme Court ruled that statutes permitting blood to be drawn without a warrant from an unconscious motorist suspected of driving under the influence of alcohol were constitutional (*Mitchell v. Wisconsin*, No. 18–6210, 588 U.S. ___ (2019). Available at: www.supremecourt.gov/opinions/18pdf/18–6210_2co3.pdf.
49 Ogundipe, Kehinde A., and Kenneth J. Weiss. "Drunk driving, implied consent, and self-incrimination." *Journal of the American Academy of Psychiatry and the Law Online* 37.3 (2009): 386–391.
50 Bentham, Jeremy. *Of laws in general*, ed. H. L. A. Hart. Athlone, 1970; Rawls, John. *Political liberalism*. Columbia University Press, 1993: 136.
51 See, e.g., Edmundson, William A. *Three anarchical fallacies: An essay on political authority*. Cambridge University Press, 1998: 79–83. For an argument to show how it is possible to be coerced in a non-consent-undermining sense, see Garnett, Michael. "Coercion: The wrong and the bad." *Ethics* 128.3 (2018): 545–573.
52 Haksar, Vinit. "Coercive proposals [Rawls and Gandhi]." *Political Theory* 4 (1976): 73.

Index